The Elephants Teach

Prentice Hall Studies in Writing and Culture

———— *Series Editor* ————
Nancy Sommers
Harvard University

PRENTICE HALL STUDIES IN WRITING AND CULTURE captures the excitement of an emerging discipline that is finally coming into its own. The writers in this series are challenging basic assumptions, asking new questions, trying to broaden the inquiry about writing and the teaching of writing. They not only raise challenging questions about the classroom—about teaching and building communities of writers—they also investigate subjects as far ranging as the nature of knowledge and the role that culture plays in shaping pedagogy. Writers in the series are particularly concerned about the interplay between language and culture, about how considerations of gender, race, and audience shape our writing and our teaching. Early volumes will be devoted to the essay, audience, autobiography, and how writers teach writing. Other studies will appear over time as we explore matters that are critical to teaching writing.

Nancy Sommers is Associate Director of the Expository Writing Program at Harvard. She has also directed the composition program at the University of Oklahoma and has taught in the English Department of Rutgers University where she was a Henry Rutgers research fellow. She has published widely on the theory and practice of teaching writing. She has received the National Council of Teachers of English Promising Research Award for her work on revision and the Richard Braddock Award for her work on responding to student writing.

Books in This Series

Nancy Kline, *How Writers Teach Writing*
James E. Porter, *Audience and Rhetoric*
Kurt Spellmeyer, *Common Ground: Dialogue, Understanding, and the Teaching of Composition*
John H. Clarke & Arthur W. Biddle, *Teaching Critical Thinking: Reports from Across the Curriculum*
D. G. Myers, *The Elephants Teach: Creative Writing Since 1880*

The Elephants Teach

Creative Writing Since 1880

D. G. Myers

Prentice Hall, Englewood Cliffs, New Jersey 07632

Library of Congress Cataloging-in-Publication Data

MYERS, D. G. (David Gershom)
     The elephants teach : creative writing since 1880 / D.G. Myers.
        p.   cm. — (Prentice Hall studies in writing and culture)
     Includes bibliographical references and index.
     ISBN 0-13-324013-4
        1. English language—Rhetoric—Study and teaching—United States-
     -History.   2. Creative writing—Study and teaching—United States-
     -History.   3. Authors as teachers—History.   I. Title.   II. Series.
     PE1405.U6M94   1996
     808'.04207073—dc20   95–15224
                                                                   CIP

Acquisitions editor: Alison Reeves
Production supervisor: Joan Stone
Manufacturing buyer: Lynn Pearlman
Copy editor: Rebecca J. McDearmon
Cover design: Bruce Kenselaar

Acknowledgments appear on page xvi, which
constitutes a continuation of the copyright page.

Published by Prentice-Hall, Inc.
A Simon & Schuster Company
Englewood Cliffs, New Jersey 07632

Printed in the United States of America

10 9 8 7 6 5 4 3 2

ISBN 0-13-324013-4

Prentice Hall International (UK) Limited, *London*
Prentice-Hall of Australia Pty. Limited, *Sydney*
Prentice-Hall Canada Inc., *Toronto*
Prentice-Hall Hispanoamericana, S.A., *Mexico*
Prentice-Hall of India Private Limited, *New Delhi*
Prentice-Hall of Japan, Inc., *Tokyo*
Simon & Schuster Asia Pte. Ltd., *Singapore*
Editora Prentice-Hall do Brasil, Ltda., *Rio de Janeiro*

To Paul Hedeen

When Vladimir Nabakov was proposed for a chair in literature at Harvard, the linguist Roman Jakobson objected. "What's next?" he said. "Shall we appoint elephants to teach zoology?"

Contents

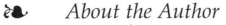 *About the Author*

D. G. Myers is associate professor of English at Texas A&M University, where he teaches the history and theory of literary criticism. He has published essays and reviews in *Philosophy and Literature*, the *Journal of the History of Ideas*, *Commentary*, the *New Criterion*, the *AWP Chronicle*, the *Sewanee Review*, and elsewhere.

Foreword

The Elephants Teach is an astonishing piece of work. The subject —the story of how we got "creative writing" into our schools, colleges, and common speech—does not sound promising, but under the author's magic wand it becomes the story of a great part of our culture since the turn of the century.

It brings before us the lives and quirks of a host of writers; the words and purport of poems by Emily Dickinson, Robert Frost, E. A. Robinson, Hart Crane, and others; the crabbed or expansive views of critics such as Barrett Wendell, Brander Matthews, Irving Babbitt, Cleanth Brooks, Lionel Trilling, and their kind; the battle over the meaning and utility of literature; the definition of prose and poetry and the boundary between them, if any; the intent and character of the artist, the means of supporting him, and the places of resort to that end—Bohemia, Yaddo, the MacDowell Colony, the university; then the democratization of the passion to write, which has inspired the curious invention of schools of writing and writing "workshops": Breadloaf, Iowa, Baker's 47, and the commercial mills.

We traverse this spacious ground after a detailed survey of the study and teaching of language and literature from the beginnings of philology early in the nineteenth century to the split of its province and the ending of its use when science made its triumphant entry into life and education. Finally, we have the spectacle of the long-lasting debate—lasting to this day—about the proper aim and way of schooling: traditional or progressive, child- or contents-centered, with teachers teaching or only "facilitating." This last scene contains the makings of high comedy beyond any afforded by the earlier topics.

In short, we have here a panorama—a pageant, rather—of the American will-to-art. Everybody who has contributed to that venture or commented on it can be seen in his place, holding his bit of ground, and with his mouth open: from William Dean Howells to Saul Bellow, from Henry Wadsworth Longfellow to John Berryman, from William Lyon Phelps to Van

Wyck Brooks, from the cantankerous Ezra Pound and the learned, sober Louise to Robert Lowell, from Charles W. Eliot to Henry Seidel Canby, from John Dewey to Hughes Mearns, from Ambrose Bierce to Jean Stafford, and so on in multiplied pairings. Offhand I cannot think of anybody who would be missing at a complete roll call based on *Who's Who*.

There is no partisanship in this recital, neither for the avant-garde of any date nor for the middle ranks and the stragglers. But the story is no mere listing and quoting and pretending to remain "judgment-free." Individual justice is meted out temperately in pleasant, readable prose. Needless to say, the research was extensive and has gone deep; there are even graphs and statistics where they can throw light. Nor is the abundance of matter diffuse. All the topics, all the names and notions form a coherent pattern. One is left with a new sense of what lies hidden in the word *creative*.

Jacques Barzun

ᐖ *Preface*

"To find out why the writing of fiction and verse has come to be called 'creative,' " Allen Tate said thirty years ago, "and to ascertain when the adjective *creative* was first so used, would be an enlightening piece of historical research." My aim in this book has been to supply that piece of research. The answer to Tate's question is pretty straightforward: the teaching of creative writing came first, historically preceding the fiction and verse that are now called "creative" and helping to determine the very categories by which this writing would be characterized and defined. The academic and not the literary usage is thus the primary meaning of the term. Like "English" it is a term that may not be universally admired, but it is pretty widely understood. "It is called 'creative writing' in most places," Richard Hugo said with some impatience. "And you know what I'm talking about."

But do we? Creative writing refers to two things: (1) a classroom subject, the teaching of fiction- and verse-writing at colleges and universities across the country; and (2) a national system for the employment of fiction writers and poets to teach the subject. The two-backed thing is one of the most striking features of the contemporary scene, academic *and* literary; this book traces its development. How did it come about? What was behind it? At one time college teaching did not seem the obvious career for a serious writer. "I can not at this moment think of a teacher of literature," said a turn-of-the-century novelist, "who has produced great literature." What happened to change people's minds? And which came first? Teaching as a career for serious writers, without which there would have been no reason for creative writing? Or creative writing as a classroom subject, without which there would have been no demand for writers who could teach? Even more important, what brought about a convergence of the twain? These are the sorts of questions I try to keep in focus as I narrate the sequence of events that has led down to the present. I must warn readers in advance, though. These days much scholarship in English is sicklied o'er with the pale cast of "theory"; the facts and propositions, that is to say, are set in relation to some currently dominant figure's system of thought. In this book I do not apply a theory in the accepted sense of the term, although that will be said to be my theory; "for a professor must have a theory," Mencken once observed, "as a dog must have fleas."

In *The Archaeology of Knowledge*, Michel Foucault says that "in its traditional form, history proper was concerned to define relations . . . between facts or dated events: the series being known, it was simply a question of defining the position of each element in relation to the other elements in the series." The post-Foucauldian historian is less concerned with merely establishing a series of events. "The problem that now presents itself," Foucault says, "is to determine what form of relation may be legitimately described between . . . different series; what vertical system they are capable of forming." My problem in telling the story of creative writing, however, has been to establish the series of events. This was not previously known, and so I have been reduced to writing history proper: history in its traditional form. Consequently, I have not been able to devise a "vertical system." To compensate for its absence somewhat I have substituted a historical argument. Although the purpose of my book is to elaborate this argument, I shall repeat it briefly here. Creative writing emerged over the last decades of the nineteenth century and the first half of the twentieth as a means for unifying the two main functions of English departments—the teaching of writing and the teaching of literature. Instead of greater unity, today's English departments exhibit a growing incongruity and disagreement between their two main functions. In short, creative writing failed to achieve its goals. And one reason is that, after the Second World War, it was put to a different use altogether: creative writing became a means for expanding the cultural role of the American university and thus found occasion for abandoning its original educational goals.

Under the title "The Rise of Creative Writing," the *Journal of the History of Ideas* published a condensed version of Chapters 2, 5, and 6 (April 1993). Officials at the universities of Alabama, California (Irvine), Iowa, North Carolina (Greensboro), South Alabama, and Virginia, Bemidji State, Bowling Green State, Central Michigan, Cornell, George Mason, Western Michigan, and Wichita State universities, and Brooklyn and Warren Wilson colleges answered my queries and supplied indispensable information. I could not even have attempted this book without the pioneering efforts of Stephen Wilbers in *The Iowa Writers' Workshop: Origins, Emergence, and Growth* (1980). And though I did not perhaps benefit from their classes in a way they might have expected (or approved of), I must also give credit to my own teachers of creative writing: Anne Steinhardt, the late Raymond Carver, and Stanley Elkin.

I have discussed my work and ideas with so many friends and colleagues that I am no longer sure what is theirs and what is mine. If I forget to name someone I hope that I'll be forgiven. Among those who improved me by their attention and criticism are Karen Belter and Will Sager, Paul Breslin, Charlene and William Bedford Clark, Frederick Crews, Dana Gioia, Anne D. Hall, John Herrmann, Amy and Mark Jarman, Douglas B. Jordan, Craig W. Kallendorf, Grace and Brinck Kerr, Scott Lamb, Jerome M. Loving, Janet McCann, Barbara Newman, Patricia Phillippy, James Seaton, and Brian H. Stagner. Deserving of special mention are J. Lawrence Mitchell, head of the English department at Texas A&M University, who arranged for a semester's leave, making it possible for me to complete the book; M. Jimmie Killingsworth, who read a substantial portion of the manuscript and recommended sending it to Prentice Hall; and Nancy Sommers, editor of the Prentice Hall Studies in Writing and Culture, whose faith in this project (and its author) gave it its final push. Jacques Barzun, whose work brings alive to me the obligation and significance of thinking historically, was generously willing to write a foreword. My thanks to all.

My deepest debts, however, are personal ones. I must express gratitude to the members of my *chavurah*—Cheryl Ackerman, Seth Adelson, Yudith and William Bassichis, Heather Gert, Deborah and Jack Miller, Beth Squerhaft, Fred Seals, Enrique and Sharon Sernik, among others—who nurtured me with *ahavat Israel*. The most profound influence on *The Elephants Teach* has been that of my mentors Joseph Epstein and Gerald Graff. As dissimilar as they are in so many ways, they are remarkably alike in intellectual integrity, independence, courage, and strength. This book is an effort to live up to their example, although by rights it belongs to an even rarer man.

D.G.M.
Bryan, Texas

Credits

Page 4: Excerpt from letter by Gerald Graff reprinted by permission of the author.

Page 30: Excerpt from Poem 1126 by Emily Dickinson reprinted by permission of the publishers and the Trustees of Amherst College from *The Poems of Emily Dickinson*, Thomas H. Johnson, ed., Cambridge, Mass.: The Belknap Press of Harvard University Press, Copyright © 1951, 1955, 1983, by the President and Fellows of Harvard College.

Pages 87–88: Excerpt from "People and a Heron" reprinted from *The Selected Poetry of Robinson Jeffers* by Robinson Jeffers. Copyright © 1925 and renewed 1953 by Robinson Jeffers. Reprinted by permission of Random House, Inc.

Page 90: Excerpt from "The Web of Life" by Ezra Pound, for which grateful acknowledgment is given to New Directions Publishing Corporation and Faber & Faber Ltd. for permission to quote from previously unpublished material by Ezra Pound, copyright © 1970 by the Trustees of the Ezra Pound Literary Property Trust; used by permission of New Directions Publishing Corporation, agents.

Pages 99–100: Excerpt from *Ph.D.s. Male and Female He Created Them* by Leonard Bacon. Copyright 1925 by Harper & Brothers. Copyright renewed 1952 by Leonard Bacon. Reprinted by permission of HarperCollins Publishers, Inc.

Page 155: Excerpt from "The Word" by Alan Swallow, in *The Nameless Sight: Poems 1937–1956* reprinted with the permission of The Ohio University Press/Swallow Press, Athens.

Page 156: Excerpt from "The Line of an American Poet," in *The Feel of Rock: Poems of Three Decades*, by Reed Whittemore, reprinted by permission of Dryad Press.

Pages 162–63: Excerpt from letter by Mark Jarman reprinted by permission of the author.

❧ *Introduction*

Like most young men and women nearing the end of college, Henry Wadsworth Longfellow was undecided about the choice of a career. "I most eagerly aspire after future eminence in literature, my whole soul burns ardently after it, and every earthly thought centers in it," he wrote to his father, seeking advice. "Surely, there never was a better opportunity offered for the exertion of literary talent in our own country than is now offered.

"To be sure," he granted, "most of our literary men thus far have not been professedly so, until they have studied and entered the practice of Theology, Law, or Medicine." But Longfellow was afraid that studying for a profession would only mean lost time. His father thought otherwise. "A literary life, to one who has the means of support, must be very pleasant," he replied. "But there is not wealth enough in this country to afford encouragement and patronage to literary men."[1]

And so in 1829 Longfellow became a professor. Although he did not publish a book of poetry until he had been teaching for a decade, Longfellow was the first American writer of any importance to choose an academic career to fill his stomach while his soul burned after literature. And though he quit the professoriate at the first opportunity—in 1854, just as soon as he could support himself on the earnings from his writing—Longfellow was an important precursor of twentieth-century writers who faced a similar economic dilemma and who arrived at a similar career choice. Unlike more recent writers, though, Longfellow did not support himself by teaching something called creative writing. He was a teacher of languages. "Poetic dreams shaded by irregular French verbs!" he scribbled in his journal. "Hang it! I wish I were a free man."[2]

This is a book about American writers' efforts to have academic careers and their freedom too—the freedom, that is, to teach creative writing. Since the Second World War, perhaps the majority of American writers have shaded their poetic dreams by teaching in universities and colleges. "Writers have become dependent on academies," observes a recent critic, "for the

1

peace and funds with which to pursue their art."[3] Once in the university, they have had to do something in return for the funds, and what they have done is to set up programs in creative writing. At last count there were more than 300 such programs granting more than 1,000 degrees a year. "Together they've probably turned out 75,000 official 'writers,' " John Barth says.[4]

Estimates peg the professional success rate for graduates in creative writing at about one percent (as compared with 90 percent for graduates of medical school), but it seems no less true that the road to professional success in contemporary literature twists through the programs in creative writing. A glance at the contributors' notes to the literary magazines or anthologies of "new" and "younger" writers confirms the widely shared impression that for an entire generation of American writers a tour of duty in a graduate writers' workshop followed by a life of teaching creative writing has been the standard training and common experience of its time. As Wallace Stegner said, "[N]early every American writer you can name is associated either with some academy or with the academic lecture-platform circuit."[5] Of the 134 poets chosen to appear in *The Best American Poetry* for 1990 and 1991, for example, all but twenty or so—85 percent—were affiliated with the enterprise of creative writing in one capacity or another, as graduates, professors, or administrators. Sometimes they were all three.

"The historical explanation for the close collaboration between American writers and American academic institutions is hard to disentangle," says a historian of modern authorship.[6] This book is an attempt to disentangle the collaboration. It pursues the teaching of writing by writers from the 1880s, when an elective course in advanced composition was offered for the first time at Harvard, down to the present day, when (or so it was predicted not too long ago) workshops in creative writing would be made "available to anyone in America within safe driving distance of his home."[7] The story is new—historically, because it begins late in the nineteenth century; but also historiographically, because it has never been told before. Several years ago a historian lamented: "We have libraries on the history of universities but very little historical work on the social and intellectual forms of modern scholarship."[8] Since then a number of books have been published on the study and teaching of English, most notably Gerald Graff's *Professing Literature* (1987). There have been volumes on the teaching of English since the sixteenth century, the study of American literature, rhetoric and basic writing instruction, the economics of English departments, professional writing instruction, the politics of English composition, writing groups, and writing across the curriculum. But a full-length history of creative writers teaching creative writing has not yet appeared.[9]

One reason for the neglect is that creative writing has more often been a subject for debate than history. The debate has been carried on with such partisan indignation that different people seem to be talking about radically different things when they talk about creative writing. On one side are those who blame it for an astonishing array of ills: the collapse of literary standards, an overproduction of homogeneously bad writing, the decadence of the age. For them, creative writing has been (according to one critic) a "catastrophe." On the other side are those who defend creative writing as a democratization of culture and a happy awakening of interest in literature and the literary life, a sign of the age's vitality. For them it has been a "service." Obviously the same thing cannot in itself be both. What is less obvious is why it should be either.[10]

Other explanations must be sought, and in this book I seek the explanation in history. What goes unexamined in the debate over creative writing are the reasons for its triumph, the original argument for the subject that apparently struck some people at one time as sound and even persuasive. The current debate starts at the end, explaining *how* creative writing now operates, but not *why*. Perhaps it would be well to return to the beginning, by means of history. The idea of hiring writers to teach writing has never won unquestioned acceptance nor has creative writing—the classroom subject—progressed much beyond apologizing for itself. Even at a time when it was growing and spreading rapidly, as Kingsley Amis recalls in his *Memoirs*, creative writing was "often ridiculed . . . by those who knew nothing of it."[11] Despite the ridicule, writers met surprisingly little resistance in taking their place on university faculties, and once it was proposed, creative writing was adopted fairly quickly as a subject of university instruction. This book is intended neither to defend the honor of campus writers nor to heap more ridicule upon them; it is merely a history, an effort to explain how writing came to be taught in large and growing numbers by writers on university campuses. Any contribution that I could make to the debate would contribute little to historical understanding. I don't mean to pretend that I am neutral on the subject. I agree with the late Lucy S. Dawidowicz that "as long as historians respect the integrity of their sources and adhere strictly to the principles of sound scholarship," their sympathies and commitments "do not distort, but instead they enrich, historical writing."[12] I readily admit that I am sympathetic to the original idea behind creative writing, the vision of literature and literary study that inspired the men and women who originated it.

But though I am sympathetic to it, I am committed neither to creative writing in its present condition nor to any plan to repair it. My concern is not that of the debater, who argues the *status quo ante* must be altered or preserved, but that of the historian, for whom the present situation arouses a curiosity to know how things got to be this way. Yet I shall be asked to declare my allegiance, to confess my bias, for these days it is the common opinion that all humanistic scholarship is written from a point of view; that is, by someone who has a stake in the outcome. And I shall not be believed if I protest that the question of bias or allegiance is simply irrelevant, since in this book I am doing something different in kind from taking sides. So, I acknowledge that I have written this book out of an allegiance to the old discredited liberal principle that knowledge is its own end, distinct from its practical effects. Not only do I have little to gain or lose from what happens to creative writing—I am not too worried about the practical effects of this historical account—but more to the point I have dedicated myself to promulgating the views of creative writing's founders. And it was for the sake of advancing the principle that literature is an end in itself that creative writing was established in the first place.

Originally the teaching of writing in American universities ("creative" or otherwise) was an experiment in education. Creative writing as such emerged out of this experiment, gradually taking shape over the six decades from 1880 to the Second World War. In the beginning it was not a scheme for turning out official writers or for providing them with the peace and funds with which to pursue their art. The goal—an educational one—was to reform and redefine the academic study of literature, establishing a means for approaching it "creatively"; that is, by some other means than it had been approached before that time, which was historically and linguistically. Over the next fifty years of its life creative writing slowly turned away from its original goal; and yet even then it retained a memory of its commitment to literature and literature's place in education. From the first creative writing was an institutional arrangement for treating literature as if it were a continuous experience and not a mere corpus of knowledge—as if it were a living thing, as if people intended to write more of it. Although the course requirements and sometimes even the exact title varied from place to place, creative writing was not merely various. Among the variety there was a principle of identity. Under the heading of creative writing, literature was conceived (in Michael Oakeshott's phrase) as both an achievement and a promise, an inheritance of texts and a flexible set of methods and standards for generating new texts. Wherever it appeared, an education in writing arose as a challenge to any other conception of literature. Creative writing was the name that might have been given to any effort that undertook to restore the idea of literature as an integrated discipline of thought and activity, of textual study and practical technique. It was the study and practice of literature (or writing) for its own sake.

Why then does creative writing now seem like anything but this integration? As Gerald Graff said after officially reviewing the program at a major university, "[T]he writers were almost all practice-oriented, hostile or indifferent to [literary] criticism, much less theory, while the critics and theorists in the English department looked down with lordly indifference on mere contemporary writing. Each component [of the department] is beautifully and completely insulated from any danger of hearing the criticism of the other—and of course that's the whole point, isn't it?"[13] In the hallways of the English department, exchanges between poets and scholars are marked by mutual hostility. The poets complain that literary study has "no point of contact with the concerns of most working poets"; the scholars dismiss creative writing as "pseudo-literature."[14] The institutional situation is a far cry from what the founders of creative writing envisioned. What happened? Briefly this: in the decades following the Second World War, as the American university expanded under pressure from several different sources—the postwar demand for more democratic access, the demand for more education to compete with the Soviet Union after Sputnik, the sheer demand for more classroom space as the baby boom generation began to make itself felt in the mid-sixties—creative writing became one of the primary engines driving the expansion. It was a means for enlarging the university's role in American society. It needed no further justification: if it was no longer undertaken for the sake of integrating literary study with literary practice, it could be pursued for its own sake—free of any other institutional responsibilities.

Now creative writing is not usually thought of in these terms. The only connection it is usually thought to have with literature and literary study is an economic or bureaucratic one—it is first an apprenticeship and then a livelihood. Even though there is no centralized control over it, creative writing seems to give every appearance of being an interlocking coast-to-coast system of patronage—a network of cash subsidies and allotments of time for writers just starting out, a quilt of academic sinecures for older, established authors. British novelist Pamela Hansford Johnson sighs enviously:

> America has been awfully lucky to have patronage through the academies, awfully lucky. I've done some of this work myself in America. Americans are very generous in looking after their writers.[15]

Writing itself may not qualify as a profession—it is neither a full-time occupation nor the primary source of income for most writers—but the *teaching* of writing, by those who have some claim to be recognized writers, looks (on this view) like the next best thing. Dr. Johnson's toil, envy, want, the patron, and the jail have been replaced by two years in graduate school, an academic job at a comfortable salary, and permanent tenure. Only envy remains the lot of contemporary writers.

Yet this description raises a question. How was *teaching* hit upon as a form of patronage? It is an odd choice to say the least. Artists have always created what their patrons have asked for, and occasionally the academic situation of campus writers is blamed for the bloodlessness of their work—as a genre (it is said) creative writing is redolent of the classroom rather than experience. Mark Harris seems closer to the truth, though, when he points out the obvious: what the teaching of creative writing creates is *students*, not commissioned works of art.[16] Creative writing arose in opposition to the German research ideal, and as such it was originally conceived not as a *Wissenschaft*—a medium for producing and expanding knowledge—but as a *Bildung*, a way of cultivating students' appreciation of the literary art.[17]

Originally, then, teaching was the goal, not production and expansion. Today writers are hired and promoted in academe on the basis of their writing—it has become their equivalent of original research—and yet they have been less successful than academics in other fields at establishing institutional peer-review mechanisms for legitimizing their own work and excluding that of others. Anyone who wants to teach creative writing must be recognized or licensed as a writer—through publication or earning the Master of Fine Arts—but no one must *teach* creative writing in order to *publish* creative writing. There is a difference between a "writer" and a "teacher of creative writing" that is not ordinarily so in the case of literary scholars, historians, sociologists, archaeologists, physicists, or oceanographers, for whom the roles of teacher and producer are combined as a matter of course. Even if it is the primary means of economic support for writers in these days, teaching remains only one possible means of support. Strictly speaking it is not a form of literary patronage at all. True enough, writers who also teach probably enjoy themselves more and fatigue themselves less than anyone who puts in a nine-to-five day for an insurance company or a bank; and they leave themselves more time for writing to boot. But if that is so their academic situation owes less to patronage and generosity than to writers' own choices and career decisions. There are other ways to make a living and some of them even demand writing. Writers who teach for a living instead of reporting the news or working in public relations or ghostwriting other people's books have chosen to do one thing instead of another. The teaching of creative writing might be more accurately described, then, as a surrogate for patronage, an occupation that has been consciously turned to (as Longfellow's father said) in the absence of wealth enough in this country to afford encouragement and patronage to literary men and women.

Why teaching? For this reason: creative writing was originally established as a discipline of education, not as a livelihood for creative writers. Now any such interpretation will be at odds with the a priori assumption of a good many intellectual historians. Ever since N. R. Hanson's *Patterns of Discovery* (1958) and Thomas S. Kuhn's *Structure of Scientific Revolutions* (1960) overturned the positivistic theory of scientific understanding, many historians have adopted the similar view—a commonplace in the sociology of knowledge—that the fields of university study as we know them are based not on scholarly discoveries but on scholarly authority; in historical terms, they took shape in the nineteenth century by a process of "professionalization."[18] Steven Turner gives an excellent short version of how the fields of study were professionalized over time:

> The scholarly community—those who wrote, read, and judged serious works of scholarship—became associated ever more closely with schools and universities. Membership in that community—the right to publish and be heard—came to depend heavily on academic licensing procedures. . . . "Serious research" became increasingly centered around the application of expertise,

whether manuscript genealogies, archival explorations, or quantitative chemical analysis; "serious scholarship" addressed itself increasingly to the narrower range of problems accessible to expertise and tended to dismiss others as illegitimate, speculative, or popular.

And Turner adds that "All of the professions, except possibly the clerical, were challenged (ultimately without success) by rival groups which coveted their status and privileges. . . ."[19] Creative writing was the rare successful challenge. It did not take shape—at least not initially—by means of professionalization; it was a *dissent* from professionalization. On one hand it remained aloof from the professionalization of literary study, which pushed forward in the name of serious research and serious scholarship. And by contrast, the new discipline stood for teaching. On the other hand, it sought to preserve writing for something other than the practical, workaday uses to which it was being put by the rising profession of journalism. By contrast, the academic discipline believed in developing young people for creative (and not merely acquisitive) work.

Creative writing, then, first saw light as a conservative reform. But though it emerged as a challenge to professionalization, it was not founded on professional resentment. Although it repudiated humanism in other ways, it was founded on the humanistic argument that literature is not a genre of knowledge but a mode of aesthetic and spiritual cultivation. Unlike the exponents of other university disciplines—such as the American Philological Association (1869), Modern Language Association (1883), American Historical Association (1884), or the American Political Science Association (1889)—teachers of writing did not organize themselves into a professional body until 1967, when the Associated Writing Programs joined in common cause. Although professional writers had established an Authors League in 1912, they wavered between seeing themselves as a trade union or a business organization.[20] For writing teachers there was no trade or professional affiliation of any kind; the new field was not defined in terms of its practitioners' expertise. Creative writing was only professionalized later, in the 1970s, after it had already been secured as a retreat from literary professionalism. And even then it remained incompletely professionalized. Although the graduate writers' workshops are sometimes described as professional schools, the creative writing establishment (if there is such a thing) has not succeeded in accrediting the schools.[21] Creative writing began with the hiring of writers to teach writing, but it was not founded upon a bid for professional privilege; it was founded upon an idea. And to put it briefly, the idea was that writing ought to be pursued for its own sake—for the sake of cultivation—and not for the purpose of gaining a livelihood or for a more specialized knowledge. If Dr. Johnson was correct in the eighteenth century that "no man but a blockhead ever wrote except for money," in the last hundred years or more—since the rise of creative writing, under the sway of its fundamental idea—men and women have blockheadedly written for the sake of writing, and have got their money by other devices; increasingly, by teaching writing.

This idea was one that had to be fought for, and still does to a large extent. Prior to the emergence of creative writing—throughout the period during which creative writing was taking shape, in fact—literature was studied in American colleges and universities as a means to some other end. Creative writing by contrast has been an effort to treat writing as an end in itself. As such, it has acted with hostility toward two different conceptions of literature and writing, which for convenience might be labeled the scholarly and the socially practical. On one side are those for whom literature is primarily a genre of knowledge—"a discipline deeply dependent upon knowledge," as one scholar says—and for whom literary learning, accordingly, is "a matter of making connections between a particular verbal text and a larger cultural text," where the cultural text is conceived as *la race, le milieu, le moment,* linguistic system, political ideology, body of theoretical propositions, or the like.[22] On the other side are those for whom literature or writing is a social practice that serves either the dominant powers or the forces of opposition; for whom literary training, then, imparts either "the limited, functional writing skills needed to complete basic documents for school and work" or "skills which might be used to subvert the status quo."[23] The one side has been content merely to *understand* literature, the other merely to *use* it. And in fact, scholarly and socially practical types have tended to reject the title of literature entirely, preferring "philology," "literary history," "critical theory," or "cultural studies" on the one hand and "rhetoric," "business English," "technical writing," or "composition" on the other.

Historically, creative writing has beckoned a third way. Although it was founded by writers, it was not created to give them (in Howard Nemerov's words) a quiet life and a fairly agreeable way to make a dollar. Instead it was an effort on their part to bring the teaching of literature more closely in line with the ways in which (they believed) literature is genuinely created. The founders of creative writing were not themselves particularly important writers, in the eyes of their contemporaries or of history. And later, when more important writers began to teach creative writing, their immediate concern was still the correction of what they saw as a false view of literature being disseminated in the universities. They wished to substitute an approach that was grounded (in the words of one of their allies) on a practical experience of writing. They sought to impart the *understanding* of literature through a *use* of it. They demanded that literature be taught (in the sensible phrase of Allen Tate) as if people intended to write more of it. They wanted "to teach the writers of the past from the writer's point of view," explained Paul Engle, director of the Iowa Writers' Workshop from 1942 to 1966, "as imaginative expressions of his agony and delight, rather than as historical instances." Creative writing was originally conceived as a means of teaching literature from the inside, as familiar experience, rather than from the outside, as exotic phenomenon. It was intended to be an elephant's view of zoology.[24]

That in any event is what I shall argue in this book, although it is not an argument much in the air these days. What I am suggesting is that historically there has been a three-way split in English departments: the terrain has been carved up into sectors representing scholarship, social practices, and what I am going to refer to as constructivism, because the other terms— art, literature, imaginative expression—as Tate once said, have all been debased.[25] It is more usual to suggest that there has been only a two-way split. The carving up, obvious to nearly everybody, is characterized in a number of ways, although perhaps the clearest (surely the most influential) has been James A. Berlin's. At the outset of *Rhetoric and Reality*, his history of American writing instruction in the twentieth century, Berlin distinguishes between "rhetoric, the production of written and spoken texts, and poetic, the interpretation of texts. . . ."[26] But though this is clear, upon closer inspection it shows itself as a rather neat-looking dichotomy. Without interpretation there would be no means of learning how texts are produced; and the production of any text is from another angle merely an interpretation—a version—of how it might be written or spoken. Production and interpretation can be analytically abstracted only in the context of what is already understood ("always already," I nearly said) as a concrete whole. After the fact they may be seen as distinct mental actions, but as a concrete experience the handling of texts—whatever the right name for it turns out to be—is a synthesis of the two. At most they are different freeze-frame instants in the same continuous loop of activity. The traditional distinction between rhetoric and poetic, still useful in our day, is not to be found here.

Again, the division in English departments is sometimes registered under the institutional aliases of composition and literary study. But these would seem merely to be translations into Latinate diction of the terms *rhetoric* and *poetic*, and in any case they do not clear away the conceptual confusion. While granting as much, Evan Watkins has suggested that they might be differentiated as economic functions. In *Work Time*, his study of English as a form of labor, Watkins argues that composition and literary study became entangled historically for the purpose of bringing about a new process of "cultural selection," a means for sorting young people into new occupations and classes.[27] Literary study may have been sufficient for civilizing gentlemen, but technological advances and the rise of the professions made it necessary to turn out workers with compound and varied skills—the social ease of a gentleman, the practical ability of a manager. Although they may be conceptually distinguished, then, composition and literary study are really partners in the same economic enterprise. This is a deft analysis, but it leaves some questions unanswered: (a) What caused this tangled process to develop? (b) If the cause is something like economic forces, is this historical analysis itself also a product of those forces? (c) If not—if Watkins stands apart from economic forces in order to describe them—why could those who originally instituted English composition and literary study also not have stood apart from them? The gerrymandered map of English studies must be accounted for in some other way.

In this book I am going to base my own historical analysis upon the premise that scholarly research in English, the teaching of practical composition, and the constructivist handling of literature are three distinct "faculties" of study, thought, and activity in English, differentiated by aim and method, by the uses to which they put their materials, at times even unrelated to one another. In my view these *partitiones scientiarum* (or something like them) are what the history of English study has been all about, and so we are in the dark about English as long as we are in the dark about how it has been divided up. Composition, the constructive art of literature, and scholarship have been separate (if not rival) attempts to give definition and meaning to the field of English, reducing it to a self-consistent order of ideas, establishing sequence and precedence, making the whole interrelated, coherent. English itself is not a consistent order; its existence is bureaucratic (or "economic," if you prefer), not logical; to adapt a remark by García Márquez, like the United States it is less a name than the designation of a plurality of interests. For historical reasons, English has become home to several logically distinguishable and perhaps even mutually incompatible modes of activity—it is a "contradiction-crossed territory," in Evan Watkins's phrase.[28] But the contradictions are logical ones; scholarship, composition, and constructive literature operate from different postulates to different conclusions; and the explanation for their differences is to be sought, then, in the thinking that differentiates one from another.

This is the *real* "excluded conflict" in our histories of English study. Historians who concentrate upon the study of literature in English departments are faulted for ignoring the antagonism between composition and literary study, but historians who concentrate upon the teaching of English composition commit a similar fault. In *Textual Carnivals*, for example, Susan Miller aligns literature with composition. Originally both were "utilitarian means," she says, of replacing the classical curriculum in nineteenth-century colleges. But then Miller re-partitions them by noticing that "the 'composition' of this two-sided unity is [an] elementary [subject], insofar as it is always thought of as *freshman* 'work,' not as the study of writing throughout college."[29] What seems to have escaped her notice is that writing *is* studied throughout college (and on into graduate school) under the name of creative writing. This suggests that Miller has slipped unknowingly from one use of the term *literature* to distinctly another. There are *three* units discernible in Miller's account. First there are composition and literature$_1$, aligned in a struggle against an established curriculum; then there are the nonaligned composition and literature$_2$, the latter of which is considered a more advanced division of the curriculum. On this exhibition neither literature$_2$ (which does not include the study of writing) nor composition (which does not include *advanced* study) bears much resemblance to creative writing. That leaves literature$_1$. She is basically correct, I think, to characterize this as a "utilitarian means"—a practical, institutional proposal, which includes the study of writing throughout college—for opposing a dominant curriculum, which does not include writing at all. Left out of account, though, is what became of the advanced study of writing on the way from literature$_1$ to literature$_2$.

The problem, I would argue, lies in a currently fashionable view of literary study, which Miller herself represents earlier in her book as "reading, and only reading, texts that constitute the quasi-religious ideal of a textual canon."[30] This view conceals two things. First, it conceals the fact that literary study is *not* "only reading"; it also consists of a productive component—a special kind of writing—that goes unexamined as a consequence. And second, it conceals the relationship of creative writing to the other sectors of the English department. In plain truth, there *are* two distinct uses of literature institutionalized within university departments of English. Literature$_1$ includes the advanced study of writing; literature$_2$ produces one kind of writing and consumes another, different kind.

What now passes for literary study often has little to do with literary texts, except as a quarry for scholarship. As Jerry Herron points out in *Universities and the Myth of Cultural Decline*, the real work of most English professors is the writing not of literary texts but of scholarly books and articles. What's more, these books and articles are almost never assigned for class, students are not expected to know them, and few scholars are even inclined to read them. If course enrollments are any indication the true subject taught by English departments—though some scholars decline to recognize it as a subject at all—is composition. Most college students never take an advanced course in literature. "And even if they do," Herron observes, "they are no more likely to encounter a recognizable subject there, within the evacuated space of the academic classroom, where no real work ever takes place."[31] In short, literature as it is taught and studied now is two-faced. It chooses its materials from one set of texts but extracts its methods from another set, which is propounded in lectures and seminars as a vocabulary for saying that literature is such-and-such but which students are never taught how to read for themselves, with independent, critical judgment. There is an almost comical incongruity about much of what calls itself literary study today. The true subject in most literature classrooms is not literature, but literary scholarship.

As W. B. Stanford observes in *Enemies of Poetry*, many of those who are known as scholars of literature do not really concern themselves with literature at all, but "treat it as a branch of some subject that interests them more." There is nothing dastardly in treating literature as a fund of information about other things—human psychology, the historical uses of a language, what orthodox Marxists like to call the "representations" of material conditions—but this is not the same as treating it as literature. Although a theoretical defense of the idea would be out of place here, it remains a historical fact that some men and women have claimed (and other men and women have believed them) that literature may be undertaken for its own sake—with its own conventions, principles, standards, criteria, rules, and rule-like propositions—rather than for the sake of information about something else. In much contemporary thought this attitude tends to be associated with the Southern new critics, but in point of fact the philosophical claim for the autonomy of literature goes back as far as the *Poetics*, and even in the history of formal literary study in the United States it antedates the new criticism by a good third of a century. In 1907, in an introductory college textbook entitled *The Appreciation of Literature*, George E. Woodberry instructed his student readers that "It is useful to recognize at once the fact that literature is not an object of study, but a mode of pleasure; it is not a thing to be known merely like science, but to be lived." Woodberry was one of the first American poets to teach full time at a university (see Chapter 4). And though his terminology may not be very sharp, the distinction he is making seems clear enough. Here in an early champion of the literary teaching of literature is an explicit plea for a third way between literature as mere knowledge and literature as mere practice. Literature is a fusion of knowledge and practice; it is to be *lived*. And this is the conception that came to be formally installed in American colleges and universities under the name of creative writing.[32]

Although creative writing leads to the production of texts, it is not rhetoric. Although some of its graduates go on to get jobs, and some of these jobs are even in creative writing, its primary function is not economic. Although it is a form of literary study, it is not a form of literary scholarship. Creative writing is the concrete representation of an idea about the best way to teach literature. And if the idea is old, the representation is new. Nothing quite like it had ever been tried before. No other age and no other country had created an institution even remotely resembling the graduate writers' workshop. Writers had been educated, and they had learned their lessons, but not in workshops. Despite the claims of some apologists, creative writing is not a more or less ancient "tradition" that brings honor to those who take it up. The poet Dave Smith says that creative writing's

> pedigree is overlooked frequently but nevertheless exists from the pre-Socratic philosophers to the Scribler Club [*sic*] of Swift, Pope, Gay, etc., to Ransom, Warren, Tate, and other Fugitives, to the Harlem Renaissance, to the Beats, to Black Mountain, and unto university programs in creative writing.[33]

This is a ludicrous hodgepodge, having more to do with Smith's yearning for custom and precedent than with anything that actually happened. The search for origins is a historical error, looking to establish the authority of current practices.34 It is an error that is repeated in more respectable form in Stephen Wilbers's quasi-official history *The Iowa Writers' Workshop* (1980). Wilbers argues that "the milieu from which the Workshop emerged was the tradition of the [amateur] writers' clubs," the local reading-and-writing circles with names like Zetagathian, Erodelphian, and Hesperian, which flourished in Iowa City from the early 1890s to the second decade of the twentieth century. The so-called "workshop method" of gathering to read aloud and exchange views on work by members of the group is, Wilbers argues, a lineal descendant of the way in which the writers' clubs conducted their meetings.35

I shall be suggesting a different source for the workshop method, but even if Wilbers were right about it the institution of the graduate writers' workshop, at Iowa or elsewhere, would owe little else to the "tradition" of the writers' clubs. Creative writing was not founded as a formal university discipline by a group of writers who wished to meet and discuss their writing. Nor does it owe its existence to rude fumbling after an institutional apparatus. Writing workshops may *look* like rhymers' clubs or literary cliques, but the academic discipline is not defined by its mode of association; it is defined by its idea of literary education. Creative writing was devised as an explicit solution to an explicit problem. It was an effort to integrate literary knowledge with literary practice. And it was initiated at a specific time and place to combat a specific disintegration in the study of literature.

To make this argument is to fly in the face of settled opinion about creative writing's origins. It is widely assumed that instruction in creative writing, in one form or another, is something that cultures have always provided its young writers—although obviously under different names. Richard Hugo insists that

> It's not new. For around 400 years it was a requirement of every student's education. In the English-speaking world, the curriculum for grammar and high school students included the writing of "verses." In the nineteenth century, when literary education weakened or was dropped from elementary and secondary education, colleges picked it up, all but the creative writing. Creative writing was missing for 100 years or so, but in the past 40 years it has returned.36

But creative writing *is* new. It didn't weaken and drop from elementary and secondary education in the nineteenth century; while it did not receive its present name until the twentieth century, it was founded in the nineteenth. Even the expression *creative writing* is of nineteenth-century origin, although it was not used to designate a field of study until the twentieth. True, in the English-speaking world as elsewhere the study of poetry was once a requirement of every student's education. And true, the study of poetry once included the writing of verses. But this study was part of a humanistic curriculum in which poetry had its place in a broader initiation in human self-understanding; it was not a special course in creative writing. "Make me a poet," Drayton remembers beseeching his schoolmaster at the age of ten; "doe it, if you can,/ And you shall see, Ile quickly be a man. . . ." And as Jonson says in drawing up his character of the ideal poet in the *Discoveries*, "[T]hat which we especially require in him is an exactness of study and multiplicity of reading, which maketh a full man." The aim of a humanistic education was to produce human beings, not poets. It wasn't adverse to producing poets, but in the humanistic order of things one became a poet in order to become a more complete person, not the other way around.37

Despite an occasional lapse into humanistic slogans, the founders and early teachers of creative writing were less interested in making men than in remaking the literary curriculum. They were less troubled by the dropping of verse-writing in their day than by the dissemination of a false view of how verses are written. They wanted literature to be taught in a more *literary* manner—from within, from the standpoint of literary creation, from the view of the elephant. And so they sought to refasten a scholarly understanding of literature to the practical use of it, installing a curricular alternative to mere scholarship and mere practice. Although it suits the rhetorical purposes of latter-day apologists to declare that creative writing is age-old and recurrent, in truth it is quite new, an invention of the nineteenth and twentieth centuries. And the reason is quite simple. The modes of study to which creative writing was originally an alternative are also new, belonging to the same period of history. The story begins with the first of these.

Chapter 1

❧   When Philology Was in Flower

On the eve of the Civil War, the study of literature in American colleges was in bad shape. The Collegiate Course of classics and mathematics (as it was known) made small provision for wide reading, intelligent criticism, modern authors, or the formation of literary taste. At Yale, for example, literary study consisted entirely of Demosthenes' *On the Crown* and Bishop Whately's thirty-year-old *Rhetoric*.

"The literatures of Greece and Rome were used solely as material for vocabulary and grammatical 'drills,' " a student of the time recalled. And the faculty offered models of nothing better. "There was not a man in the faculty who had ever done anything in pure literature," the student complained. In theory the study of the classics was to lead to a reading of the classical authors. But in practice it rarely progressed beyond historical grammar. Students did not learn to read the authors; they learned, in a phrase of the day, to "work them up"—that is, to prepare passages for classroom recitation and examination. Although they were assigned sixteen "literary exercises" a week, the only literary element in these exercises was the scansion of the classical poets' meters—if that can even be described as literary. The poet Edward Rowland Sill, who was attending Yale at the time, did not find it so. He made up his mind to ignore the curriculum and pursue literature instead. "Please sir, I don't scan," he informed his professor one day when called upon to recite. The comment may sound priggish, but it gamely steps off the distance between college literary work and a young poet's sense of what he required in the way of training.[1]

Within a few years Sill would become one of the first poets to teach college English, serving from 1874 to 1882 as a professor at the University of California, where he took—the words are his—"a great and growing interest in being the cause of writing in others," helping to supply the literary training he himself had lacked.[2] By that time, however, the literary curriculum had undergone a complete overhaul. The period from the enacting of Reconstruction to the beginnings of the Populist movement—from the late 1860s

15

to the early 1890s—was the period of the classics' decline and the rise of English in American colleges. Although English literature had adorned college registers and catalogues since the first quarter of the century, its relative importance (and its place in the collegiate order of things) is suggested by the full title of those who were entrusted with the teaching of it—the professors of rhetoric, oratory, and English literature. Not until the final third of the century was English permitted to stand apart from rhetoric and oratory.

Even then, however, the study of English *literature* was subordinated to the study of the English *language*. Again, professors' full titles suggested as much—the new chairs were invariably set up in "English language and literature" (in that order). But what is more to the point, English as it emerged as a separate discipline of study in the late nineteenth century was guided and impelled by a positivistic Germanic ideal of linguistic scholarship. Literature was read (if at all) merely as source material for the new science of language, which went by the ancient and impressive name of philology. The witness, again, is E. R. Sill, who spans in a single lifetime the gulf between one educational régime and another. As he wrote in a letter to Henry Holt in February 1880, Sill was greatly concerned with education, "and especially literature as a means of it. . . ."[3] But he was also greatly disturbed by what had become of literary education in his day. Toward the end of his teaching career at Berkeley, he complained that

> so far as the real authors of our literature have been studied at all, it has been with too much exclusive a regard to philology. . . . The outside shell of literature, the language, has been taught with much acumen and nice scholarship; but the substance, the thing itself, has been neglected.[4]

For those who were devoted to literature as a thing in itself, the passing of classical study and the coming of English philology meant little in the way of real change. It merely replaced one kind of pedantry with another.

The story of writers teaching writing in the American university begins with philology and the opposition to it. It was English philology that prepared the ground for the later arrival of creative writing not only in setting English on foot as a separate course of study but also in establishing a dominant régime of study, which some of the men and women who were drawn to college English would seek to depose. As much as anything, creative writing owes its existence to an antischolarly animus that was originally directed against philology. The rise of creative writing belongs to the conflict between positivism and idealism that raged in many fields of endeavor in America after the Civil War. Creative writing enlisted on the side of idealism; its origins lie in the complaint that an austere and uninspiring literary scholarship, obsessed with the ideal of scientific knowledge, had treated literature as mere material for analysis instead of what it was—the most spiritual of subjects. Both the nature of the despised scholarship and the substance of the complaint against it are keys to understanding why creative writing came into being. And the explanation begins with the emergence of English philology, beginning in the late 1860s.

This was a period of rapid expansion in higher education. Although statistics on the number of four-year institutions and student enrollment are unavailable, the census bureau's figures on the rising number of professors in America give some indication of how quickly colleges were expanding: faculty numbers increased by 109 percent from 1870 to 1880, by 37 percent from 1880 to 1890, and by 51 percent from 1890 to the century's end (see Fig. 1). Moreover, this growth almost certainly must have been in response to pressures from within the institution itself, because when measured as a percentage of the general population the size of the faculty in American colleges displays a similar climbing pattern over the same period (see Fig. 2).

There are many reasons for this expansion, including the growing hunger for modern science, stimulated by Darwin. But the primary *internal* reason was the increasingly widespread adoption of an elective curriculum, which was partly a concession to the importance of modern knowledge and partly an effort to transform colleges into universities (which comes to the same thing). The old Collegiate Course placed strict de facto limits on knowledge. As Harvard president Charles W. Eliot pointed out, under a compulsory system the entire curriculum could be handled by twenty professors, and it was impossible to find work for more than twenty, restricting what a college could offer its students. As Eliot said,

> The limitation of teaching is an intolerable alternative for any institution which aspires to become a university; for a university must try to teach every subject

FIGURE 1 Number of faculty in U.S. colleges, 1870–1900

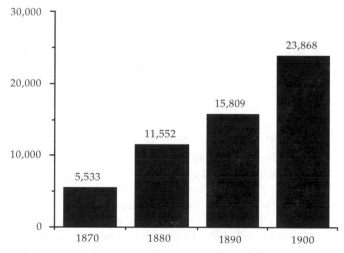

Source: Historical Statistics of the United States, Colonial Times to 1970, Series H 689–699.

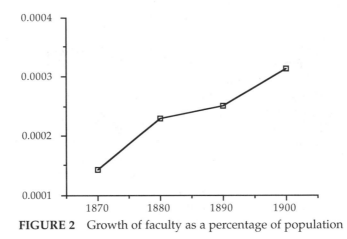

FIGURE 2   Growth of faculty as a percentage of population

. . . for which there is any demand; and to teach it thoroughly enough to carry the advanced student to the confines of present knowledge, and make him capable of original research.[5]

The last three decades of the nineteenth century were a time of expansion in the sheer number of subjects that were taught, and one subject for which there was an increasing demand was English—though it would take several attempts to satisfy the demand. As the *Atlantic Monthly* observed editorially in 1874, if nothing else the elective system at Harvard led to a "proportionate increase in the amount of instruction offered the students."[6]

Before leaving these figures, it may be worth remarking upon a coincidence. The two biggest jumps during the period—in the 1870s and again in the 1890s—correspond to the two stages of English's debut as a field of study. The 1870s were the decade of its separation from classical studies, when it appeared likely that philology would answer the demand that, if they were going to replace the classics, English writings would have to be "studied and analyzed" (as the president of the University of Missouri said at the very beginning of the decade) "with the same severe attention which is given to Greek and Latin classics."[7] The 1890s were the decade when an altogether different approach to English writing—something less severe, more creative—was installed in the curriculum.

While I don't mean to imply that the events are causally connected, I do want to suggest that each stage in the development of English as a field of study has been motivated and defined by demands for recognition on the part of faculty members for their own peculiar way of dividing up the field. English has surged forward by means of additions to the curriculum and not necessarily because of contributions to literary or linguistic knowledge; it has depended more upon the arguments that could be made on behalf of the new subjects than upon research and scholarship as such. Standards and definitions of what constitutes English work have counted for more than the quality of the work itself. To account for the development of English as a field of study—the emergence of philology, the seeding of the later growth known as creative writing—it is necessary and sufficient to see how the agents of that development constructed their arguments, how they defined their goals.

"English" first appeared in the Harvard catalogue to designate a separate course of study in 1868–1869, but the term had been used in American colleges before then, and for two antithetical purposes.[8] On one hand it denoted the embryonic form of modern literary study: a tiny portion of the curriculum devoted (at most) to lectures *about* English literature. On the other, it referred to a new and separate curriculum altogether, an early effort at expansion, a practical alternative to the Collegiate Course of classics and mathematics. Neither of these was English as we understand it today; neither provided a satisfactory conception of writing or criticism. Yet both were significant precedents, as much for what they lacked as for what they promised.

As a catchphrase in higher education, *English literature* dates from the earliest part of the nineteenth century. But though "English literature" was a part of professors' titles as early as the first quarter of the century, professors' duties did not include the teaching of English literature to any great extent or in any recognizable form. At the University of Kansas, for instance, a solitary professor taught grammar, composition, etymology, rhetoric, and early and modern literature, along with ancient, medieval, and modern European, and American history.[9] Under such a system, no one subject—especially not literature, cleaved roughly into early and modern sections—could receive much attention. More often than not it received no attention at all. As a student at Miami University in Ohio complained in 1850, "English literature was never alluded to, and the general impression among us was that nothing good had been written since Homer and Virgil."[10] At the same time, the term *English* was also used as a special name for a new alternative to Homer, Virgil, and the classical curriculum—the so-called "English course." Brown University, for example, announced in its catalogue of 1847–1848 that

> There has been established in the University, in connection with the regular Collegiate Course, an English and Scientific Course, designed for the benefit of those who do not propose to enter either of the learned professions, but who desire to prepare themselves, by a thorough education, for some of the more active employments of life.[11]

The English course spelled the doom of classical study. For as Frederick Rudolph has argued in his history of the American undergraduate curriculum, the new course was founded upon a confidence in scientific progress and practical utility, which entailed a shift from the study of the past to an absorption with the present.[12] Thus the new curriculum was one of the steps by which in the next century English would become the lingua franca of modern science and business. But the new course was significant for more than its reliance upon English as the language of instruction. Even more important was its implicit devaluation of historical learning and the classical authors. Although the English course was also known (here and there) as the literary course, in motive and design it was sharply opposed to the ancient ideal of literary education as founded upon the study of the classics.

As an academic term, then, *English* originally denoted two countervailing tendencies in American colleges. On the one hand it registered an institutional awareness that English might be as legitimate a subject for study and teaching as classical literature, capable of withstanding "the same severe attention." On the other hand it pointed away from literature altogether, toward "the more active employments of life." Although the two uses of the term are incompatible—a fact that helps to explain the incongruous course offerings of most English departments even today—there is some overlap. In both senses of the term, *English* implies modernity. It is one name under which the latest knowledge and some of the most pressing demands for adjustment to contemporary life have been brought to bear upon the curriculum.

Since so many professors' titles included English language and literature, it is not always easy to tell when the actual teaching of English began. Many schools must have been like Beloit College in Wisconsin, where the Rev. Henry J. Whitney initiated the teaching of English philology when he succeeded to the chair in rhetoric and English literature in 1871. Although Amherst had created a chair in rhetoric, oratory, and English literature in 1825, it did not set up a separate chair in English language and literature for another six decades—until 1889. When Michigan lost the literary historian Moses Coit Tyler, its professor of rhetoric and English literature, to Cornell in 1881, it appointed a successor to a renamed chair in English literature and rhetoric. These events punctuated a stretch of time during which English was put on a separate footing in many different places: Yale and Georgetown in 1870, Minnesota, Carleton, and Furman in 1874, South Carolina and Rutgers (with mining income donated by a Newark church) in 1880, Vanderbilt in 1881, Dartmouth and Kansas in 1882, the University of Texas upon its founding in 1883, Eastern Michigan in 1884, NYU in 1888 (after a benefactor had given $20,000 for the purpose), Penn State in 1889, and Brown in 1890. At Texas A&M, English was listed separately in the catalogue as early as 1877–1878, although literary study (such as it was) consisted wholly of the reading (in the junior year) of *Shaw's Complete Manual of English Literature*, a textbook that emphasized the lives of English authors (and not always accurately), followed by selections from Shakespeare and Milton in the senior year. At the University of Illinois, where in 1870 students had petitioned the Board of Trustees for a series of lectures on English literature, two-and-a-half decades later there were still only four courses in the subject to be taken: a general survey, Shakespeare, nineteenth-century poetry, and eighteenth-century prose.[13]

The basic outline of nineteenth-century English study (and its basic conservatism) may be illustrated by the curriculum at a school that was slower to change. As late as 1892, the English department at Muhlenberg College in Pennsylvania "begins its work"—the description is a contemporary's—"with simple, but fully illustrated, lectures upon the art of composition." The student then proceeds to the philology of the English language, with "selections from authors of the present century read for application of the principles learned. . . ." And finally English literature, in which a "series of carefully annotated text-books is studied, beginning with *Piers Plowman*, and Chaucer, and ending with Shakespeare and Milton."[14]

In this light it is perhaps easier to understand why English, when it was first established as a separate field in the 1870s and 1880s, originally meant the study of the English language. There was an increasing demand for something better than classical study, although few men (and fewer women) had been trained to teach the better thing. When students pressed for and governing boards decreed an alternative to the classical curriculum under the name of English, they seemed to have the study of literature vaguely in mind, although no one seemed to be very sure what the study of English literature might entail. What they got instead was linguistic study, for which a growing number of scholars had been trained by the second half of the century.

A comparison of two different schools' experience is instructive in this regard. When English was added to the curriculum at the University of Virginia in 1882, the Board of Visitors announced that the new course would concentrate upon four areas of study: (1) the structure of the language, (2) correctness in speech and writing, (3) principles of style "as disclosed by master-pieces of the English language," and (4) the history of the language. These remained the focus of the course for over a decade. Then in 1893 English literature was formally separated from linguistic study. And significantly enough, the incumbent professor of English—James M. Garnett—was reassigned at that time to the language side. The university's historian explains that Garnett's course in language and literature "had signally failed to win the popularity confidently expected of it," but the reason for its lack of popularity was probably Garnett's near total neglect of the literature side.[15]

Similarly, the Johns Hopkins University sought to promote the study of both literature and language. In 1875 it offered the chair in English to Francis J. Child, the Boylston Professor of Rhetoric and Oratory at Harvard; and this was one of the clearest indications that English had emerged from the shadow of rhetoric and oratory. For Child, whose wooing has been described as perhaps the first "outside offer" in academe, bargained for release from his duties as Boylston professor, and stayed on at Harvard as the first professor of English.[16]

Four years later Hopkins was still searching for its first English professor. University president Daniel Coit Gilman explained that he was looking for a "man who has both literary [and] philological aptitude—a future Child. . . ." And he would not settle for someone who neglected literature for the philology of the English language, although he was willing to consider someone who neglected philology. In 1879, the poet Sidney Lanier was appointed as a part-time lecturer on literature, a stint that resulted in *The Science of English Verse* (1880) and *The English Novel* (1883). This promising experiment was cut short when Lanier died in 1881. The next year Richard Watson Gilder (editor of the *Century*) suggested the hiring of another working writer. He observed that William Dean Howells had resigned as editor of the *Atlantic Monthly* the previous year and was unable to live on the earnings of his novels. Gilman liked the idea and offered Howells a three-year contract as full professor at $5000 to come and "awaken [at Hopkins] as much love of literature as there is of science." James Russell Lowell—who held a similar position at Harvard—urged against it, and though the offer was extended more than once, Howells steadfastly declined, saying "he desired to make his work as a writer his chief vocation." Next Gilman tried Robert Browning and Edmund Gosse without success. He wanted a man like Lowell or Matthew Arnold, he said, but they seemed to prefer "the freedom of their own libraries to the fetters of a professorship." Finally, in 1893, the university named its first professor of English. He was the university's own first Ph.D. in English, James W. Bright, who had originally been hired in 1884 as a part-time lecturer on Anglo-Saxon grammar. And if he did not have an aptitude for literature Bright seemed to be capable of philology, publishing classroom readers in Anglo-Saxon and Old English as well as editions of the Gospels in the medieval West Saxon dialect.[17]

A thirst for the study of literature (among university officers as well as students) may have created the demand for new chairs in English, but even where the duly appointed professor of English was popular his course was unlikely to satisfy the literary thirst. At Princeton, for example, the Rev. James O. Murray was named Holmes professor of belles lettres, English language, and literature in 1875. And though Murray was a well-liked instructor, his approach to the subject may be inferred from an enthusiastic student's comments. English literature under Murray, the student said,

> was a revelation to me. . . . I was not content merely to hear and read about the great writers; so far as my very busy life permitted, I read their works, which, of course, made the lectures doubly interesting.[18]

Like Murray, the early professors of English were content merely to lecture *about* literature—the actual reading of it was extracurricular. As a turn-of-the-century humanist said, looking back on his college years, "the study of things about literature left him no time to study literature itself. He was athirst and famished: literature, literature everywhere, and not a moment for it."[19]

English was established with confident expectations in the early 1870s, but by the early 1890s the confidence had begun to wane as the new subject failed to deliver on its implied promise of modernity and relevance. This was the period of English philology's reign, which may be dated almost exactly as stretching from 1871—when Hiram Corson was officially recognized as professor of English at Cornell (he marked the occasion by promptly writing an Anglo-Saxon handbook for use in his classes)—to 1889, when upon his urgent request Corson was finally released from having to teach the language.[20] During this period the study of language almost exclusively usurped the name of "English"; but what is more important, an ideal of scholarly research—scientific knowledge at the expense of aesthetic cultivation—was firmly implanted in the heart of the discipline. So even when the teaching of philology as such passed out of fashion, the philological ideal remained in force. But what *was* philology?

As Irving Babbitt observed in *Literature and the American College*, his 1908 attack on the literary curriculum, the term *philology* was "strangely elastic." Generally speaking it denoted what Babbitt described as the study of "the phenomenal relationships of language and literature." It was not the study of literature as such. It was, as the Corpus Professor of Latin Literature at Oxford observed in 1889, "really a subsidiary branch of history and philosophy." And though these might seem to be loose statements of approval or disapproval rather than precise definitions, a recent historian of scholarship goes along with them. The meaning of the term in the nineteenth century was vague, he says: "Rather than denoting a particular method or technique of analysis, it usually referred to a historical attitude toward language and written sources."[21]

The root of the confusion is that the term *philology* was made to do double duty. Sometimes it meant historical linguistics; at other times, something like cultural studies. As language study, philology saw itself as an exact science, standing among the *Naturwissenschaften* rather than as one of the *Geisteswissenschaften*: it was confident that, as the historian of linguistics Geoffrey Sampson puts it, "a 'language' must be some kind of entity which can be described objectively along with the rest of the furniture of the natural world." Linguistic (or comparative) philology was distinguished by method—the "comparative method" of describing linguistic change on the basis of resemblances between words in different languages—and so it was antispeculative and a posteriori, painstakingly accumulating data rather than theorizing from general principles. It was interested in literature (if at all) merely as a linguistic phenomenon, open to scientific explanation, rather than as a human utterance requiring interpretation.[22]

As cultural study, though, philology was almost precisely the opposite—historical and hermeneutic, seeking to understand rather than to explain. It was not particularly concerned with languages as such, treating them as mere repositories of culture. The ultimate objective of philology on this view was to trace the evolving "spirit" of a culture through its written works. The slippery and intangible notion of a culture (or its various substitutes, such as an age's "world picture" or a national "mind"), the conception of a more or less stable entity that exists apart from written works and yet can be reconstructed out of them, is itself philological in this sense of the term. Cultural philology—or classical philology, so called because it was inaugurated as an effort to gather all the remains of classical antiquity, literary and otherwise, into one learning—also believed itself to be a science. As a method, Anthony Grafton explains, it sought to "control all the evidence" necessary for a fully contextualized understanding of written works. From this angle the philological ideal might be defined, in Grafton's words, as "read[ing] literary documents historically, in the light of the situation, needs, and values of their original audience."23

By the next century the two senses of "philology" had broken off and migrated into separate disciplines. Comparative philology developed into modern linguistics, although under the pressure of its neopositivistic and scientific ideal it exchanged historical and textual study for the structural analysis of speech. Classical philology developed into modern literary scholarship with its emphasis upon the restoration, in one form or another, of a total framework for understanding—a thick description of literary backgrounds, if you will. Even in the nineteenth century, however, these contradictory impulses were apparent. In the first volume of the *American Journal of Philology* (1880), William Dwight Whitney of Yale described the study of language and literature as being in a state of semi-chaos. Different scholars approached their subject in logically inconsistent ways. And though few were as clearsighted as he in observing it, Whitney noted the problem was that the very word *language* was susceptible to being used in logically inconsistent ways:

> we use [it] to signify, on the one hand, the capacity or complex of capacities, a part of our endowment as human beings, whereby we are enabled to acquire, use, modify, and make spoken expression of our thoughts; and, on the other hand, any one of the existing bodies of signs and modes of their employment, established methods of expression, habits of speech.24

From which it follows that study can go forward either into language as a mode of expression or into language as an existing body of signs. In the nineteenth century, *both* of these studies were called "philology," even if they were logically incompatible. What seems to have happened is that, despite its historical associations with the science of language per se as it was originally set on foot in Germany in the second decade of the century by such scholars as Franz Bopp and Jacob Grimm, the term *philology* was retained even when scholarly interest began to drift from language into literature.25 The term merely shifted its meaning without freeing itself of its linguistic connotations. According to a twentieth-century linguist who wished to banish it from his discipline, "philology" was esoteric when used to signify literary and cultural study; it was "the mark of a professional dialect; not even the official terminology of our Universities was affected by it."26 There was no other word, however, for what literary scholars thought they were doing.

In short, philology was the study of literature in the name of linguistic science. What is more, "language" and "science" were the slogans of American philology, despite the fact that it was not really interested in language as a sign-system and did not closely resemble a natural science. The words were the keys to philology's self-understanding, although its redefinition of them—to say nothing of how it conceived of literature under their influence—committed philology to principles that were ultimately difficult to explain and defend.

"Science" referred to the Germanic ideal of systematic research in a subject as opposed to desultory reading. And in Germany the research ideal was operating in the disciplines of classical and comparative philology long before there was anything like the modern sciences of physics, biology, chemistry, or geology. In America, philology assisted the "Germanization" of higher education in the 1880s, a process that was characterized by the establishment of graduate study and fellowships, the seminar as a form of teaching, peer-reviewed scholarly publication, and national scholarly associations. These changes had a profound effect on professors in several fields, who increasingly began to identify themselves with a discipline instead of a campus, redefining their chief task as research (not teaching) and making the esteem of their peers (not the achievement of a local reputation) the mark of professional success.27 If anyone asked whether such a system turned out anything of importance (as the University of Wisconsin classicist Grant Showerman sardonically recalled),

> Every truth was important, he was told, and the slightest contribution to knowledge a legacy of inestimable value, whatever its apparent insignificance; and besides, this was the way it was done in Germany. He soon learned that the appeal to Germany was considered final, and even made use of it himself when it came handy.28

The appeal to Germany was indistinguishable from the appeal to "science" or "knowledge" or "research" or "scholarship." For the philologist, these were self-evident goods.

A telling example of how the linguistic and scientific appeals were brought together in the rhetoric of American philology is to be found in the thinking of Johns Hopkins's Basil Gildersleeve, founder of the *American Journal of Philology*. Gildersleeve coined the term "historico-philological science" to describe his field, maintaining that despite the arguments of some—including his colleague W. D. Whitney—philology *was* a science. The difference between natural science and "historico-philological science" was not to be located in their methods, because each relied upon experimentation, the verification of research, the certainty of results, and the exclusion of error. "The difference," Gildersleeve said, "is simply in the material." Natural science is the exact study of natural phenomena; historico-philological science is the exact study of the works of man. For Gildersleeve the crucial difference was between those who studied the same literary material in two different ways: *littérateurs* (in his sneering term) versus philologists. The first were florists; the second were botanists. The "florist's conception of literature," Gildersleeve said, is that "aesthetic charm" is the prime determinant, the value that qualifies a text for classification as literature. In truth, however, "aesthetic charm is beside the question." For a working definition of their subject, all that honest students of literature are "to insist on is the conservation of verbal groups by a voluntary act of the individual or of society. . . ." In other words, literature is a historical accident; its substance is to be found not in its aesthetic value but in its verbal nature. And to insist that only the aesthetically charming be known and read is to abridge the knowledge of literature arbitrarily. On the philological showing, literature is the merely accidental remains of a historical process of language change. "One undeniable effect of linguistic study," Gildersleeve noted—one consequence of calling literary study philology—"has been the widening of the term 'literature.' "29

The scientific bias of philology made it possible to exclude an aesthetic appreciation of literature from the university study of English. And the main reason, according to a recent feminist scholar, is that science sounded masculine, while literature hinted at femininity, softness, emotionalism, passivity. On this view philology was "a powerful tool for effecting [a] defeminization of literary study. . . . [T]he philologists' impassioned creation and defense of a 'science' of English was a particularly effective way of establishing its 'hardness' and dispelling the aura of the feminine that clung to the subject."30 There is much to be said for such an explanation. In its rhetorical effect, Gildersleeve's division of literary study into botany and flower arranging lends credence to it. But it is not the whole of the story. There is also a philosophical principle involved, which can be grasped whether or not one approves of it.

As a principled approach to the study of literature, philology seeks completeness rather than selection. This is implied by the very name. As Curtius shows in *European Literature and the Latin Middle Ages*, for the medieval Schoolmen *philologia* meant something like "all knowledge."31 When specifically narrowed to literary study, the philological ideal continues to imply knowledge of the whole of a literature—as when, in "The Idea of an 'English School,' " C. S. Lewis explicitly calls for a historical and national curriculum founded upon the knowledge of everything that has ever been written in England, as opposed to a curriculum in literature in general, founded upon a selection of masterpieces. In a characteristically memorable analogy, Lewis compares the curricula to two styles of tourism:

> In the one you turn the young out into a single, untidy country to make what they can of it; in the other you take them to what their elders think the five or six most interesting places in a whole continent. It is the difference between knowing, say, Worcestershire inside out, while remaining ignorant of the rest of the world, and knowing four or five European capitals while striking no roots in any single European soil.[32]

Here are two alternative conceptions of literary study. But if the one is philological, the other (as Lewis makes clear by immediately citing Matthew Arnold's axiom "the best that has been known and said in the world") is founded upon *criticism*. It is important to bear this in mind. Criticism was the sworn enemy of philology and, in seeking to depose it, would eventually join forces with another enemy of philology—creative writing (see Chapter 6). Critics argued that the philological ideal of completeness in literary study does not really solve the problem of selection so much as conceal it, because philology never addresses itself to the question of what literature distinctively is. For the philologist, literature is simply *everything* that has been known and said in the world. There is no way, though, to teach everything. In a literary curriculum organized upon philological premises, then, there must be a practical expedient—a rough-and-ready method of selection—for reducing the whole of literature to manageable proportions. And the time-honored methods have been those of the national canon, the major figures, the historical period, and the chronological survey, each of which (as our own day has rediscovered) raises more problems than it solves.

Despite arguments to the contrary, the philological model of literary study is founded upon selection, not completeness. And from one angle its principle of selection appears just as arbitrary, just as open to question, as that of a curriculum built upon a critical selection of masterpieces. Although his rhetoric may have obscured it, Gildersleeve struck closer to the heart of the matter when he distinguished philologists from *littérateurs*—scholars from critics, as his opponents would say—by defining the former as those "who insist on knowing what the letter means before they let themselves be carried away by the spirit."[33] The distinction between letter and spirit, fact and value, semantic meaning and aesthetic transport—the hostility of positivism to idealism—is what was more genuinely at issue in the dispute between philologists and their opponents. Given that any literary curriculum is a selection of everything that has been known and said (in the world, in a single, untidy country, even in a multinational language like English), what shall be the basis and objective of study? Philology took the side of letter, fact, and science, curling its lip at the mention of spirit, value, and art.

It was precisely this emphasis in philology upon linguistic fact at the expense of literary value that awakened opposition to it. In a Phi Beta Kappa address, the Rev. Phillips Brooks of Trinity Church in Boston (the author of "O Little Town of Bethlehem") warned that "That which is a lofty ambition when it deals with large, living things—the love of facts as facts—becomes but miserable pedantry and dilettantism when it comes to waste itself on little dead trifles." Its apologists might reply that philology trained students of literature in a discipline of mind, but Brooks was not convinced. By this phrase, he said, "we all now understand something more than the discipline of the memory by roots and conjugations."[34] And at times philology appeared to be little more than that. According to a student who had been introduced to literature by its means in the 1870s at Harvard, the philological method was "to scrutinize every syllable [of a literary text] with a care undisturbed by consideration of any more of the context than was grammatically related to it."[35] What is more, philological study commenced with the earliest English literature, starting as far back as Anglo-Saxon, said another Harvard man,

> apparently on the ground that the earlier the English the purer and better worth knowing it is, and the more barren the literature the less probability that a student will be diverted by some literary *ignis fatuus* from the study of the forms of words.[36]

Students were unlikely to be diverted from the study of words, especially if they were worried about what was going to be on the exam. A typical English examination from the University of South Carolina in 1874, for example, put to students the following six problems:

> (1) What is English Grammar?
> (2) Define a sentence and give an example. What must every sentence contain?
> (4) Give the feminine of *hero*. Compare *full*.
> (6) Parse the following sentence: "The accusing angel flew up to Heaven's chancery with the oath, and blushed as he gave it in."[37]

Even when literature and not the study of words was the announced subject of a course in English, it was likely to be reduced to what could be accounted for in exact linguistic terms. Even philology's friends admitted as much. Louise Pound, a founder of the American Dialect Society who taught at the University of Nebraska, recalled a seminar in Chaucer she had taken from Professor George Hempl while a graduate student at the University of Michigan. "I do not recall that Chaucer's poetry loomed large in the course," she said, "save as regards his pronunciation."[38] If this marked the upper limit of philological teaching, the lower reaches were not far below. Undergraduate teachers of literature, touched by the philological mood if not trained in the philological method, travestied the scientific ideal, substituting factual accuracy for exact knowledge. In 1888 a newcomer to English recalled how she had been instructed in literature a decade before:

> A small biographical history of literature served for a textbook and an interrogation mark for a teacher. The lesson was so many hard dry facts—dates, names, and titles—all to be piled up in the memory like bricks. Even the day of the month of the author's birth and death, no matter how unimportant his work might be, must be carefully memorized. The titles of all the works each writer had composed, with the dates of publication, must be religiously committed to memory. Great emphasis was laid upon such good mouth-filling names as *Areopagitica*, *Novum Organum*, or the *Leviathan*. That these words might mean anything or contain ideas which we could understand never once dawned on us. Why one man was called a better writer than another we made no attempt to find out. We memorized the opinion of our textbook with painstaking accuracy, and that always satisfied the question mark.[39]

The philologically colored teacher could be identified by his attention to words and facts at the expense of ideas. In one account—perhaps it is apocryphal, but it captures the popular image of the philologist—a teacher's practice was to call upon his students to read aloud from the work of a great poet, stopping them at certain words to trace the etymologies. One day in class a student looked up from his reading to ask, "What does this mean, sir?" "Mean?" the teacher roared. "It means what it says!"[40]

Their opponents charged that the philologists were not merely bad teachers but worse writers; terrible models for students of literature. The critic Brander Matthews catalogued the literary sins of philological scholarship: it contained "endless quotations and endless citations and endless references"; the essential facts were "entangled with a heterogeny of other facts," encumbering pleasure and comprehension; the argument was handed over to "the least important technical details," shamelessly indulging a taste for "interminable controversy over minor questions"; and the ruling assumption was that every reader of a scholarly text had an "acquaintance with the preceding stages of the discussion." Their own literary practices suggested the extent to which philologists neglected any consideration of such problems as style and form. The philological study of literature, critics charged, had little to do with judgment or expression. It was a mere heaping up of facts, and fact-gathering (as the essayist Barrett Wendell pointed out) did nothing to awaken the critical faculty. As students of literature, Wendell said, "Our true task is not one of accumulation but of synthesis, of philosophy."[41]

Under the influence of philology, literature was studied and taught as a source of knowledge about language—or, at best, as factual backgrounds

to reading—but not as itself a ground and context for synthesis and judg
ment. Linguistic, historical, and biographical facts were treated as prior to
literature and therefore given. Any treatment of a literary text as something
created rather than determined, a transcript of individual choices and not a
specimen of larger forces, was left out of account. As a consequence, literary
education under the auspices of nineteenth-century philology contributed
little to students' experience of literature as such, abandoning them to their
own devices (or to trust to luck) in developing themselves as critics and writers, stumbling along and falling short of what they might have been *taught*
to do. "American education pays little heed to aesthetic and spiritual cultivation," complained the poet Katharine Lee Bates, who taught at Wellesley.
The literary spirit had departed the collegiate life, said a New York University professor; it had been killed by the methods of "the philological
dissector"; and "discipline," he lamented, had "taken the place of inspiration."[42]

The opposition of philology to the literary spirit might almost be described as one of the central myths of nineteenth-century American literature. Emily Dickinson retells it in a poem that reflects upon the writing of
poetry.[43]

> Shall I take thee, the Poet said
> To the propounded word?
> Be stationed with the Candidates
> Till I have finer tried—
>
> The Poet searched Philology
> And when about to ring
> For the suspended Candidate
> There came unsummoned in—
>
> That portion of the Vision
> The Word applied to Fill
> Not unto nomination
> The Cherubim reveal—

On one level, this little poem is merely a restatement of the Platonic
theory of poetic inspiration in terms of Hebrew prophecy—a commonplace
since Sidney's *Apologie*. On another level, though, it is a shrewd complaint
about the direction in which literary thinking was headed in the nineteenth
century. Distinguishing between philology's handling of words and poetry's, Dickinson suggests it is not the attention to words as such that, *pace*
its critics, makes philology of little use to someone whose primary interest is
in poetry. Poetry too addresses itself to words, but subordinates them to vision. The difference lies in their mode of handling them—the different ways

in which poetry and philology modify words in the handling of them. For philology words are material; they are "Candidates" that are nominated to a ready-and-waiting office. Dickinson's pun on "nomination" is itself philological, implying that the grammatical procedure by which a word becomes a noun is far different from the means by which a vision is revealed. For poetry words are ideal, hinting at the existence of a realm *hors de texte*. A naive view perhaps, it suggests that for the nineteenth-century American poet language was anything but a prison-house.

And this is the view that clings to the center of the argument for replacing philology with a species of literary education that is more visionary, or perhaps more creative. The argument opens with Emerson's 1837 Phi Beta Kappa address "The American Scholar," which apparently contributed the phrase "creative writing" to the language. It is not immediately clear what Emerson means by the phrase: "There is then creative reading as well as creative writing," he says.[44] But the context of the passage is significant, because it introduces not merely the phrase but also the terms by which creative writing will be discussed for decades to come. What Emerson is doing when he comes to utter the famous remark is building a case for creative learning, and to clarify what he means he characterizes with scorn the work of academic literary scholars, "the restorers of readings, the emendators, the bibliomanics of all degrees." Although he does not explicitly name them, the philologists deserve a place on this list. Academic scholarship, or so Emerson implies, is the polar opposite of creative activity.

In *Emerson's Fall*, her 1982 reinterpretation of the essays, Barbara L. Packer insists that "what Emerson is really concerned with has nothing to do with scholarship."[45] But in fact the case for creative learning—Emerson's figure of Man Thinking—positively demands an attack upon academic scholarship; that is its essential precondition. In scholarship, Emerson says, "[t]he sacredness which attaches to the act of creation, the act of thought, is transferred to the record." It is the mind embodied in any great literary text that makes it great, but instead of paying respect to the mind by studying the creative activity of which the text is a mere record, scholarship sanctifies the record, treating it like a holy relic. Thus in scholarship creation yields ground to reason, upon which colleges are built. The first lesson of creative learning is freedom of mind and the independence from received opinion upon which such freedom is based. By contrast, the fundamental principle of academic learning—its ground plan, to speak in Emersonian terms—is the uncritical acceptance of other men's views. In their published writings, accomplished scholars "set out from accepted dogmas, not from their own sight of principles"; young scholars, training themselves for a life in the stacks, "believ[e] it their duty to accept the views which Cicero, which Locke, which Bacon, have given."[46]

Despite his own unhappy experience as an undergraduate at Harvard, Emerson was not unforgiving toward the college as an institution. The academic regimen, he said charitably at the beginning of his address, is a "sign of the survival of the love of letters amongst a people too busy to give to letters any more."[47] But as the sole institution devoted to literature in a nation busily trading and making money, the college was simply insufficient (he believed) to found and sustain the uniquely American literature that cultural nationalists were calling for. Something more was needed. What Emerson sought in "The American Scholar," as Stanley Cavell argues, was to persuade his listeners of two things: first, that literature demands a labor of its own; and second, that this special form of labor has not been adequately accounted for, either by academic scholars or by busy tradesmen. A genuine devotion to literature—the labor of creative learning—demands a *break* with scholarship and practical concerns. It depends upon a recognition that, although we may profess a love for literature, neither in the college nor the marketplace are we yet engaged in the *creation* of literature.[48]

On this showing, the usual interpretation put on Emerson's use of the word *creative*—it is a synonym for "original" or "nonimitative"—now seems unduly restrictive. Emerson appears to conceive of "creative reading as well as creative writing" as a third way of thinking that is distinguished from rationalistic, fact-gathering scholarship on the one hand and the conventions of day-to-day behavior (including money, "the prose of life," as he calls it elsewhere) on the other. Emerson is not always consistent when he describes the two opposing modes of experience, inveighing sometimes against tradition and historicism (as in the opening paragraph of *Nature*), at other times against a scientific naturalism that is unable to transcend time and space because it is dependent on them. The general pattern of his thought is clear enough, though. By "creative reading as well as creative writing" Emerson means that reading as well as writing is a creative activity because it entails an active working through and not merely the passive reception of a text. Not only is it an ontological mistake to assume that the contents of a text are given rather than constructed; it is a moral failing to accept the contents of a text without struggling to master them. Interpretation cannot be abstracted from production without loss; true scholars *create* knowledge in the process of acquiring it, not in the economic sense of producing a commodity (scholarship) with exchange value, but rather in the sense that something new has been brought into the world—a distinct and individual understanding that did not exist before, even if the text that is newly understood is itself quite old—something that is lost if the text is assumed to be merely given and accepted as such. As a theory of literature, this postulates an outside-the-text, a transcendental frontier of understanding that is constantly pushing beyond texts. Instead of imagining the human spirit as a material signifier lost in a cosmos of textuality, Emerson thinks of the text as continually being reabsorbed into the realm of spirit. In a "creative" literary education, then, the study of literature is subordinated to something higher—the incessant creation and re-creation of literature. The literary act, not the literary record, is the basis and objective of study.

So the case for creative writing begins with the objection of idealism to positivistic literary scholarship. Speaking for many who shared his belief, Grant Showerman said: "I am objecting to the fraud of a system which treats the most important of the humanities as if it were the most material instead of the most spiritual of subjects. . . ."[49] Under the system of philological scholarship, literature was treated as a stockpile of raw materials for study—an uninspiring approach that impressed its critics as having isolated the study of literature from the human experience. At best, philological scholars were satisfied merely to understand literature without asking themselves how anyone had ever used it. They did not conceive of literature as the most important of the humanities, because they did not put their minds to the question of what literature is *for*. They studied the outside shell, not the thing itself. Although it arose in the nineteenth century as a counteractive to the classics, English did not improve the teaching of literature in American colleges and universities; or not at first. It was motivated by a different drive altogether: the scholarly drive to extract and systematize the knowledge contained in the English literary record.

Literary scholarship starts from the reception of texts—reception is its first principle—and for this reason it stresses accumulation, thoroughness, exactitude, connections between text and language or text and culture. And these positivistic ideals have never lost their attractiveness for scholars in English. The opposition of philologists to *littérateurs*—of fact to value, letter to spirit, scholarly discipline to aesthetic cultivation—was not settled with the slow decline and eventual disappearance of philology by the time of the Second World War and the concurrent rise of creative writing. While literary scholarship has oscillated between scientific explanation and hermeneutic understanding, it has remained distinct from—even opposed to—the ideology of the aesthetic. A devotion to literature has aroused suspicion (and stirred contempt) on the part of literary scholars for a hundred years and more.

And for nearly as long this has struck devotees of literature as a very strange attitude. In their view literary scholarship could never explain how anyone had created a work of literature in the first place. For them any discussion of literature must begin with the acknowledgment that it is not an object of study but an occasion for astonishment and delight; not to be known merely, but to be created and re-created. Philip Larkin once gave vent to such an attitude when an interviewer asked him what he had learned from his study of the English poets. "Oh, for Christ's sake," Larkin replied, "one doesn't *study* poets! You *read* them, and think, That's marvellous, how is it done, could I do it? and that's how you learn."[50] Scholars have treated literature as if no one were ever going to do it again. And in this way (their critics charged) they have severed the literary record from the literary act. A different sort of literary education was called for—something less scholarly, more creative. The English department was the best home for such an education, because from the beginning of its history as a field of university study English had implied up-to-dateness, relevance to students' lives, the devaluation of historical learning and classical authors. Philology failed to deliver on this implied promise. So late in the nineteenth century a rising generation of English teachers—represented by some of the most prominent critics of philology, including Barrett Wendell, Brander Matthews, and Katharine Lee Bates—sought to carve up the field in a different way. They did so by adding a new subject to the English curriculum. This is where the next chapter begins.

Chapter 2

❧ *The Founding of English Composition*

Early in the nineteenth century, Emerson had hoped the American college would somehow transform itself into an institution that was genuinely devoted to creative writing as well as creative reading. Half a century later, nothing of the sort had happened. The colleges did not seem interested in original literature. As a Chautauqua lecturer noted in 1891,

> With few exceptions, the men who have made American literature what it is have been college graduates. And yet our colleges have not commonly been, in themselves, literary centers. . . . Even in the older and better equipped universities the faculty is usually a corps of working scholars, each man intent upon his specialty and rather inclined to undervalue merely "literary" performance. In many cases the fastidious and hypercritical turn of mind which besets the scholar, the timid conservatism which naturally characterizes an ancient seat of learning, and the spirit of theological conformity which suppresses free discussion, have exerted their benumbing influence upon the originality and creative impulse of their inmates. . . . The professors of literature in our colleges are usually persons who have made no additions to literature, and the professors of rhetoric seem ordinarily to have been selected to teach students how to write for the reason that they themselves have never written anything that any one has ever read.[1]

In the nineteenth century the American campus was less a literary center than a seat of literary learning. The scholarly examination of literature had dampened the impulse to create it. The scholars themselves were anything but literary men. And the professors who were hired to teach writing were not much better. The study of literature—creative reading as well as creative writing—was divided between a fastidious and hypercritical scholarship on the one hand and a rhetoric that was distant from the genuine creation of literature on the other.

Scholarship was divorced from practice, and behind the breakup was a corrupt view. To borrow Gilbert Ryle's distinction: the conception of literature as a knowledge *that* (as represented by philological scholarship) was cut off from any conception of it as a knowledge *how*.[2] Literature was approached as an order of hard dry facts (or, by later scholars who shared the philological assumption often without being aware of it, it was approached as a banquet of rich meanings) abstracted from any recognition or mastery of the skills by which meanings are formulated and facts given value. Under the influence of philology, literature was not conceived as a means of saying anything. Even where the official slogan was "the best that has been thought and said in the world," it was not taught as what might *yet* be thought and said.

The constructivist approach to literature—if I may now begin to use that term—was neglected. Nowhere was literature studied, as urged by one advocate, in such a way that "the mind [of the student] must reproduce in some measure the processes and fundamental mood of the creative mind."[3] Nowhere was it studied as a discipline in itself that could enable its students, if they possessed the necessary talent, to *do* something in literature. Even where it assumed a place in the curriculum, the higher study of literature did not include writing for its own sake or any account of the processes of mind by which literature is constructed. The constructive aspect of literature was the province of rhetoric. But rhetoric was not literature. As one teacher observed, looking back on her college days, literature and rhetoric

> were taught as distinct branches. One was an account of the lives of literary men; the other was a summary of conclusions as to good usage of language, based on their writings. Neither was, properly speaking, a study of literature. From a literary standpoint, neither was of much value, and the latter was almost devoid of educational value.[4]

The story of creative writing began with the opposition to philology and resumes with the effort in the 1880s and 1890s to restore literary and educational value to the teaching of rhetoric. The effort was sufficiently organized to be called the New English in some quarters. Searching for a New English—an alternative to scholarly unconcern with literature as a creative act—the opponents of philology turned to rhetoric. Finding the old subject in disrepair, they rebuilt it from the ground up; and they renamed it English composition.

What now passes for composition in American higher education is a heterogeneous, even amorphous field, but its subsequent career should not be permitted to obscure its initial singleness of purpose. English composition was the first widely successful attempt to offer instruction in writing in English not merely as an insignificant and subordinate part of the college curriculum but (in the words of its chief founder) as a "thing apart." It was formulated at Harvard in the last quarter of the century out of a constructivist belief that the ideal end of the study of literature is the making of literature. And as such it was, an observer noted a few years later, "only the first of a long line of demands for literary fluency."[5] Indeed the subsequent heterogeneity of composition can largely be explained as the result of success-ful attacks on it for being *too* literary—something less elitist (as we would now say) was called for. By that time, however, the demand for literary flu-ency was already beginning to be satisfied by creative writing. English com-position established the autonomy of college writing and created a demand for courses in writing from a literary and constructivist point of view. And these were necessary preconditions of creative writing's acceptance as a sub-ject of serious study. Until about the 1920s, though, there was small need for creative writing per se, because English composition and creative writing were one and the same thing. Creative writing only arose as a distinct sub-ject when, under attack, English composition was redeployed to other than literary ends. The former might even be described as a reappearance of the latter under a more distinctive literary banner and oriented toward compo-sition's original (but increasingly abandoned) goal.

The name of English composition had occasionally been used before the 1880s, but the composition that was previously taught in American col-leges was entirely different from the subject that assumed its name. Throughout much of the century, "composition" was normally understood as referring to Latin composition. And it was normally conceived as a lesson in the study of Latin. A student wrote a paper to apply the rules of gram-mar—or, at best, the principles of order and style learned in his reading of the classical authors—and occasionally he even wrote in English. But his purpose was the same as if he had written in Latin. The motive in writing was to demonstrate mastery of the language. Writing as such was subordi-nated to grammatical exercises, spelling drills, and the memorization of rhetorical precepts. Even when writing was the main focus of the course, the qualities sought in student compositions were correctness, neatness, promptness, accuracy, and completeness of treatment. Students were not en-couraged to risk their ideas or imaginations in a venture of writing, but merely to avoid errors. In this way, complained one observer, "composition is made the basis of language study. . . ."[6]

The new English composition was a continuation of rhetorical study only in the sense that it built upon the institutional foundations of rhetoric, elbowing into the place that rhetoric had carved out for writing instruction in the American college. Otherwise there was little about the new composi-tion that could be described as traditionally rhetorical. It was not concerned with the tropes, persuasion, the social context of discourse, seeking a practi-cal result, or the traditional subdivisions of invention, order, style, memory, and delivery. In fact English composition might be termed (if it were not so ugly a term) the constructivization of writing instruction, entailing a rejec-tion of the typical classroom practices associated with rhetoric in the nine-teenth-century American college. First it did away with handbooks of usage and therefore with the emphasis upon correctness and then it did away with oral delivery and therefore with the emphasis upon communication. English composition was not merely the old college rhetoric under an improved, up-to-date label. It was the creation of a new discipline altogether.

English composition was a literary reformation of rhetoric. In *Nineteenth-Century Rhetoric in North America*, Nan Johnson says something similar, arguing that much of the century's rhetorical theory was founded on the "belletristic assumption that to acquire critical insight is to achieve greater mastery over discourse and a deeper aptitude for the profound. . . ." What is more, the belletristic assumption encouraged a "comprehensive definition of rhetoric," Johnson says, expanding its field from the arts of argument and public speaking to the more literary kinds of discourse.7 To be even plainer: English composition was the name under which a belletristic conception of rhetorical study—or what I am calling constructivism—was institutionalized in American higher education. And it was belletristic in conceiving of writing rather than oratory as the efficient cause of discourse, and expression rather than correctness as the final cause.

Thus the shift to the new composition involved two significant institutional changes. First, the practice of assigning the subjects of student papers was dropped. And second, the new compositions were never declaimed aloud in class. Under the old system, students were asked to organize their thoughts on such questions as "Can the Immortality of the Soul Be Proven?" or "Whether the Soul Always Thinks." Under the new system, a genre or certain techniques might be assigned, but the subjects of their papers were left up to the students. To cast this in the traditional terms of rhetoric, *invention* was not taught in the new composition course; it was considered a matter of individual taste and talent, a practical concession to the romantic doctrine of creative genius. Correctness and assigned themes were accordingly de-emphasized; what was encouraged was original work. Moreover, since the new compositions were never declaimed, the traditional rhetorical problems of *memory* and *delivery* also disappeared. Writing and not speech became the customary discourse situation.

It is not surprising that the origins of speech instruction belong to the same period as the rise of the new composition, beginning in the late 1870s as noncredit courses in Kansas and Missouri colleges and spreading by the early 1890s to the regular curriculum in other parts of the country.8 As I argued in Chapter 1, the partitioning off of literary and linguistic study from oratory, under pressure from philology, split the art of discourse into two halves. And it was perhaps inevitable that the early partisans of speech education should feel a certain hostility to literary discourse, which had usurped the chair of rhetoric. "One of the great mistakes in rhetorical training," said Henry Allyn Frink, professor of logic, rhetoric, and public speaking at Amherst, "has been the failure to make the necessary distinctions" between writing to be prepared for oral delivery and the "purely literary type":

> Literature proper which appeals to the thought, the imagination, the sensibilities, simply through the eye, is but slightly subject to the rules of rhetoric. The essential elements of literary power and beauty are indefinable, illusive; and are not to be communicated by formal instruction.[9]

In the next century this would be routinely offered as if it were a knockdown argument against creative writing: Writing cannot be taught. Any such argument merely plays a variation on the late classical aphorism "poets are born, not made," which earlier in the nineteenth century had received the blessing of science in the British eugenicist Sir Francis Galton's assertion of the principle of "hereditary genius."[10] "Genius," "imagination," "power"— these were the watchwords of essentialism; they were invoked to conceal the neglect of the purely literary in education. They were also words that tended to be used, at least in literary thought, in connection with the adjective *creative* (see Chapter 5). From early on the new composition took the opposite side. It was understood as the teaching of literary composition (or what would now be called creative writing); it embodied a constructivist and anti-essentialist view of literature, believing that "power" and "beauty" were not given but obtainable; and it was resented on this basis. If resented, though, it was also defended on this basis. "At last," said one defender, "it has occurred to some that it might be a good plan to set pupils to writing, and make the subject they were trying to teach the subject of instruction."[11] The partisans of oratory were correct: the new writing instruction was not rhetoric but something else entirely, because it did away with everything else except instruction in pure writing.

And one thing it did away with was formal rhetoric, as represented by textbooks of precept and usage. Students, it was felt, ought to express themselves "first-hand, without the intervention of books."[12] So writing teachers were urged to "[a]bolish all such extraneous helps as language lessons, manuals and hand-books of rhetoric and composition. If you cannot make up your minds to do this," rapped the principal of Boston Girls' High School, with no trace of irony, "you are still in the bonds of iniquity."[13] The new composition was an effort to recover the original conditions for writing—a writer facing up alone to the question of what he or she has to say—which may have set the first rhetorical theorists to reflecting, but which had been increasingly lost sight of as rhetoric developed into a massive superstructure of theory and dogma. Gertrude Buck—a leading figure in the New English and a historian and theorist of literary criticism at Vassar—put the case succinctly:

> The precepts of formal rhetoric as a guide to writing have been discredited and abandoned, the art of composition in our schools has been conditioned more naturally by a real occasion for writing and a real audience to be addressed, such theory as must be involved in the criticism of the student's writing has grown steadily less complex and dogmatic because springing more directly from the writing itself; in short, the tendency of every recent reform in

composition teaching has been to free the student's act of writing from all artificial conditions, and to substitute for these such conditions as accompany a genuine act of writing outside of the classroom.[14]

The promoters of the New English disliked formal rhetoric because they believed that it neglected the practice of writing in favor of its theory. "No amount of theoretical work," asserted one composition teacher, "can give an intelligent appreciation of the principles of literary art." The art of literature is only to be known from within, by practicing it. What was wanted was a bringing together of theory and practice—"a development of the one out of the other. . . ."[15] And this was the goal of English composition.

English composition has been recognized before now as a precedent for creative writing. It has long been known that the Harvard composition staff—Adams Sherman Hill, Barrett Wendell, Le Baron Briggs, Charles Townsend Copeland—would occasionally accept poems and stories for credit in their classes. According to Wallace Stegner, who himself founded the program at Stanford, creative writing

> began with Dean Le Baron Russell Briggs of Harvard, who early in the century began teaching a class that required a daily theme. (Those were the hard old days, before rigor was relaxed.) Many, many American writers came out of Dean Briggs' class. . . . Charles Townsend Copeland, also at Harvard, followed Dean Briggs' lead. Between the two, they must have trained half the American writers of their time.

The facts are more complicated; my purpose is to say how. For the moment, though, the important point to make is that the debt to Harvard belongs to creative writing's autobiography, the discipline's understanding of itself. The debt may have been given currency by John Reed's dedication of his 1914 book *Insurgent Mexico* to Copeland, which can be interpreted as an acknowledgment that Copeland taught him how to write. Others who studied under Copeland included Conrad Aiken, John Dos Passos, Alan Seeger, Robert Benchley, Bernard De Voto, Walter D. Edmonds, John P. Marquand, and Van Wyck Brooks. Departing slightly from Stegner, Aiken credited Copeland (not Briggs) with being the founder of creative writing. The question of who exactly deserves thanks for being the founder is of less significance than the general recognition that someone at Harvard deserved thanks for getting creative writing started.[16]

At Harvard, it may be said, creative writing was accepted for academic credit in an American university for the first time. The claim is valid—so far as it goes. Yet the facts have been misinterpreted if what is being inferred from them is that the founders of creative writing acted upon the hint of earlier teachers and elaborated it into a full-blown system. The literary form of the writing that is done in creative writing classes is not what gives the discipline its distinctiveness. The name *creative writing* came to be extended as a term for a certain kind of writing—poems and stories, fiction in general—because the academic discipline of writing was sharply differentiated from philological research and thus from the specific type of nonfiction that was produced (and esteemed) by the name *scholarship*. But the key is that it was differentiated from literary scholarship. English composition cleared the road for creative writing not in accepting poems and stories as academic work but in showing that literature could be used in the university for some other purpose than scholarly research.

Although it did not acquire the impetus and notoriety of an educational movement until later, English composition may be traced if not *ab ovo* then to the appointment of the thirty-five-year-old Charles W. Eliot as president of Harvard in 1869. Eliot's inaugural address sounded the trumpet for an awakening of English studies. The American university, Eliot said, is "literally centuries behind the precept of the best thinkers upon education. A striking illustration can be found in the prevailing neglect of the systematic study of the English language."[17] Not one to recommend a reform without seeing it through, Eliot nominated Harvard's first full-time instructor of English composition in 1872; and for the academic year 1873–1874 Harvard adopted its first entrance requirement in English.

Harvard composition grew out of a displeasure with the older way of teaching writing. And this took two forms. On one hand (as we have seen) rhetoric and oratory themselves were rejected by the new teachers of composition. But on the other hand, the displeasure was professional, reflecting the desires of the philological professoriate to be relieved of the duty of teaching rhetoric and oratory. When Eliot was appointed president, the Boylston Professor of Rhetoric and Oratory was Francis J. Child; and he had been since 1851. Child was precisely the sort of man that Eliot had in mind when calling for attention to the systematic study of the language. Graduating from Harvard in 1847, Child was immediately hired as an instructor in English. The next year he published his first book—an edition of four obscure English plays from the sixteenth century, accompanied by an introduction, complete scholarly notes, and a philological glossary—which seems to have won for him a leave of absence to study in Germany. He sat raptly through lectures by Jacob Grimm at the University of Berlin, then moved on to Göttingen to study under two lesser-known philologists, Friedrich Schneidewinn and Karl Hermann. Although he was appointed Boylston professor upon his return in 1851, Child would have preferred to spend his time collecting Scottish ballads to correcting student papers, which he considered drudgery. Sophomores, juniors, and seniors were expected to write sixteen "themes" a semester, which means that Child was confronted by more than a thousand bundles of student writing every year. "Get out of this subject, young man, as quickly as you can," he advised jurior colleagues.10 Anyone who repeats this detail about Child's life is in some risk of being charged with elitism, as if it were self-evidently more populist to teach composition than to study ballads. Yet the drudgery was real enough and Child was not alone in feeling so. Joshua Lawrence Chamberlain—later a hero of Gettysburg and a key player in Ken Burns's film *The Civil War*—complained that during his first year as professor of rhetoric, oratory, and English literature at Bowdoin College in 1856–1857 he had had to correct over eleven hundred student themes. It may only be, as Briggs was to suggest in the next century, that complaints about grading papers reveal the difficulty of some scholars in adjusting their research specialties to the needs of general education.19 But it may also be that the complaints point to an unhappiness with the prevailing method of teaching the subject prior to its reform at Harvard—that is, by *correction*. In later years Child confided to a friend that during his tenure he had been peppered with questions about the abysmal quality of student writing: "What," he was repeatedly asked, "is the Boylston Professor of Rhetoric and Oratory doing?" What he had been doing was correcting student themes and hoping for a chance to concentrate exclusively upon literary scholarship.20

As I have argued, the professional desires of the philologists opened a division between the study of English language and literature on one hand and the study of rhetoric on the other. When Johns Hopkins offered Child a chair in English, and when Harvard matched the offer, Eliot needed to find a new type of man to take over the teaching of rhetoric. His first choice was Adams Sherman Hill (1833–1910). A former Washington correspondent for the *New York Times*, Hill had been a classmate of Eliot. His ideal of rhetoric was a newspaperman's: for him it was a special skill in the use of words for passing on detailed information that was gathered from investigations and studies divorced from rhetoric. Thus Hill's plans for teaching composition at Harvard entailed a break—a small break perhaps, but a break nonetheless— with the teaching of rhetoric in the nineteenth-century American college.21

At first glance Hill does not appear to be a pathbreaker. Historians such as Albert R. Kitzhaber, James A. Berlin, and Nan Johnson place him smack in the main current of traffic. Stressing his similarities with other writers on rhetoric, Johnson observes that Hill's *Principles of Rhetoric* (1878) is founded upon the belletristic conviction that the elements of literary style are suitable for nearly every occasion of writing and speech. The book offers exempla from English and American literature and close analyses of literary selections, and it emphasizes what Johnson calls the principle of adaptation to the audience, defining writing primarily as a means of communication.22 And yet the belletristic conviction and the principle of adaptation may be in contradiction with each other. If student writers are invited to think of every writing assignment as a literary occasion, they are being asked to adapt not to their audience but to the demands of literature. By contrast, the leading exponent of adaptation in college writing subordinates literature to audience. John F. Genung of Amherst opened his *Practical Elements of Rhetoric* (1886) by asserting that

> Literary discourse, properly considered, does not exist for itself alone; it is not soliloquy, but a determinate address to readers or hearers, seeking to impart to them some information or thought, with accompaniment, as occasion requires, of emotion or impulse.

Accordingly, any piece of writing "must strive after such order and expression as is best fitted to have its proper power on men"; and its general aim is to present its thought in such a way "that it shall have power on men, which aim is most satisfactorily expressed in the term adaptation."[23]

In similar fashion, Hill echoes De Quincey in saying that rhetoric belongs to the literature of power rather than the literature of knowledge. And yet he goes on to discuss the doctrine of adaptation only in discussing persuasion, four pages from the end of his 400-page book. Anyone reading the *Principles* could easily fall into the belief that writing *is* soliloquy. In explaining why rhetoric belongs to the literature of power, for instance, Hill says that if in writing "the communication of knowledge is not the sole aim, or if the reader's attention cannot be taken for granted, the language should be not only clear but effective."[24] He does not account for effectiveness in terms of a determinate effect upon a determinate audience, however. He proposes merely that one *word* is more likely to be effective than another, perhaps because it is univocal, short, specific, familiar; perhaps because its sound suggests its meaning; perhaps because it is natural and not a trick of style. Hill's entire approach is intrinsic rather than extrinsic, a question of literary or even aesthetic judgment—an attitude of constructivism—as opposed to the rhetorical calculation of an audience's level of expectation or readiness.

"Throughout the nineteenth century," Johnson says, "rhetorical expertise was equated with an understanding of fundamental rhetorical principles. . . ."[25] And at first Hill seems to be in line with this view, especially since he named his book the *Principles*. Yet in Hill the discussion of fundamental principles is at best vestigial and routine. Although he sets forth the tropes and figures of speech, he tends more to illustrate than to define them, quoting canonical authors like Shakespeare, Milton, Dryden, Austen, Wordsworth, George Eliot, Hawthorne, and Thoreau, supplementing them with contemporary figures like Robert Louis Stevenson, Matthew Arnold (from a recent essay on America in the *Nineteenth Century*), Kipling, W. H. Mallock, Thomas Hughes (author of the Tom Brown novels), Mary E. Wilkins, and both Henry and William James, plus selections from American newspapers and intellectual reviews like the London *Spectator*, the *Athenæum*, the *Atlantic Monthly*, the *North American Review*, and the *Critic*. As this list of exemplars suggests, the principles of rhetoric (in Hill's system) "should serve not as shackles but as guides to judgment."[26] The purpose in studying them is to school the judgment; not to lock them into place, but eventually to dispense with them.

After Hill the whole tendency of Harvard composition was to elevate judgment above principle. And the emphasis upon writing as communication—that is, upon the doctrine of adaptation—must not blind us to the fact that this doctrine was being conceived differently at Harvard than in formal rhetoric. For Harvard, adaptation did not mean the knowing concealment of doubts and hesitations to aid persuasion, but rather a lissome conformity to the practices of great and contemporary literature, to aid intelligibility. Harvard stressed good usage, although good usage was defined not by abstract grammatical rules but by the best that was thought and said in the world—especially at present. Over and over in their books on composition the Harvard teachers scoff at rule-bound dogmatism and conservative efforts to fix usage such as spelling reform. "These marked failures," Hill observes, "should warn the student of language, whether he fills a professor's chair or sits at a pupil's desk, not to try to stem the current of usage when it strongly sets one way." The current of usage, as reflected in the best writing of the day, is the final court of appeal. And adaptation, then, is a liberal principle. It gives writers the freedom to decide for themselves upon good usage, because every such decision "is an expression of personal opinion, not an authoritative decision: it binds nobody, and it is frequently overruled." It seeks intelligibility in writing for its own sake, not for the sake of rhetorical community or linguistic purity. And it defers to the judgment of the present when this comes into conflict with the judgment of the past.[27]

None of which is to imply that A. S. Hill was a radical. Despite his best efforts to reform the teaching of composition, his own classroom method seems to have been the prevailing one of correction. As a former student described it:

> The essence of Hill's method was common sense ruthlessly applied; surgery; wounds which left scars, and at first, it may be, bitterness toward the operator. . . . A smart undergraduate characterized him as "pungently Philistine." No man could take the conceit out of a pupil more rapidly, or with more memorable phrasing. . . . [T]he discerning pupil soon discovered in him a mind as quick in responding to the significant and genuine as in exposing and damning the empty and insincere. . . .[28]

It is a little difficult to see anything definite in these phrases, but they seem to suggest that Hill spent much time in class criticizing the style of his student writers, overruling their word-choices on the strength (not of an authoritative decision, surely) but of personal opinion.

Whatever his classroom method, though, Hill was an academic reformer. His plans for English composition at Harvard were motivated at least in part by an antiphilological zeal. He publicly ridiculed the study of

Anglo-Saxon, and in the *Principles* he approvingly quotes a passage from one of Walter Savage Landor's *Conversations* in which Dr. Johnson is imagined telling John Horne Tooke, the eighteenth-century British philologist, that grubbing at the roots of words indicates an atrophy of mind. Philological scholarship had narrowed the study of English. In its "widest sense," Hill says, English may be studied as language, as literature, or as "a means of communication between man and man"—that is, as writing. But it is not "either practicable or desirable to teach English in one sense without teaching it in the other senses also." Any student who honestly wishes to pursue the philology of the English language or to devote himself to scholarship of English literature should have "all the opportunities and all the facilities" a university can provide. But in "a prescribed curriculum," English composition furnishes "the greatest good to the greatest number." And therefore it "should be a prescribed subject," Hill concludes, "in every college curriculum in which any subject is prescribed."[29]

Yet the purpose of "the English mill" is not to "produce 'finished writers,' whatever may have been put in the hopper." Although he retains traces of essentialism in his thinking—he identifies a native gift for writing with the possession of "something worth saying"—Hill is beginning to move in the direction of constructivist anti-essentialism by suggesting that writing is one means by which human beings construct themselves. The business of the writing teacher is not, he says, to show untalented writers "how to hide poverty of thought in 'finish' of style." His job in a nutshell is to "interest his pupils in what they are writing so deeply that they put their best selves into their work." There is some confusion here. The use of Arnold's phrase implies that, in Hill's conception of it, composition was to be a merger of Arnoldian humanism and utilitarian reformism ("the greatest good to the greatest number"). Yet the basic direction is clear: writing is not a body of essential elements and principles but a mode of construction. And this explains why Hill put a stop to the assigning of themes, which he deplored as "the practice of forcing young men to write on topics of which they know nothing and care to know nothing—topics, moreover, that present no salient point for their minds to take hold of." The practice he inaugurated at Harvard was to accept anything a student felt energetic enough to write—even original stories.[30]

It is easy to miss the undertones of reform and innovation in reading Hill today. In the context of nineteenth-century rhetoric, his divergence is not wide. And yet the genre of composition that Hill established at Harvard has at least four features that distinguish it from the older rhetorical composition and that continue to distinguish the genre, now operating under the name of creative writing. (1) It is literary rather than rhetorical, conceiving of communication otherwise than in light of the expectations belonging to a specific and restricted audience. (2) Instead writing is thought of in terms of its intrinsic demands—that is, the formal demands intrinsic to the piece of writ-

ing under hand. Thus (3) it is a constructive activity that depends upon flexibility of judgment, the capacity to devise an ad hoc solution to a unique
problem of literary form, and not upon tested and essential principles, which
are better suited to the comparatively more limited number of rhetorical sit-
uations. Finally (4) composition is a liberal art, an effort to retrieve English
study from the illiberal influences of philological science and rhetorical dogmatism.

From 1872 to 1885, English composition was taught twice weekly to
sophomores, and it was the only course required of Harvard students after
their freshman year. Then, in 1885, Hill succeeded in getting it adopted as a
three-days-a-week requirement for freshmen—he hoped it would encourage
the development of writing instruction in the secondary schools—and freshman English was born.[31] An elective course in advanced composition was
created to fill the void. It was the invention of advanced composition that
marks the true beginnings of creative writing. And this course was invented
(or at least perfected) not by Hill but by his first assistant—Barrett Wendell
(1855–1921).

Wendell joined the Harvard faculty in 1880. Born in Boston, the son of
a wealthy yard-goods manufacturer, he was himself a Harvard man, graduating in 1877. During the intervening three years he prepared himself for the
bar. One day, as he recalled, he met his old teacher A. S. Hill on the street in
Boston.

> He asked me what I was doing. I told him I was reading law. He asked whether
> I liked it; I said no. And on his duly inquiring what kind of job I should prefer,
> I am said to have answered, "Even yours." Somehow the incident stuck in his
> memory.

A good thing too, because Wendell failed the bar. In the meantime, Hill had
found that he needed help in reading sophomore compositions, and so he
proposed Wendell's name to President Eliot for a job as his assistant. Upon
Eliot's agreement, Hill telegraphed to Wendell with an offer. "The telegram
decided my career," Wendell recalled; he remained at Harvard for thirty-
seven years.[32]

Wendell had no intention of making a career out of teaching writing.
Ever since he had received a complete set of Thackeray for a birthday gift at
the age of thirteen, he had longed to be a creative writer (he used the phrase
as early as 1886 to distinguish one type of writer from another). Like
Longfellow before him, he turned to college teaching as a means of supporting his literary habit. When his gothic romances *The Duchess Emilia* (1885)
and *Rankell's Remains* (1887) flopped—a parodist in the *Harvard Advocate* attributed them to the author Whendull Bearit—he put away his creative writing and gave his full attention to teaching. But he did not merely teach. He

completely revamped the teaching of writing at Harvard, publicized end-
lessly on its behalf, and created a cadre of disciples such as George Rice
Carpenter and the novelist Robert Herrick, who spread his ideas and methods to universities such as Columbia and Chicago. His 1891 book *English
Composition*, which went through thirty editions, changed the name of
rhetoric. "[I]n this subject," his Harvard colleagues eulogized him after his
death, "he made himself felt through the whole country."[33]

Wendell's *English Composition* was not the first book by that title. The
first was evidently that of David Irving, published in Philadelphia in 1803
and reprinted in 1825. The phrase then reappeared in the titles of books by
Richard Green Parker (1835 and 1846), one Dr. Brewer (in London, 1859),
James R. Boyd (1860), I. H. Nutting (1860), Alexander Bain (1866 and 1871),
Walter Scott Dalgliesh (in Edinburgh, 1868), and William Swinton (1870).[34]
Even so, it was Wendell's book that gave the new discipline its permanent
name, because it was Wendell's plan of instruction that was adopted at
Harvard and other schools, giving official sanction to Wendell's ideas.
English composition was also creative writing's first name; and though the
name was later changed, the initial conception—the original motive behind
English composition and creative writing both—belonged to Wendell.

Most accounts of him highlight Wendell's personal eccentricities. He
was a dandy who wore spats and a red Vandyke beard, parted his hair carefully in the middle, brandished a walking stick, and kept a watch on a chain,
which he would twirl in class as he spoke in a rapid staccato voice, pacing
back and forth, delivering ex cathedra pronouncements. He was a campus
character whom students liked to mimic and whose courses they flocked to.
By 1885, the second year it was offered, his course in advanced composition
had an enrollment of 150. The *Harvard Monthly* was founded the same year;
an editorial in the first issue declared that "There can be no doubt that the
study of English composition at Harvard has come out of the second and
into the first rank of studies now offered"; Wendell's course in advanced
composition was given the credit.[35] Before long the circle around Wendell
and the *Monthly* became an informal writers' club. Wendell himself encouraged his legendary status as a teacher, remarking that most of his successes
in the classroom were due to his indiscretion. But he was not without his critics. Although they were friends—Wendell persuaded Scribner's to publish
The Sense of Beauty in 1896—Santayana was unimpressed by him, saying "he
had no real distinction in himself," his mind was confused, "his force spent
itself in foam," and something admirable in him—a capacity for deep emotion, perhaps even passion—was wasted. "He was a good critic of undergraduate essays," Santayana allowed; "but not . . . a learned man; and his
books were not worth writing."[36]

And yet, he went on, Wendell's work as a teacher of composition was
useful work. Who knows how much it contributed to raising the tone of

American literature? Clearly the question in evaluating Wendell is what his achievement is considered to be. Most of those who knew him considered his personality to be his greatest achievement. Santayana—more perspicacious than most—saw that his personality interfered with Wendell's very real gifts. If he is judged not as a personality but as a teacher, and not as a campus character but as someone who (in Santayana's words) devised and carried out a new way of teaching writing—a way of teaching, moreover, that may have raised the tone of American writing—then Wendell's achievement begins to look considerable indeed. The triumph of English composition was later attributed to the tendency on the part of other colleges and universities to follow Harvard's lead blindly.[37] But the real reason was probably that Wendell's success at teaching writing at Harvard made it seem like something worth duplicating.

Wendell's approach to the subject can best be described as a writer's approach to writing. Although his books may not have been worth writing, Wendell was perhaps the first professor of rhetoric in America who taught students how to write on the basis of his own ambition to write. He came to the subject with the habits and concerns of a working, published writer. Against the current practice in college rhetoric, Wendell held that good writing is "agreeable, as distinguished from correct"; against the current practice in literary scholarship, he held that a real writer was "living in a real world as distinguished from a world of books."[38] For perhaps the first time it had occurred to someone that it might be a good plan to set pupils to writing, and make the subject he was trying to teach the subject of instruction.

In later years, Wendell set forth the original rationale behind English composition. It had been, he said, an "educational experiment" the aim of which was to enable "everyday students" to write with "habitual and unpretentious skill," while "exceptional pupils" would "become skillful creative artists—poets, if they truly be poets, of refreshingly confident technical power."[39] And this talk of refreshing the technical power of poets indicated something that Wendell believed was sorely lacking in college English—the study of literary technique. He was not alone in believing this. As we shall see in the next chapter, Brander Matthews, George Pierce Baker, and others also devised plans for remedying the neglect of technique in literary study. Wendell's plan was the more widely adopted, however. Although the training of poets was not his first concern, in Wendell's view the only education available to them was of little use to them as poets. Whatever else they got out of their classes in English, poets-to-be would not have been likely to learn very much about acquiring "technical power." The experiment of composition was also conceived as a counterirritant to the scholarship of the day. Something was needed at Harvard, Wendell said, "to help men who are willing to be helped" toward "larger thinking"—a need that "Germanized scholarship" had checked. Wendell was contemptuous of the "plodding scholar, burrowing in detail until he cares mostly for technical exactitude."[40]

The contrast of poets' technical power to scholars' technical exactitude suggests much about how Wendell envisioned the teaching of writing, but he seems also to have in mind what others had taken to abusing as formalism in education—that is, the expectation that the end of study was the mastery of knowledge that did not look to the production of anything.[41] For Wendell the whole point of education was that it should inspire the desire to work: "The test of living study is that it shall stimulate curiosity, aspiration, a willing, almost spontaneous effort." The real purpose of the study of any art, he said, "is the production of some piece of work." Even a blue book could be a work of literature: "In its own lesser way a letter, an examination book, a college thesis—or whatever else your poetaster would most disdain—may surely be a work of art, and as a work of art a thing of beauty." Every teacher of English ought to teach the forms of writing, even the most instrumental and mundane, as if they were "fragment[s] of literature." For "if all went well here below," Wendell concluded, "the ideal end of the study of literature would be not only the enjoyment of poetry, but the making of it."[42]

Wendell taught advanced composition by assigning a daily piece of writing—the "daily theme," as it came to be known. He later recalled that the original idea for the course

> was suggested to my mind by talking with a friend who was connected with a Boston newspaper. He remarked the fact that whoever becomes a reporter, no matter how ignorant he began, learned by the very effort of reporting to express himself in a readable way, in a way that the public would like; and, at the same time, that reporting enormously stimulated observations of life, precisely the thing which I found my pupils in Harvard College to lack.

Acting on this suggestion, Wendell began requiring a single page of writing from every student every day. The basis of the theme was to be the student's observations during the day:

> It may be something he has seen, it may be something he has thought about. The only requisites are that the subject shall be a matter of observation during the day when it is written, that the expression of it shall not exceed a hundred words or so, and that the style shall be fluent and agreeable.[43]

The purpose of the daily theme, according to Katharine Lee Bates, who introduced it into the curriculum at Wellesley, was "to quicken observation and give as much practice as possible in the sifting and grouping [of] facts of personal experience, and in . . . clear, concise, and cogent statement." The novelist and critic John Erskine, who took advanced composition from George Rice Carpenter at Columbia and then taught it himself at Amherst, praised the method. "The writing of short pieces constantly either left you with not another idea in your head, or it taught you how much there is to say if you keep your eyes open and think about what you see." Critics satirized it as "jotting down daily what the student saw on his walk to the post-office."[44]

A more recent critic, echoing the sort of politically radical argument that Richard Ohmann made acceptable in *English in America* (1976), is even more scornful of the daily theme. "The method," he says, "saved the student and teacher time (time, after all, is money) in preparing for class." By reducing instruction in writing to the very effort of writing, and by excluding any more theoretical discussion of other methods and rational categories, Wendell's genre of advanced composition "encourages a mode of behavior that helps students in their move up the corporate ladder—correctness in usage, grammar, clothing, thought, and a certain sterile objectivity and disinterestedness."[45] This is unfair. Wendell's intention was not to make his job easier by saving himself time. Although he eventually wore down after years of reading student compositions, he enjoyed reading them; he compared it to reading Pepys's diary. What is more, the students in Wendell's classes did not write daily themes to the exclusion of everything else. They also wrote formal essays every other week. The daily themes were supposed to have the same relation to the formal essays as "sketches to finished paintings."[46] Hardly a time-saving plan. Nor was Wendell on a mission to convert students into organization men. He wanted to foster the very quality that is usually stamped out by corporate life—individuality of expression. It is more characteristic of corporatism (or collectivism, for that matter) to low-rate the merely personal element in experience; to dismiss as trivial what a person sees on her walk to the post office. For his part, Wendell preferred the trivial and personal; at least they are the basis of firsthand experience and as such an expression of genuine knowledge. "I confess to a growing belief," he said, "that the best thing any one can do, when occasion serves, is to tell us what he himself knows. It may be of small value, but at worst it is not second-hand."[47]

Correctness was secondary and subordinate to expression in his classes; Wendell's first concern was teaching students how to write. And though he expected their formal essays to be polished and technically correct, Wendell wanted to see these things only *after* the daily theme had already been written and judged on different grounds. Learning to write, he announces at the very beginning of *English Composition*, has little to do with matters of detail or correctness in usage—"by far the greater, and incalculably the more important part are [sic] concerned with what I may call matters of discretion." Writers do not need to learn the difference between right or wrong so much as they need to learn judgment; they will have to judge how closely their language comes to expressing what they want to say; and they must learn to judge this for themselves. In writing as in dress, Wendell says, "there is no more absolute rule than the one which prudent people habitually exemplify; namely, that a wise man should keep good company, and use good sense." The slight stuffiness may obscure the fact that Wendell is endorsing flexible literary judgment ("good sense") over strict rhetorical principle. The trouble with most rhetorics, he complains, is that they endorse principle: they "consist chiefly of directions as to how one who would write should set about composing" and "in every case these directions are appallingly numerous." They balk and perplex young writers instead of aiding them in invention; they are misleading as to the real question in good writing. What is to be sought is not conformance to rational general principles but something a writer can judge only for himself. "The real question before any writer is what effect he wishes to produce," Wendell concludes.[48]

This is still a largely rhetorical conception of writing, defining the criterion of excellence as an effect upon an audience rather than as, say, the perfection of the text. But it is rhetorical only in the sense that Longinus too is rhetorical: the audience is shadowy and indefinite, and the *rhetor* is more clearly conceived; he or she is distinguished by the power to create an effect. The shift from audience to artist is a commonplace in nineteenth-century literary theory, but in literary education it was a reversal of standard procedure. Before Wendell, teachers of writing demanded little more from students than mastery of the course materials; they did not expect students to produce an effect. "A learner should not be asked even to show off what he can do outside the teaching of the class," warned Alexander Bain, professor of logic and English at the University of Aberdeen in Scotland. "If you depart ever so little from the principle of testing pupils on your own teaching, and on nothing beyond, you open the door for any amount of abuse."[49] Wendell shifted the weight from teaching to student performance; from testing to self-cultivation; from the classroom to the world outside. And this prepared the ground for a more literary conception of writing instruction. The aim, as he put it in *English Composition*, was to teach a young writer to recognize and grasp the individual nature of experience. "It is perception of what makes one moment different from another that marks the sympathetic character of the artist," he said; "and nothing can do more to make life interesting than the deliberate cultivation of such perception."[50] This is pretty much the aesthetic impressionism of *Marius the Epicurean*. As it was restated by one of Pater's friendlier American critics—a contemporary of Wendell— "receptivity, the most alert and varied powers of taking in impressions, is the one aim of cultivation."[51] The aim, in other words, was to get students to develop habits of mind not unlike those required for literature. And by literature was meant something aesthetic (at least in Pater's sense), not rhetorical:

descriptive writing full of sensory detail. This did not preclude the writing
of poems and stories. Yet the innovation of accepting poems and stories was
institutionalized by the doctrine of the deliberate cultivation of perception.
And it was the substance (perception), not the form (poems and stories), that
was of first importance. Poems and stories were merely ready vehicles. It
was perception, not the formal qualities of poems and stories and certainly
not the calculation of an effect upon a specific audience, that was the object
of study.

Wendell stood between the idealism of Emerson's "symbolic sight" (by
which poets reveal the spirit within matter) and the new literary realism that
was beginning to emerge at about this time, although his understanding of
the new realism was influenced by aesthetic impressionism. On one hand he
believed the business of writing is "to translate the evanescent, immaterial
reality of thought and emotion into written words," creating on paper
"something that in just that form was never on paper before."[52] On the other
hand he preferred the seen to the unseen, associating writing with newspaper reporting, which he identified with the taking in and reproducing of impressions. From this point of view Wendell reinvented the teaching of writing, establishing it upon many of the principles by which it would be
distinguished for a century or more. (1) Writing itself—not the study of previously written texts—was made the subject of instruction. (2) It was conceived not as an academic exercise, in service to other departments of the
curriculum, but as a unique and intrinsically valuable occasion for expression, (3) requiring aesthetic self-cultivation ("perception") and literary judgment ("discretion," "good sense") rather than mastery of a body of materials. (4) Writers are the best ones to teach the subject, because (5) the purpose
is not the scholarly examination of writing, but the making of it. Even more
significantly, Wendell established the *importance* of writing instruction, suggesting that it was perhaps the most important of the humanities. "A dull
business this seems to many," he described it—prior to his reinvention of
English composition it *was* a dull business—"yet after ten years' study," he
went on,

> I do not find it dull at all. I find it, rather, constantly more stimulating; and this
> because I grow more and more aware how in its essence this matter of compo-
> sition is as far from a dull and lifeless business as early matters can be; how he
> who scribbles a dozen words, just as truly as he who writes an epic, performs—
> all unknowing—one of those feats that tell us why men have believed that God
> made man in His image. For he who scrawls ribaldry, who as just as he who
> writes for all time, does that most wonderful of things—gives a material body
> to some reality which till that moment was immaterial, executes, all uncon-
> scious of the power for which divine is none too grand a word, a lasting act of
> creative imagination.[53]

In Wendell's hands, Emersonian idealism and descriptive realism were knit together into a constructivist philosophy that has served creative writing ever since as both an aesthetic creed and a defense of its place in the curriculum: in good writing, physical perception is made into an image of human reality by "a lasting act of creative imagination."

Later teachers of English composition at Harvard consolidated Wendell's gains. Le Baron Briggs (1855–1934) is sometimes assigned the credit for Wendell's achievement, probably because he was better liked than Wendell. For a quarter century he was an administrator (dean, first of the college and then of the faculty, and president of Radcliffe). Originally, though, he had been a writing teacher—one of the first at Harvard, joining A. S. Hill's staff in 1883—and he never deserted the classroom, succeeding Hill as Boylston professor in 1904. Briggs pioneered at least one writing course; from 1889 to 1925 he taught the history and principles of versification to graduate students who wanted to write verse under criticism. This led to the misconception that he was a professor of creative writing, which is how James D. Hart described him in the old *Oxford Companion to American Literature*.[54]

Aside from the fact that he never held any such title, Briggs belonged to the moralist rather than the constructivist tradition in American thought; and consequently he was out of the mainstream of creative writing's development. For him the purpose of instruction in writing was "to make moral character more efficient through mental discipline." In *To College Teachers of English Composition*, the fifty-page pamphlet he wrote in 1928 after retirement, he insists the goal is not to turn out great writers but to teach "an art which at its best is great"; and this requires as many moral as artistic qualities. Quoting Ruskin's *Modern Painters*, he says that the teaching of writing "cultivates in [the student] those general charities of heart, sincerities of thought, and graces of habit which are likely to lead him, throughout life, to prefer openness to affectation, realities to shadows, and beauty to corruption."[55]

Briggs's contribution to the development of creative writing may have been his own reputation as a beloved teacher. Although his motives were those of an administrator, Briggs promoted teaching at the expense of research—cultivation at the expense of learning, to use his own and the traditional humanistic terms—and because he was widely known for his teaching of writing, even credited in some quarters with having invented it, Briggs added a strong and commanding voice to what was becoming the chant of creative writing: it is more important for young writers to cultivate the right qualities—charities of heart, sincerities of thought, graces of habit—than to be learned in the literature of the past. "[S]cholarship, admirable as it is," Briggs said, "threatens poetry as theology once threatened religion, substituting stern intellectual requirements for the direct answer of heart to heart, measuring the unmeasurable, handling the intangible, materializing the spiritual."[56] It is doubtful that Briggs would have endorsed the abandonment of literary learning altogether, but he did admit that in many writing classes there was not always time to get around to it.

Like Briggs, Charles T. Copeland (1860–1952) contributed his reputation to the development of creative writing. Copeland inspired an almost slavish loyalty in his students, whom he would invite to his rooms in Hollis Hall to meet visiting writers, actors, and politicians. Like Hill, he had been a newspaperman—a staff reviewer for the *Boston Post*—before returning to Harvard at the age of thirty-three as a teacher of freshman English. According to his student Van Wyck Brooks, Copeland was uninterested in the creative imagination; he trained young writers not to be artists but to be reporters, urging them (as if he were their editor) to get out and see life.[57] One young writer who took his advice was John Reed. In dedicating *Insurgent Mexico*, he wrote to "Copey":

> I remember you thought it strange that my first trip abroad didn't make me want to write about what I saw there. But since then I have visited a country which stimulated me to express it in words. And as I wrote these impressions of Mexico I couldn't help but think that I never would have seen what I did see had it not been for your teaching me.
>
> I can only add my word to what so many who are writing already have told you: That to listen to you is to learn how to see the hidden beauty of the visible world; that to be your friend is to try to be intellectually honest. . . . [58]

Copeland had urged him to "see," and yet Reed insisted that what Copeland had really taught him to see was "the hidden beauty of the visible world"— which sounds closer to the spirit of Harvard idealism than to the editorial practices of the *Boston Post*. The combination of reporting and idealism was the trademark of Harvard composition; Copeland was retailing a familiar line of wares. Although Van Wyck Brooks wished to set "seeing life" in binary opposition to "the inner eye," at Harvard they belonged to a unified structure of belief; and Copeland fully adhered to it. Something like this must have been what Conrad Aiken meant when he praised Copeland as "the founder of a tradition, the tradition itself, and the inheritor of the tradition."[59] If he was not the founder he was a significant inheritor.

Copeland inherited Wendell's course in advanced composition in 1905 and succeeded Briggs as Boylston professor in 1925. He himself was not a true writer; he wrote a brief life of Edwin Booth and coauthored a teaching manual, *Freshman English and Theme-Correcting in Harvard College*; he is best described as a modern Ion who created chains of the inspired by reading aloud from great literature, in public performance and private conference.

(Two anthologies of his favorite readings were published during his lifetime.) This may not strike us any more forcibly than it struck Socrates as a rational method, but his students testified that Copeland had taught them how to write. Perhaps the point to make is that, like Briggs, Copeland had doubled back to retrieve the values of humanism: cultivation as distinguished from learning in the case of Briggs, aural appreciation as distinguished from an exclusively literary culture in the case of Copeland, teaching as distinguished from research in both their cases. Although there was little about the new teaching of writing that was traditionally humanistic, the reputations of Briggs and Copeland had the effect of defending it conservatively in terms of *Bildung* rather than *Wissenschaft*; and this camouflaged its actual newness. What is more, these rearguard actions built humanism into the thinking of creative writing, which would become important at a later date when a new humanism would join forces with creative writing as part of an advance guard fighting to reform academic literary study (see Chapter 6).

The renovations put into effect at Harvard reverberated throughout the country. "As the Frankish tribes in the sixth century submitted to Rome," John Jay Chapman said, "so the Americans in the nineteenth submitted to Massachusetts."[60] By the end of the century Harvard composition had become the dominant mode of writing instruction. The dominance was fated not to last. Within two decades, it was reported, the daily theme had been dropped in perhaps the majority of U.S. colleges.[61] And yet Harvard's influence was lingering, because despite its shortcomings English composition established an alternative method for the higher study of literature. The exact nature of this method was steady (daily) writing in which flexibility of judgment, the capacity to devise an ad hoc solution to a unique problem of literary form, was emphasized over correctness as a means of giving order to descriptive perception and firsthand experience. As such the method was founded upon the conviction that literature is not merely a body of knowledge; it is a constructive activity. Though composition might come under attack, its principles would prove firm enough to supply a foundation for an even newer subject of study. "[It] is not that our courageous experiments in the teaching and study of composition as a thing apart have been fruitless," Wendell said in later years; "it is rather that they have led to unforeseen conclusions."[62] One of the unforeseen conclusions would be creative writing, but there would be a ways yet to go before it came into full view.

Chapter 3

 The Problem of Writing
in a Practical Age

In 1903 John Lane published an anonymous satire of the writing life, *The Literary Guillotine*, dedicated to the proposition that contemporary literature was controlled by editors. Names were named: William Dean Howells and Henry Mills Alden of *Harper's Monthly*, Richard Watson Gilder and R. U. Johnson of the *Century*, Edward Bok of the *Ladies' Home Journal*, W. C. Brownell of Scribner's. These men were portrayed as a sort of central committee with dictatorial powers over literary taste and literary production. Although more than one of them were writers themselves, they were said to share a contempt for writers; that's what made them editors. In one scene, speaking for the group, Gilder objects to "the malign tendency of the writers of today." Writers insist on truth to nature; editors know what is really important. And so the writers must be brought to heel. Gilder says:

> We are the ones to check them. My colleague and myself, as you are doubtless aware, always carefully avoid all approach to nature, and the *Century* is the richest periodical in the world. I have given you the major and the minor premise, draw the conclusion for yourselves.

Just in case we are unable to do so, however, Gilder hastens to explain that what the editors seek is nothing less than "the emasculation of literature." To accomplish this end, he urges, "let us divorce in our minds literature and business—" "It can't be done," Howells sputters.[1]

Literature and business were going through a divorce, first economically and then on the level of ideas. Self-consciously literary artists were beginning to see themselves as a separate and distinct class; literature and journalism were becoming separate and distinct occupations. As the new magazine the *Writer* editorialized in 1888 at the end of its first year of publication, only a comparatively small number of those actively engaged in writing were "people with whom literature is the chief occupation.... The writer with a small 'w' is abroad in the land."[2] Abroad in the land, and no longer known by sight. If Jane Tompkins is right that the literary community

of the earlier nineteenth century had been close-knit, almost familial, toward the end of the century and in the early years of the twentieth it became increasingly anonymous as it was reorganized to keep in step with market forces. One consequence of this, oddly enough, was the passing of anonymous authorship in magazine publication and the appearance of the writer's *name* as a commodity with commercial value. As Henry Seidel Canby observed, editors began "to buy names and sell names to their subscribers. . . ." The old literary guard disliked the new practice. "Names are bandied about as mere tokens, with no reference to the essential values which have made them significant or interesting," Henry Mills Alden groused. The commodification of authorship signified a revaluation of it: celebrity cut ahead of achievement. "It was never so easy as now for an author to be named in print irrespective of what he has done," George E. Woodberry said. "He is known, if his works are not."[3]

This pointed to a change in the economics of literature. As the century wound down, New York emerged as the center of American publishing; and as it did so writing faded out as an avocation for gentlemen and began to be professionalized—the "commercial motive," as Woodberry called it, replaced the "internal impulse," the purely aesthetic motive.[4] The transition was largely complete by 1890 when Howells's novel *A Hazard of New Fortunes* officially recorded the shift from Boston to New York. By 1897 Katharine Lee Bates was saying that "literature tends at present to be a craft rather than a calling"; it had gone from being a form of leisure to a business; and this had had an effect on the quality of American writing. "American men of letters are too busy nowadays to achieve the best," she said. "Sucked in ever greater numbers into the vortex of New York, they are spun about, like mere bankers and brokers, in the whirl."[5]

Along with the move to New York, American publishing was putting itself on a sounder financial basis. International copyright, adopted in 1891, was a mere stopgap measure, artificially inflating profits by protecting publishers from the so-called "cheap books," the ten to twenty-five cent paperback editions of pirated foreign titles. The collapse of Harper & Brothers in 1899, despite loans that amounted to survival capital from J. P. Morgan, put a scare into the literary community. "It was as if I had read that the government of the United States had failed," Howells said. Harper was the leading publisher in America, perhaps the world; if it were capable of going under, no house was safe. The general opinion in the trade was that Harper had failed to keep its business practices up-to-date. Publishers had to improve the way they did business. So they tried several things: they invented the nonfiction series; they came up with anthologies; they scoured the magazines for new talent; they aggressively procured new books, asking for advance proposals rather than waiting for what came in unsolicited; in general, they became less worried about literary merit and more about salability as the ultimate criterion in accepting a manuscript.[6]

Perhaps the change that measured the distance that American publishing had strayed from literature to business was the growth of book advertising. The very idea did not sit well with the old literary guard. "What I want to do," said George H. Mifflin, "is while giving strength and vigor to our advertising keep it free from methods associated with patent medicine and Pears Soap, which some publishers seem to be striving to equal or surpass." Even so, Houghton Mifflin kept up with the competition, raising advertising outlays from $30,000 in 1881 to $67,000 in 1895 to $99,000 in 1901.[7] The new advertising methods seemed to work. Despite the Panic of 1893 and the three-year depression that followed, the *fin de siècle* was a boom time for American writing. In 1895 the first bestseller list was printed in the *Bookman*, suggesting how far salability had gone to replace merit as a standard of judgment. There was money to be made from writing. For fifteen days in 1899, Paul Leicester Ford earned $1000 a day in royalties on his Revolutionary War novel *Janice Meredith*. In one year—1903, the year she published *Rebecca of Sunnybrook Farm*—Kate Douglas Wiggin made over $38,000. Starting the same year, Harper guaranteed Mark Twain an annual income of $25,000 for staying with the firm. Publishers were also doing well—even the formerly cash-strapped Harper. For the eight-year period after it entered receivership, Harper reported a trading profit of $2,000,000 before depreciation.[8]

Similar trends affected newspaper and magazine journalism. Led by Cyrus H. K. Curtis—publisher of the *Saturday Evening Post*—American magazines begin to shift from circulation to advertising as their primary source of income. As Edward Bok editorialized in the *Ladies' Home Journal* in 1898: "It is the growth of advertising in this country which, more than any other single element, has brought the American magazine to its present enviable position in points of literary, illustrative, and mechanical excellence."[9] Bok did not exaggerate; the growth of advertising changed the clientele of magazines from its readers to its advertisers; and one effect of this change was a new relationship between the magazine and its contributors. In the 1880s, an editor like the *Atlantic Monthly*'s Thomas Bailey Aldrich could wait for manuscripts to come in over the transom, confidently expecting the reputation of the magazine to attract interesting writing.[10] But now magazines needed to be able to show potential advertisers a more reliable product. The idea of gathering a "stable" of regular contributors dates from this time; it was an idea that originated with the *Saturday Evening Post*.[11] And this is of the utmost importance in the history of American authorship, because it suggests that the magazine was being converted from a literary outlet to a business organization. The same was true—perhaps even more true—for the turn-of-the-century newspaper, which (according to the contemporary social critic Hamilton Wright Mabie)

> has passed through the preliminary stage of purely individualistic enterprise and, in many cases, has taken on something approaching institutional stability

and continuity. The age of the newspaper created and directed by one strong man of marked individuality who made his journal a personal organ has passed; a first-class newspaper of to-day is a highly organized enterprise conducted by a group of men, the majority of whom are often men of university training.[12]

It was not only advertising and new business and editorial practices that were leading to a reorganization of the literary life. Technological advances also played a part. The shift-key typewriter, introduced in 1878, made it easier and faster to prepare manuscripts, and may even have contributed to the breaking down of traditional literary styles. Dana Gioia argues that it gave a boost to free verse by allowing writers "to predict accurately for the first time the *look* of their words on the printed page rather than just their sound."[13] Although it is more likely that the typewriter assisted the development of journalism, this is an enormously fruitful suggestion; new printing technologies were developing too quickly not to have an effect on literature. In 1885 the Mergenthaler linotype was perfected, improving typesetting rates by from 25 percent to 40 percent. Other improvements in printing throughout the 1880s and 1890s—cylinder presses, automatic sheet feeders, paper folders, cutters, and new machines for sewing book signatures—also sped production and lowered costs.[14] Without these advances there would have been no profession of modern journalism and big-money publishing would have been impossible. What is more to the point, the rise of modern journalism and big-money publishing changed the way in which writing—including the study of writing—was conceived in America.

Two different ideas of writing emerged in conflict with each other. On one side was writing conceived as a social practice, whether it was defined as a profession (in connection with journalism) or as basic proficiency in the ordinary use of language (in connection with college writing instruction). On the other side was writing conceived as an art. Although it would eventually triumph as an ideology, the aesthetic was a distinctly minority view of literature. Journalists, as Barrett Wendell observed, were "far and away the most prolific and most widely read of modern men of letters."[15] Their ranks swelled and swelled throughout the twentieth century, while the number of authors grew at a much slower pace (see Fig. 3). Moreover, "artistic" writing did not appeal to as many readers as journalism did; and for the same reason, then, the kind of education associated with the literary art seemed impractical and pointless to a good many Americans.

In the opinion of critics, the rivalry between art and journalism was ruinous for American writing. Henry Seidel Canby warned that literature was being divided between two extremes, which he called the extremes of strenuous professionalism and delicate aestheticism. On one side was "[t]he bulk of our circulating library and news-stand literature," "loud-voiced, aggressive, marvelously lush in its growth and loved of the multitude." Its themes

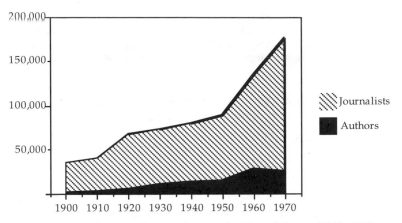

FIGURE 3   Authors and Journalists in the United States, 1900–1970

Source: Historical Statistics of the United States, Colonial Times to 1970, Series D 233–682.

were adventure, business, romance, pathos, or humor. It was not "literary"; it was conventionalized and formulaic; and yet it "contained much real literature, in which American conditions are mirrored . . . with a shrewdness that almost makes up for depth." On the other side was a literature of which the multitude was largely ignorant. And "though not hardy in our practical America," it too was typically American—"the delicate, scented variety of writing." Canby's description of it is worth quoting in full:

> In occasional contributions to the general magazines, in a hundred "paid-for-by-the-author" books, and in thousands of essays, stories, and poems read before clubs or printed for the few, there is a gentle, highly personal, highly polished style of composition which, if not literature, is certainly literary. People with no story to tell write it excellently and call it art; people with nothing to say polish their style and call it literature. As if by some survival of the curse of Babel, careful writing, discrimination in words, restraint, grace, beauty—all that goes to make a style—have become associated in America with the privately printed or the sparingly read.[16]

The problem of not being taken seriously as literature is what has baffled professional writing since the turn of the century, while a lack of economic viability is the problem that has always faced writing for writing's sake.

A two-sided division was also apparent, at least to contemporaries, in American education. It was said to be divided, as Michigan professor Irving King observed, between the extremes of professionalism and truth-seeking. Truth-seekers attacked professionalism by arguing that it was merely a seeking after personal gain, but King argued that the dichotomy was false. As a pragmatist he held that the dispute between them could be resolved by correctly understanding the concept of *practice*. "The truth-seeker," he said, "is really the person who chooses, definitely and habitually to abandon the careless attitude in the sphere of activity in which he is engaged."[17]

And yet there remains a conflict between a practical and professional attitude on the one side and an aesthetic or constructive attitude on the other. Either might be careless; the difference between them is caught in another word that was popular at the time: *efficiency*. To use the word in its Aristotelian sense, however, one attitude is efficient in looking at writing and education as means to an end; the other gives them a certain finality, looking upon them as ends in themselves. Whether this too proves to be a false dichotomy—whether the terms *professional* and *truth-seeking*, *practical* and *aesthetic*, or *means* and *end* are finally preferred—some such conflict as this is what motivated thinking about writing and its place in education around the turn of the century. "[T]he steadily advancing standards of efficiency in all fields of endeavor," as Hamilton Wright Mabie said, "have compelled the reorganization of the methods of higher education."[18]

During the period from 1900 to 1925 college instruction in writing was put on a different footing as the constructive, developmental, and professional aspects of it diverged. Creative writing was formed by amputating "expression" from a concern with the communication of ideas and proficiency in usage. The latter is recognizable as the subject that is now taught under the name of English composition, and it was during this period that it was formed. At the same time, the cry was raised for the specialized training of professional writers. "[W]hile all other arts have their professors and accredited teachers, while the greatest masters have had their following of disciples, the author alone makes no attempt to impart his methods," an observer remarked in 1906.[19] English composition was unlikely to satisfy this demand. And though creative writing, when it finally got under weigh, was launched as the explicit attempt by one author to impart his methods, in no respect was it intended—at least at first—as a specialized training. In the early years of the century, expression and training were also bracketed off from each other: expression would become the province of creative writing, while the demand for training was soon supplied by a new institution—the journalism school. When it first emerged as a separate study, creative writing took shape by distinguishing itself from the increasingly basic proficiency of English composition on the one hand and workaday journalism on the other. In the meantime, college writing instruction was reorganized to make it more efficient, practical, and professional.

"Whatever else may be said in disparagement of this enterprise," Albert Jay Nock quipped about the teaching of writing, "there is certainly enough of it."[20] Actually, the reverse was true—at least in the minds of many people. This was a period of rapid expansion for college writing instruction. It *was* widely disparaged, though—which paradoxically did much to secure its place in the university. The antagonism to it often took the form of a call for a different kind of writing instruction altogether. More often than not the new plan either traded on the name of English composition or depended upon the assumption, which looked natural as long as composition was part of the curriculum, that the teaching and study of writing rightfully belonged in the university. Thus the period of expansion in the teaching of writing coincided with a period of demands for its consolidation or restructuring. At the very moment it was becoming an unquestioned part of the curriculum there was little else about it that was not called into question. Critics accepted the institutional status of writing as a given and sought a merely conservative reform carried out from within. Broadly speaking, there were two objections: the teaching of writing was either said to be too literary, too remote from the actual needs of real students; or it was said not to be literary enough, not sufficiently concerned with literature and the growth of students' literary knowledge and abilities. It is no accident that both creative writing and the journalism school belong to the first quarter of the new century. English composition had brought writing into the curriculum, but in neither an aesthetic nor a professional sense was it an adequate conception of writing.

Discontent with English composition began to be voiced not long after its adoption and continued to build throughout the next three decades. No other branch of the curriculum was said to involve so much time and energy with so little to show for it. The problem, according to its critics, lay with the theory and practice of the writing course. Its theory that (to use Wendell's phrases) "observations of life" and the "perception of what makes one moment different from another" were the basis of good writing was mistaken. And its idea of practice—steady, daily composition—was ill-conceived to bring about any real improvement in college writers.

Even Barrett Wendell came to have doubts about his invention. Although the professor of what he described as "a radical and practical subject," by 1908 Wendell had arrived at an eleventh-hour endorsement of the Collegiate Course, "the old system of classics and mathematics, in comparison with anything newer." The progress of his radical and practical subject was unsatisfactory. "Twenty years ago, composition, studied by itself, appeared full of unforeseen possibilities," Wendell lamented; "now, as a subject of study, it has come to seem exhaustible by a single and not very arduous effort." From the teacher's side composition offered few rewards; from the student's, few benefits. It neither turned out professional writers nor improved those who only occasionally wrote. "[A] student who emerges from a course of earnest instruction in English composition with perceptibly, or at least incontestably, firmer command of his pen for general purposes than he had to begin with, has hardly yet had the benevolence to cross my path," Wendell said. What was likely to be offered as the reason for its lack of success was that composition was ill taught. It is just as likely that the subject is one "which [nobody] on earth knows how to teach."21

On the theoretical level, composition was attacked for raising expression above knowledge and meditation upon knowledge. "[A]mong the platitudes that have escaped challenge is the current notion that everyone should be taught to express himself," said Cornell professor Lane Cooper. And lest anyone accuse him of undemocratic elitism, Cooper hastened to add that "Even in a democracy it may now and then be true that silence is golden, and long, barren silence better than personal talk." The trouble was that the new writing pedagogy conceived of physical observation and perception as substantial rather than instrumental activities of mind. The observations were not expected to grow increasingly faithful to a specific reality within a definite province of knowledge; nor were writers expected to compare their observations and draw inferences from them. They were not taught to *think* about what they saw. Although observation and perception may serve as aids to expression, they are useless as means of imparting insight. At best they can train young hands to turn out superficially readable writing suitable for the daily press. Quoting the English positivist Frederic Harrison, Cooper concluded that "It is the business of a university to train the mind to think, and to impart solid knowledge, not to turn out nimble penmen who may earn a living as the clerks and salesmen of literature."22

On the practical level, composition was attacked for its neglect of literary study. As early as 1896, William Lyon Phelps objected to

> the supposition, very generally accepted in some high circles, that the pupil, in order to write good English, may profitably neglect literature, if he only steadily write compositions. We are told that the way to become a good writer is to write; this sounds plausible, like many other pretty sayings equally remote from fact. No one thinks that the way to become a good medical practitioner is to practise; that is the method of quacks.

The best way to become a writer, other than by being born to the right parents, is by wide reading. The wide reader "writes well," he said, "principally because he has something to say, for reading maketh a full man. . . ." Phelps's Yale colleague Thomas R. Lounsbury agreed wholeheartedly, arguing that the method of "constant practice" to the exclusion of anything else may actually inhibit the growth of literary ability. "Clearness or effectiveness or felicity of expression can never be created by it," he said, "nor can they be developed by it satisfactorily unless the proper foundation has previously been laid." And the proper foundation can only be laid by "cultivated taste begotten of familiarity with the great masterpieces of our literature. . . ." The fallacy behind the teaching of writing was that the ability to write had been confounded with the ability to learn. In the absence of literary study, Lounsbury said, "A useful but subsidiary part of instruction has been exalted into one of paramount importance."23

Such attacks may be dismissed as the grumblings of a verificationist positivism and a foundationalist humanism that were going ignored in the teaching of writing. But even so they were not entirely wide of the mark. They clearly identified college composition as a *style* of composition, a style that (to repeat Canby's description of it) if not literature was certainly literary. It was distinguished by personal talk; it sought readability, even at the expense of imparting knowledge; it did not always have something to say. Such criticisms suggest that the proponents of the "literary" style had not given sufficient thought to some rather obvious challenges. What finally is the point of reproducing one's personal perceptions? Why should anyone care to read the result? And what exactly is the relationship between the practice of writing and the study of writing, especially other people's writing? Even from a literary point of view, then, the new writing pedagogy could be seen as inadequate. In another sense, though, the criticisms suggest that the teaching of writing had survived a difficult birth. For by the second decade of the new century it was no longer an untried experiment; it had developed into an inquiry. By then it was more than what could be taught. It was not merely something that went on in classrooms; it was something that could be *discussed* by experts in the instruction of it.

Under these circumstances there was little chance that writing instruction would be curtailed, even if no one was very clear about why it was continuing unabated or whether it was successful. "Have all our methods of teaching English composition failed?" asked a Colorado State professor in 1921. His conclusion was indeed they had—at least as measured by their usefulness for life after college. In the eyes of most students "a course in English composition may be all right for those who intend to follow a literary pursuit, but they believe that they can get along without it."[24] The dissatisfaction with composition was usually given the form of an unhappiness with its literary orientation. Although writing instructors repeatedly demurred that it was not their business to produce literary artists, critics charged that the whole tendency of writing instruction was in a literary direction. This was revealed by the course in advanced composition, the crown of writing studies in the university. The literary nature of this course, it was said, contaminated the teaching of lower-level composition. As a Stanford professor observed,

> Where the colleges give any training in advanced composition, it is usually of [a] quasi-literary type, as a result of which the student who later becomes, not a great author but a teacher, has, as at least the subconscious aim of all his teaching, the producing of literary artists. Hence he is often satisfied with an extremely frothy product. Because of him and his kind, there is in educational work a supercilious attitude toward "business English."[25]

It was "business English," or at least not "artistic English," that students were increasingly said to require. The emphasis on literariness (or quasi-literariness) had led to the writing course's being badly misconceived, and as a consequence its failure had also been misjudged. It was indeed a failure if judged by literary standards. But these were not the right standards to judge it by. "The aim of the college course in composition today," Canby wrote in 1914, only five years after Wendell had asserted the contrary, "is not the making of literature, but writing; not the production of imaginative masterpieces, but the orderly arrangement of thought in words."[26] Canby's definitiveness belied the confusion of aims that was everywhere apparent. "In every textbook, in every magazine article, in every paper before a convention," another observer remarked, antagonists seem "dazzled by the assumption that the purpose of composition work is to inspire some measure of grace and charm. College theme-writing is a failure, it has been argued, because college graduates are no more literary than they used to be."[27]

It was the initial assumption that was mistaken. The arguments of composition's antagonists were irrelevant, because the reason for teaching writing was *not* to teach literature. Or so at least it was beginning to be argued. The purpose of instruction in writing was proficiency, defined as the "[a]bility to write a decent theme, on a topic not based on reading," which was "free from common, typical, fundamental errors in spelling, punctuation, syntax, and arrangement of material."[28] The new champions of the teaching of writing were not opposed to the teaching of literature. They simply believed that, as a course required of all students, writing should not be run as if it were a course for would-be authors. When they complained that the subject had become too literary, then, they were (like their critics) condemning the tendency on the part of some teachers, as it was put by an advocate of proficiency, "to imitate the procedures and results of purely literary activity before there is a proper foundation for them."[29] Unlike their critics, however, they did not believe that the proper foundations lay in a familiarity with the great masterpieces of literature. It was foundations of grammar and usage that students required. What students did *not* need were lessons in purely literary activity—lessons in how to write a story, for instance. "[I]t is an open question," the proficiency experts said, "whether the writing of fictional narratives, at least on a large scale, has any proper place in a general course." What was largely needed was a course in basic English proficiency cut loose from "the encumbrance of 'literature.' "[30]

Those who wanted to cut writing loose from literature got what they wanted. A comparison of composition textbooks from three different periods reveals a steady decline in the attention given to the forms of discourse and the literary genres and a steady increase in grammar lessons and practical activities (see Fig. 4). Institutionally too the trend was toward a splitting of writing and literary study. In the 1920s at least two land-grant universities, Penn State and Mississippi State, created separate departments of English literature and English composition with separate department heads for each.

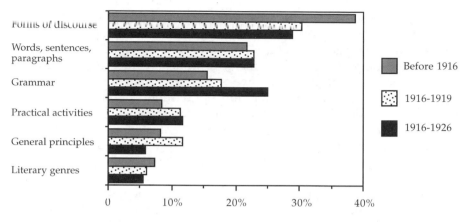

FIGURE 4   Distribution of subject matter in composition texts

Source: Roy Ivan Johnson, *English Expression: A Study in Curriculum Building* (Bloomington: Public School Publishing, 1926), p. 98.

And as remarked upon by more than one observer of the academic scene, the tide had begun to drift away from Harvard-style courses in the daily theme, suggesting a progressive abandonment of the "literary" teaching of writing.[31]

There were some people, though, who still wanted to encumber writing with literature. While English composition was pulled in the direction of proficiency, starting to become what we would now call a service course, expression was left homeless but in demand. Courses in composition had aroused a thirst for literary expression that composition itself could no longer satisfy. Many teachers of writing were men and women of letters like Wendell, Katharine Lee Bates, Brander Matthews, Gertrude Buck, Robert Herrick, George Rice Carpenter, and John Erskine. Their interests were unlikely to be satisfied by courses in proficiency. Perhaps more significantly, courses in composition had introduced the writing of fiction and poetry for academic credit, provoking a curiosity to see whether fiction and poetry writing could be taught by themselves. And yet—and this is important to note—many of the first efforts to teach fiction and poetry writing were *practical* efforts, experiments in offering formal instruction in current styles of literary practice. "Everywhere," said the critic Fred Lewis Pattee, "the emphasis was upon the mechanistic, upon manner, upon a technique that one might learn from books."[32]

In 1902 Lewis Worthington Smith, a professor at Drake University, published *The Writing of the Short Story*, a handbook for college teachers who wished to offer instruction in story writing. Smith was not the first to teach the short story on the university level. He was preceded by Edwin Herbert Lewis, father of the poet and novelist Janet Lewis (and father-in-law of the poet and critic Yvor Winters), who held seminars on the story at the University of Chicago in the 1890s. While Lewis's interest was in a genre that had been neglected by critics and scholars, though, Smith's interest was in a form that prevailed in the real literary world among writers and editors. Lewis's interest was historic, Smith's (to use his own word) was "constructive." In conceiving his course, Smith may have avoided the crassness of a later educator who proposed the teaching of magazine writing for the sake of motivating composition students (by reminding them that magazines pay) and improving their "chances of 'landing.' "[33] At the same time, though, he was attracted to the story because it was undeniably commercial and as such it was fashionable, up-to-date, a living part of the current culture.

In his plan, a "complete story" was the end product of a course in daily themes. Students were to analyze stories in current magazines by means of a complicated system that involved the use of marginal symbols: "F" for statement of fact, "In" for incident, "As" for anticipatory suggestion, "m" for mood, and the like. They wrote daily themes on suggested topics: "1. A sunset sky. 2. A group in the park. 3. A spring freshet. 4. The man at the threshing machine. 5. The city across the river: night." And finally the complete story: three thousand words on a plot supplied by the teacher and employing "methods of treatment" suggested by him or her. Even though it reduced the writing of stories to the following of formulas, Smith's course in the constructive study of the story was a step forward in literariness from English composition, because it made a form of fiction its exclusive concern.[34]

Smith's was one of several attempts to develop a course in practical methods. Columbia professor George P. Krapp observed in 1913 that "the increased commercial value of certain kinds of literature today," primarily the short story, the novel, and the drama, had created "a tendency on the part of some college instructors to place great stress on the teaching of a practical technique in literature"—that is, to teach it as an art "which the student shall be able to put into practice with the hope of immediate pecuniary profit." The tendency on the part of some college instructors paralleled tendencies outside the college. In 1901 Frank Norris reported in the *Chicago American* that he had heard that two different schools had opened "for the purpose of instruction in the art of novel writing." One school was on the West Coast and the other was in New York. Norris said he knew nothing else of the schools, though he believed the West Coast operation was "conducted by W. C. Morrow." I haven't been able to learn anything else about these novel-writing schools either, though a four-book author by the name of William Chambers Morrow is listed in the 1922–23 *Who's Who* as "Director of creative writing in Cora L. Williams Institute, Berkeley."[35]

The technique of story writing, taught by correspondence, university extension, or self-instruction, was much in demand. It "was the era of the short-story handbook," Fred Lewis Pattee said; the story "was found to be peculiarly teachable." The teaching books included Sherwin F. Cody's *How to Write Fiction* (1895), Charles R. Barrett's *Short Story Writing* (1898), Clayton Hamilton's *Materials and Methods of Fiction* (1908), Evelyn May Albright's *Short-Story: Its Principles and Structure* (1907), J. Berg Esenwein's *Writing the Short-Story* (1908), Ethan Allen Cross's *Short Story: A Technical and Literary Study* (1914), and Robert W. Neal's *Short Stories in the Making* (1914). It was also the era of the first classroom anthologies of stories like those edited by Charles Sears Baldwin (1904) and Brander Matthews (1907). Criticism of the story came of age with treatises by Bliss Perry (in the closing chapter of his 1902 *Study of Prose Fiction*) and Henry Seidel Canby (in 1902 with another in 1909). In magazine publishing, the story rose as the serialized novel declined. Editors were beginning to realize that serials might be good for prestige, but did little to increase circulation. Horace E. Scudder, editor of the *Atlantic Monthly* from 1890 to 1898, preferred 5000- to 6000-word stories and believed readers did too. "A race of modern readers like ours," Scudder said, "educated upon . . . the scraps into which newspapers are degrading is particularly caught with stories to be taken down with a gulp." The growing market for stories is one explanation for the growing number of story courses. Another explanation, though, is to be found in the peculiar teachability of the form. Anything that was so widely practiced practically taught itself.36

Everywhere the creative was being adapted to the practical. And not only in the short story. As George Krapp observed, the teaching of practical techniques in dramatic writing was also to be found on campus. The most famous of the attempts to teach playwriting was George Pierce Baker's "47 Workshop" at Harvard, the forerunner of the Yale Drama School. Baker (1866–1935) won fame as the teacher of Eugene O'Neill, Philip Barry, John Dos Passos, and Thomas Wolfe (who sketched a portrait of him as Professor Hatcher in *Of Time and the River*). He began his career at Harvard in 1888 as a teacher of debate and argument, primarily to law students, but his passion was theatrical history and stagecraft. Promoted to full professor in 1905 on the strength of *Principles of Argumentation* (1895) and *Forms of Public Address* (1904), Baker at last had sufficient stature to gain approval for the course he had long been contemplating: a graduate course in advanced composition, "The Technique of the Drama," intended to offer almost a kind of professional training for which he could demonstrate a growing need.37 Although a trial run was conducted for Radcliffe women the previous year, the first meeting of English 47 was held in 1906. From then until 1925, when he was lured to Yale by the chance to head a theatre, Baker taught courses at Harvard that were intended, as he said, "for professional dramatists, professional scenic designers and professional and amateur producers."38 What had begun as an English course—a course in advanced composition—ended as something else. By the time he published *Dramatic Technique* in 1919

Baker's goal was "by showing the inexperienced dramatist how experienced dramatists have solved problems similar to his own, to shorten a little the time of his apprenticeship."[39] Hence the name *workshop*. As the popular playwright Bronson Howard had prefaced a lecture to Harvard students in 1886,

> I invite you today to step into a little dramatic workshop instead of a scientific laboratory, and to see a humble workman in the craft trying, with repeated experiments . . . not to elucidate the laws of dramatic construction, but to obey them, exactly as an inventor . . . tries to apply the general laws of mechanics.[40]

This was Baker's conception of the workshop too. Its idiom was that of advice, not explanation; the instructor's concern was not to be understood but to be followed. Small wonder Baker came to feel that "[m]ere lectures, no matter how good, will not make the students productive."[41] Productivity, not mere knowledge, is the thing. In a workshop, experienced workers show the inexperienced how things are done—hands-on training, as it would now be advertised. Baker's concerns were not theoretical but practical; and not merely with what works, but with what *succeeds*.

Still, Baker's standard for dramatic success was a historical one. Monetary success cannot be the measure; "aiming to hit popular taste," he warns, "is like shooting at a shifting target"; the likes and dislikes of the theatrical public are too unpredictable to be studied with profit. Far more reliable is the study of plays that have been tested before the public and have succeeded. "[T]he history of the drama has shown again and again," Baker says, "that a dramatist may owe something to the plays of a preceding period and achieve success." He does not mean, however, that the plays of the past ought to be sedulously aped. What historical study will reveal is a discrepancy between "the essentials of the drama throughout time" and the use in every play, even Shakespeare's, of "methods and devices effective for the public of its time, but not effective at present." The problem facing a current dramatist is how to *adapt* the essentials to the public of his time. If this sounds rhetorical Baker does not flinch: "the dramatist shapes his material more and more in relation to the public he wishes to address, for a dramatist is, after all, a sort of public speaker." Baker stood well within the Harvard tradition; the principle of adaptation did not mean "truckling to an audience." The dramatist engages in historical study to gain a close familiarity with the practices of past and present drama to assist in the objective of "persuasion," by which Baker really means plausibility: the audience's applause at the dramatist's intended effects.[42]

And this is the sense of the term *technique*. After Baker it might be defined as the convergence of the principles of history and practice, where practice is distinguished on the one hand from what will sell and on the other from what ideally ought to be good but, given the very real constraints of time, the theatre, and an audience, just will not work. "The technique of any dramatist may be defined, roughly," Baker says, "as his ways, methods, and devices for getting his desired ends." He is not an untutored genius; he does not have technique "as a gift at birth"; nor is he merely a student of composition, acquiring a knowledge of dramatic technique "merely by writing plays. He reads and sees past and present plays," Baker adds, "probably in large numbers." And in this way the genuine dramatist is marked off from the scholar, whose *only* interest is in the drama of the past; and from the "hack playwright," whose *only* interest is in practical methods for getting desired ends.[43]

Everywhere, though, technique was being confused with practice. At Columbia, Brander Matthews (1852–1929) taught a course in what he called "metrical rhetoric." At first he described the course as "an attempt to give practical instruction in metrical composition," but this led to its being misconceived. Matthews's purpose was not honestly practical; a few years later he set the record straight. The course, he said, "was designed to parallel the prescribed courses in the theory and practice of rhetoric, my intention being to tempt the students into various kinds of verse-making, not with any absurd hope of developing them into poets, but mainly because I believed metrical composition to be an excellent discipline for prose-writing." In 1911 he published *A Study of Versification*, a textbook derived from twenty years' experience of teaching the course. The purpose of the text, he announced in the preface, was to lead students "to a richer appreciation of poetry," and the purpose of the verse-writing exercises in the back of the text was "chiefly to increase [students'] appreciation and understanding of the masterpieces of the major poets."[44]

Matthews's *Study of Versification* was not a practical treatise and his course in "metrical rhetoric" was not designed to give practical instruction in the writing of poetry. What concerned Matthews was the problem of technique, which had been grossly neglected in the university study of literature, even though the true writer "cherishes" it, "is forever thinking about it and enlarging his knowledge of it," and knows that it is "almost the only aspect of [his] art which can be discussed profitably." Literature should be taught as he himself taught it at Columbia—"by an incessant consideration of its ever-advancing technic." What Matthews wanted was to give students the use of literature through acquiring an understanding of it. The plan is a little confused: on one hand it considers literature as an integrated, self-moved discipline (a technique rather than a fund of information), but on the other it is general culture (the ultimate goal is "appreciation" and the hope of making poets is abandoned as "absurd"). Yet even with its confusions Matthews's effort was important, because it conceived the exercise of technique as an aid to the study of literature.[45]

Matthews was not alone in seeking to join literary study to the exercise of technique. It was usual, when the study of poetic meter was incorporated into a course of advanced composition, as in Lewis Worthington Smith and James E. Thomas's *Modern Composition and Rhetoric* (1900), for the aim to be an increased appreciation and understanding of the formal qualities of poetry rather than creative writing; the aim was to enforce knowledge by means of a reproduction of the objects of knowledge. And though Matthews said that even by 1917 the course in metrical composition was "not as frequent as it might be" in American universities, it was frequent enough. Le Baron Briggs, it will be recalled, taught a similar course at Harvard (see Chapter 2); and versification was also taught at Fordham, Middlebury, Iowa, and Missouri. But wherever it was taught it was taught along not-very-practical lines. At the University of Virginia the course was devoted to the theoretical study of poetic form divorced from practice, except in as far as "[c]lass exercises [were] assigned from time to time"; and at Indiana University the one-semester course in "metrics" *accompanied* the historical course in poetry.46

Upon close examination, practical instruction in story writing and the "rhetorical" teaching of metrical and dramatic composition can be seen as countervailing movements. The one was based on current practice, the other on the need to emphasize the historicity of a practice; the one was given impetus by the desire of a great many people to acquire a skill that could be plied for pay, the other by the intention of showing that a historical knowledge of literature is entailed in the exercise of literary technique. But from a wider perspective the two departures can be seen as belonging to more or less the same movement—the movement to improve the teaching of writing by making it more literary, more faithful to the true character of literary activity, past or present. The conflict was over what conception of literature was more faithful to its true character: the practical or the historical?

And so late in the century there began to be talk of making the university a place for creative or constructive work. Indiana University offered a course in magazine writing, for example, although the chairman of the English department, Martin W. Sampson, said that "current magazine writing is not held up as ideal literature"—it was held up as a model of possible attainment—"nor, on the other hand, is the production of literature deemed a possible part of college study." The fact that he even had to say so implies that others were deeming otherwise. And in fact the same year Charles Mills Gayley announced the University of California's intention of offering a graduate course in literary composition. "Academic scholarship does not look with favor upon the attempt to stimulate or foster creative production," Gayley observed. Cautiously, though, he endorsed the plan: "constructive literary effort may surely find a place in the curriculum of an exceptional graduate—never, of course, unattended by other study with informative or disciplinary purpose in view." Two decades later (as we shall see in the next chapter) Gayley would act less cautiously, without appealing to the gods of information and discipline, in bringing the first poet in residence to the Berkeley campus.[47]

The split between art and journalism was beginning to show up in the different kinds of plans being offered for the training of writers. In 1899 a School of Literature and Composition was organized at Bessie Tift College in Georgia. "The purpose of the school," according to the college catalogue, "is to aid those who wish to enter the field of Journalism and Literary Composition. We cannot hope to create genius, but rather to discover, develop, and direct it." In 1901, W. E. Mead reported the findings of a survey to the Modern Language Association: some English professors, hoping for rhetoric to become a subject of graduate instruction, "seemed to think that a graduate school might be made to serve as a school for critical or creative genius, but their plans for the conduct of such a school were not very definite." Neither the Tift College venture nor the plans of Mead's respondents came to much. But what is interesting about them is this. Even though the proposals were for different kinds of schools—a school of journalism on the one hand and a program in rhetoric on the other—both were framed in the same terms: that is, in terms of a school to aid and develop genius.[48]

In 1903 the novelist H. C. Chatfield-Taylor (*An American Peeress, The Idle Born*) proposed a more definite plan to aid the development of genius—a "studio system of instruction" for young writers, a European system of "ateliers." Chatfield-Taylor called upon his fellow novelists to take in pupils. The young painter has the opportunity of being taught by a master; not so the young writer. "And where in all this wide, cruel world can he go," Chatfield-Taylor asked, "to learn the art of word-painting?" In a studio, with a novelist like William Dean Howells passing among the desks, a young writer might learn in a year "what otherwise he might not in a lifetime." Without a school to attend the would-be writer is "obliged to grope . . . in the darkness of his own ignorance," doing little more than reading good books and trying his best "to write like the great authors he has read." In a school he might be improved; if any good he might even be perfected. "The principles of novel writing," Chatfield-Taylor insisted, against the general opinion, "certainly can be taught, such as the value of words, the proportion which description should bear to dialogue, characterization, and above all, construction." The universities were not doing the job. "Mechanical writing is taught," he granted, "but not perspective, [formal] composition, colour, light and shade."[49]

What Chatfield-Taylor proposed was to adapt the individualist system of the master's private studio to the institutional system of university education. And even if these two systems were capable of coexisting in harmony, the proposal underplays the improbability of their being brought together in an age of increasing state control over the universities.[50] A more politically realistic statement of the case for the training of writers—and a remarkably prescient vision of what was to come—appeared in 1907 in the fiftieth anniversary edition of the *Atlantic Monthly*. It was written by Walter Hines Page (1855–1918), a journalist who commanded wide attention. Page, a Southerner, was a newspaperman on the New York *World* and *Evening Post* before editing in succession the *Forum*, the *Atlantic*, and the *World's Work*. With Frank Nelson Doubleday in 1900 he founded one of the leading New York publishing houses. Later, during the First World War, he served as Wilson's ambassador to Great Britain. His interest in the training of writers was both professional and political.[51]

In Page's view, the training of professional writers was a problem of more than literary concern. Although they made up a profession, ranking second or third in size, writers were incompetently prepared for their careers. And because the intellectual life of the American people was largely shaped by current writing, the lack of training among them was a cause of dangerous political conditions. The only available training was an apprenticeship in those "writers' workshops," the editorial offices of newspapers and magazines. University study was of little use. Writers who graduate from college, Page says,

> have not been prepared by a reasonable amount of practice even to understand what writing, day by day, means. They have their heads full of "literary" notions, which are, as a rule, very false notions. They are not prepared for the orderly practice of a useful art.[52]

University study fills pupils with academic superstitions instead of principles; it goes little farther toward training someone for a career in writing than undergraduate courses in theoretical mathematics go toward training him or her to be an engineer. Something better was needed. Even Page's vocabulary—"writers' workshops," "the orderly practice of a useful art"—suggests the broader changes in thinking on questions of literature and literary training that were occurring at this time. But Page is not merely an example of a drift. He had a specific proposal, with recommendations on admissions, staffing, and curriculum.

What Page proposed was a course of postgraduate study for those who intend to make their careers by writing. Students will only be admitted after getting a good general education and earning a B.A. The teachers will themselves be writers; if they are scholars they will not be *mere* scholars. And though the curriculum will not overlook the study of literature, its chief component will be practice. By itself reading does not make a writer; the belief in the sufficiency of reading is a fallacy as shopworn and outdated as a belief in divine inspiration. A writer *can* be made, and by practice; but not by the small amount of practice afforded by courses in the daily theme. Every student will be required to write ten times that much—a thousand words a day. The kinds assigned for practice will be various: biography or history at the start, followed by the writing of a novel and then a play, and including the forms of verse, including a sonnet a day. The key, though, will be a genuinely effective amount of practice. Page points out that

> A student who should write a thousand words a day would in a year of three hundred working days gain such practice as the writing of three books of the usual size of a novel would give. In three years he would have written as much as nine such books contain.[53]

Students will bring their writing to class where it will be submitted for criticism to their teacher and fellow students. The criticism will be of a special variety; not literary criticism meant for public consumption, but helpful criticism. "Helpful criticism," Page explains,

> is a personal and friendly and intimate service that can best be done in private; and public criticism usually hardens a writer in his wrong ways by arousing his resentment. . . . The time to criticise writing, for artistic improvement, is before it is published; and the only criticism that helps a man to write better is his own criticism and that of fellow workmen while still writing.[54]

Again, a school for writers will not overlook the study of literature. But it will not pursue the usual method of college literary study either. Because it is dominated by philology, running to such tasks as the tracing of medieval legends from one language to another, literary study has neglected the art of expression, even showing a contempt for it. And this has had terrible effects on scholarship and the university. Publishing scholars "think it a mark of weakness to try to write well. They regard it as their sole business to be accurate," Page observes. "They do not regard it as their business to be graceful." The result is learning written up in a ponderous and impenetrable style, which cuts scholars off from the rest of the community and separates universities "from the life of the people," leading to "their loss of control and even of authority over the intellectual life of the nation." A school for writers, by promoting the study of literature not as a closed chapter of the human experience but as a vital part of actual human lives, will help reverse the decline of learning as a cultural force in American life by restoring the balance in universities between the acquisition and expression of knowledge. And it will do so by teaching literature not merely as something to be investigated but as something also to be *practiced*. This, Page says, "is the best method of developing a man for creative (and not merely acquisitive) work."[55]

The idea of a school for writers was given a mixed reception. George Krapp said that the "question of the relation of the study of literature to creative literary composition" was a perfectly legitimate one. "From the psychological point of view," he went on, "it certainly seems unjustifiable that a student's mind should be kept in the receptive and appreciative attitude throughout his whole consideration of a subject." At the same time, though, writing stories and plays to meet a commercial demand fell "obviously under the head of technical rather than liberal training," and did not belong among courses in English. Henry Van Dyke, the Princeton professor and moralistic essayist, went further. No school could train professional writers, he warned; nor should it if it could:

> In the first place, the world would not support them; in the second place, the flood of books with which our intellectual integrity is [already] somewhat threatened would be increased vastly, horribly; and, in the third place, the magazine editors would be driven either into an early grave or into a sanitarium.

Marion Dexter Learned, head of the German department at the University of Pennsylvania and president of the Modern Language Association, agreed that American writers were uneducated, but believed that only literary study—only the historical study of literary theory—lay the proper foundations for literary practice:

> It is—to use the language of my native heath—a "sorry sight" to see the scores of young writers essaying to create literature for this great people, but ignorant of the first principles of literary construction—novelists whose eyes are blank when the relation of novel and short story is under discussion; dramatists who have never seen Lessing's *Hamburgische Dramaturgie* or read Wilhelm Schlegel's *History of Dramatic Literature*; poets who would balk at the study of Schiller's *Briefe über die æstätische Erziehung der Menschen* or his essay *Ueber naive und sentimentalische Dichtung*.[56]

Such criticism may have indicated very little more than a confusion over whether a school for writers would be run along practical and professional or literary and artistic lines. Conceiving of writing as an art—a light and winged and holy thing—critics of professional training could not imagine how anyone could be professionally trained for it. As his own magazine the *World's Work* observed editorially in endorsing Page's plan, those who criticize the training of writers

> project the discussion into the region of "genius." Because any man cannot possibly hope to write with "genius," therefore he were foolish to give time to training. . . . Nobody seems to regard [writing] as a craft that can be taught.[57]

This was an exaggeration to make a point; many people in fact were starting to regard writing as a craft that could be taught; Page had proposed what others like George Pierce Baker, Brander Matthews, and Lewis Worthington Smith had already begun to do. By the time of his death in 1918, schools for the teaching of the profession of writing had become almost commonplace. Of course the new schools were not exactly what Page had envisioned: they were schools of mere journalism. The first journalism school unlocked its doors at the University of Missouri in 1908, and perhaps the most famous—Columbia's, which had initially been endowed in 1903—opened in 1912. Between 1908 and 1915, in fact, seventeen accredited university programs in journalism were founded.58

The *World's Work* was right, though. Genius had been detached from craft by the early years of the century. "Genius" referred to the portions of an academic subject that were excluded from consideration (see Chapter 2); what remained—the teachable element—was "craft." In the university teaching of writing what was increasingly neglected was self-expression. Composition classes sought the attainment of proficiency in English, while journalism schools devoted themselves to training young men and women for paying jobs on newspapers and magazines. Some other method would have to be found of developing young people for creative (and not merely acquisitive) work. In the meantime, genius would have to shift for itself.

Chapter 4

❧ *An Index of Adagios*

As the literary life became professionalized in the last years of the nineteenth century and the first years of the twentieth—as the writer with a small "w" moved abroad in the land, diverting literature from a calling to a craft—the poet, the writer for whom literature remained the chief excuse for existence, was left without visible means of support. The problem of getting a livelihood became his first concern. And when he found something—as Hart Crane did, being hired as an advertising copywriter in the J. Walter Thompson agency—he was "forced to be ambitious in two directions, you see, and in many ways it [was] like being put up on a cross and divided." Yet what else was he to do? "The situation for the artist in America seems . . . to be getting harder and harder all the time," Crane said. "If you make enough to live decently on, you have no time left for your real work—and otherwise you are constantly liable to starve." Real work and starvation, or being fed materially and going hungry artistically: these seemed to be the only options. Small wonder the poet dreamed of a place (in Edwin Arlington Robinson's words) "to unroll/ His index of adagios." To do the real work of poetry—"to console/ Humanity with what he knows"—the poet was convinced that he needed to be at leisure; literally, to live adagio.[1]

So the turn of a new century was witness to several attempts by poets to find a solution to the problem of living; a solution that would still afford them the leisure—the freedom from professionalism—to be poets. Two *modi vivendi* suggested themselves: bohemianism and the academic life. In truth, these two were more closely related than it might be thought, because both were related to the ideal of creative freedom, which can be understood either aesthetically (as freedom from artistic restraints) or socially and economically (as freedom from professional responsibilities). Operating under the influence of the latter, several poets—Ezra Pound, Robert Frost, William Vaughn Moody, Witter Bynner—tried short stints as professors before, like Longfellow, getting out at the first opportunity. At pretty much the same time, the California writers George Sterling and Mary Austin tried to devise a bohemian alternative for themselves, their friends, and younger postulants to the life of art like William Rose Benét and Sinclair Lewis. Such attempts were short-lived, because they were mere stopgaps; but within a few years they were absorbed into American higher education, where they were given an institutional structure; and what began in expediency wound up as a permanent fixture.

Resistance to the professionalization of poetry is over a century old. In 1885, George E. Woodberry lamented in the *Atlantic Monthly* that "the calling has no longer that fine indifference to mortal circumstance which gave it character when the favorite of the gods was honored of all men." The old tradition of inspiration and the *sacer vates*, Woodberry said, serves

> to set in bolder relief the book-making, money-getting, reputation-sustaining, in a word the professional poets, of the modern time; for if it be not altogether a new thing, certainly to a greater degree now than ever before do the acknowledged poets, the "kings of song," exercise their power out of mere habit.

Whether out of economic necessity or the desire to keep their names before the public, too many poets had begun to make a practice out of publishing "a new book of verses each year. . . ." Under such a regimen "an imaginative poet has little opportunity to select; he must print nearly all he writes that reaches respectability. . . ." The professional practice of poetry encourages the "substitution of routine in execution for a living art." In a lawyer, this takes the shape of a reliance upon legal formulas; in a poet, of reliance upon "the poetical blanks of verse-form, the set terms of his distinctive vocabulary . . . but more subtly in the very form of his customary thought." Thus professionalism "favors mediocrity in a man by cultivating content with what he is usually able to work out day by day, instead of discontent with all save what he can achieve at the full height of his nature in some fortunate moment; and hence for the true lyrist," Woodberry concluded, "it is a snare." Of course this view of the "true lyrist," discontent with professionalism and mediocrity, is the product of a particular point of view—that of romantic aestheticism. Even if it is mere ideological sloganeering, though, what it suggests *in practice* is a search for other than professional means to support the lyric motive.2

Woodberry himself turned to the university as a means of support, although it was for him only a temporary means. After teaching briefly at the University of Nebraska in his twenties, he was named professor of comparative literature at Columbia in 1891 at the age of thirty-six upon the recommendation of James Russell Lowell. He held the chair until 1904, when he quit in a dispute over pay—his teaching assistants' pay, not his own. He was a complete man of letters, writing poetry (and being ranked by the *Dial* at the turn of the century as one of the country's two greatest living poets) in addition to criticism. But though his students described him as a great teacher—John Erskine said that "the importance of his teaching lay precisely in the fact that he treated all literature as creative, as poetic, in the larger and truer sense"—Woodberry did not think of himself as much of a teacher at all. Something of his teaching method (and his attitude toward teaching) is captured in an anecdote. One day in class Woodberry interrupted a discussion of Keats. "Of course," he mused,

> if young Keats were sitting among you he would probably be ranked lowest in the class, but assuredly he would have the best time. You see, he was a poet. If I were running a college I would work out an experiment whereby the boys who had the best time would get the highest marks. But then, I suspect I am not a real professor.

The importance of Woodberry as a historical figure lies precisely in the fact that he was *not* a real professor. As he said in his "New Defense of Poetry"— a forthright defense of aesthetic idealism—the question that faces the young poet is "how to live as well as how to express life," and the answer is "to make one's life a poem, as Milton dreamed of the true poet. . . ." The answer, in other words, is not a real one. For the poet, something other than a practical, professional life was to be sought.[3]

Thus the search was less for a career, some kind of sustained and remunerative work, than for a *situation*. And thus the tendency was to think in terms of places rather than professions. This is the truth of the matter, I believe, about Edwin Arlington Robinson's great poem "Hillcrest," which was named after the house in which he lodged every summer at the MacDowell Colony in Peterborough, New Hampshire, from 1911—four years after the Colony's opening—until the last year of his life. In the poem Robinson spins out a vision of the ideal working situation for a poet. As a meditation on the relationship between poetry and its circumstances in the world, "Hillcrest" is an effort to create (and defend) a place for poetry in modern America—just as the MacDowell Colony itself was an effort to do much the same, in a more practical way, for individual writers and composers. Here is the poem in full:

> No sound of any storm that shakes
> Old island walls with older seas
> Comes here where now September makes
> An island in a sea of trees.
>
> Between the sunlight and the shade
> A man may learn till he forgets
> The roaring of a world remade
> And all his ruins and regrets;

And if he still remembers here
Poor fights he may have won or lost—
If he be ridden with the fear
Of what some other fight may cost—

If, eager to confuse too soon
What he has known with what may be,
He reads a planet out of tune
For cause of his jarred harmony—

If here he venture to unroll
His index of adagios,
And he be given to console
Humanity with what he knows—

He may by contemplation learn
A little more than what he knew,
And even see great oaks return
To acorns out of which they grew.

He may, if he but listen well,
Through twilight and the silence here
Be told what there are none may tell
To vanity's impatient ear;

And he may never dare again
Say what awaits him, or be sure
What sunlit labyrinth of pain
He may not enter and endure.

Who knows today from yesterday
May learn to count no thing too strange:
Love builds of what Time takes away,
Till Death itself is less than Change.

Who sees enough in his duress
May go as far as dreams have gone;
Who sees a little may do less
Than many who are blind have done;

Who sees unchastened here the soul
Triumphant has no other sight
Than has a child who sees the whole
World radiant with his own delight.

Far journeys and hard wandering
Await him in whose crude surmise
Peace, like a mask, hides everything
That is and has been from his eyes;

And all his wisdom is unfound,
Or like a web that error weaves
On airy looms that have a sound
No louder now than falling leaves.4

"Hillcrest" develops a vision of the poetic life that is closely wedded to withdrawal from the world. At first it may seem as if the poem were intended merely to decorate the conceit of the tower, the monastic retreat. And indeed Robinson characterizes the MacDowell Colony as being far from the storms that shake the ancient edges of civilization: "Old island walls," "older seas." By contrast the artists' colony lies inland—an "island in a sea of trees"—a modern refuge from the modern world, the "roaring of a world remade," where the artist can forget the "ruins and regrets" of experience. What is being endorsed here, however, is not an escape from experience but a withdrawal into the privacy of experience, where the poet "may by contemplation learn/A little more than what he knew. . . ." The key word is *contemplation*—the traditional name for the poet's style of cognition. It enlarges knowledge, but requires a withdrawal into silence, where the poet may be given to overhear what is not told to "vanity's impatient ear." *Vanity* is meant here in Dr. Johnson's sense of "busy scenes of crowded life"—the professional world of book-making and money-getting and reputation-sustaining. Only if he gets away from this world will the poet have the courage to confront his "duress," the inevitable unhappiness of human experience. Retreat to such a place as Hillcrest, then, trains a poet in stoic acceptance and endurance of his fate. Since he must learn to endure his private tragedy— that is one thing which sets him apart from other men—the poet positively *needs* a place like Hillcrest. But though it is necessary, it is not sufficient. Anyone who comes "unchastened here," who sings "the soul/ Triumphant," is little better than a child "who sees the whole/ World radiant with his own delight." Genuine delight—the genuine effect of genuine art—is reserved for those, not who sing their souls, but unsparingly examine them. The business, the crowdedness, of an active life is foregone; but the goal is not simple "Peace," because this would merely be the consequence of escaping the inner torment of self-understanding. Those who will go to any lengths to avoid the truth are those who say they long for peace; the longing is a "mask" for the flight from truth. In short, life at the MacDowell Colony taught Robinson that the poet needs a working situation that provides him with a retreat from which to scrutinize and evaluate his suffering. The last verse paragraph draws the contrast. For the person who flees when stymied by a problem self-understanding is permanently out of reach: "Far journeys and hard wandering/ Await him. . . ." The self-deluded seek the peace of self-ignorance, and plunge into the noisy world to escape themselves. The poet needs a place "No louder now than falling leaves" to undergo the throbbing anguish of contemplation.

George E. Woodberry and Edwin Arlington Robinson exemplify the main choices that were available to poets at the turn of the century. As the years wore on an increasing number of teaching jobs became open to poets, many of whom continued to hold out for a better situation—one in which they could devote themselves to their real work, even if the money was not as good. In 1898, for instance, through the intervention of a friend, Robinson obtained a clerk's job at Harvard. By then he had published two books—the privately printed *Torrent and the Night* (1897) and *The Children of the Night* (1898)—but he was as obscure as Jude and probably would not have been considered for a teaching post even if he had wanted one, which he did not. He wanted nothing to interfere with his writing. Upon the death of his father in 1899 he moved to New York to write poems and live in poverty. In 1905 his work came to the attention of President Roosevelt, who was moved to create a $2000-a-year sinecure for him as a special agent for the Treasury; he held the post until 1910, when President Taft eliminated it. By then, however, he was able to scratch out a living on the earnings from his writing—in large part because he summered at the MacDowell Colony, living rent free.5

The devotion to poverty while hoping for a better situation, a retreat from the busy scenes of crowded life, was also at the root of bohemianism, which displayed itself as a repugnance for professionalism and business. In the first decade of the new century, the "king of San Francisco bohemia"— the now forgotten poet George Sterling (1869–1926)—founded the first rural artists' colony in the United States at Carmel, California. Sterling's original intention was not to set on foot a new American cultural institution, but merely "to find out for myself whether or not one can exist on little money and less 'society,' " while creating art. Sterling wished only to realize, for himself, the vision articulated in Robinson's "Hillcrest." What the artists' colony at Carmel became, however, was the concrete representation of a nonprofessional way of life, and a model for subsequent attempts to devise an artists' alternative to professionalism—including the writers' workshop.6

Sterling feared that he would come to be known as "the man who made Carmel famous" rather than a poet, which was how he wanted to be remembered. Unfortunately, this is exactly what happened. Although the town is better known today as the home of Clint Eastwood—it is more of an upscale celebrities' preserve than a bohemian artists' colony—Carmel became famous as a result of its association with Sterling, who enjoyed notoriety in the early part of the century after Ambrose Bierce praised him in an article in *Cosmopolitan* as "a very great poet—incomparably, the greatest that we have on this side of the Atlantic." Sterling drew many other writers to Carmel, some for longer stays than others—Mary Austin, Jack London, Upton Sinclair, Van Wyck Brooks, William Rose Benét, Sinclair Lewis. So much talent gathered in one place that at least to residents it seemed only a matter of time before California became the locus of American art, with Carmel as its center. In retrospect, though, it is an open question whether Carmel attracted notice because of the art that was being created there, or perhaps for some other reason. In an article published in the *Los Angeles Times* in May 1910, Willard Huntington Wright—later the editor of the *Smart Set* and after that the mystery novelist S. S. Van Dine—described Carmel as a "hotbed of soulful culture" and a "vortex of erotic erudition."7

George Sterling was born in Sag Harbor, New York. While at St. Charles College in Maryland he studied under a priest-poet named John Bannister Tabb, a fairly good epigrammatist in the Herrick manner. And though Father Tabb coddled the young man, directing his reading and believing in his talents, Sterling said later that he did not experience "the urge to become a poet" until "the scandalously mature age of twenty-six." By that time he had been working for five years as the right-hand man to his uncle Frank C. Havens, a multimillionaire land developer in the Bay Area. Sterling lived in the Piedmont Hills above Oakland and commuted to San Francisco for work—a bohemian on the weekends, a businessman during the day. It was his craving for the full bohemian experience in fact that pushed him toward poetry. His friend Jack London accused him of living a lie. The businessman's existence, London said, was

> Just somebody else's way of thinking and living you've taken over, and it's not what you want. If it was satisfactory, you would stay close to Piedmont over the week-end and make money the rest of the time. You have everything to make you a financier and you want to be a poet.

What then did London recommend as an alternative? Not the university; that much was certain. London, who had studied briefly at Berkeley, sneered at academic life in terms that would have been familiar to Thorstein Veblen:

> Benjamin Ide Wheeler is put at the head of the [U]niversity [of California] because he knows Greek. His Greek impresses the legislators who don't know a word of it. The legislators appropriate vast sums of money. For what? To develop promising materials into scholars? To make the embryonic creative artist secure during his period of great growth? No, to build buildings.

If a young man hoped to develop himself as a creative artist he had to break with business and the institutions of American culture. It may be wondered, though, whether art was the motive for the break—at least in Sterling's case—or a byproduct of it, an effort to justify rebellion after the fact. It is not clear whether, for Sterling, poetry demanded a bohemian existence, or bohemianism poetry. Sterling explained that "There are two elements, at least, that are essential to Bohemianism. The first is devotion or addiction to one or more of the Seven Arts; the other is poverty." He appeared to want to write poetry, in other words, because he did not want to be a businessman. "Above all," said his friend Joseph Noel, "he hated being a commuter and a good provider. They seemed to contain elements of genuine failure."8

In 1905 a land developer named Frank Powers offered Sterling a lot on the cheap, hoping he would establish an artists' colony that would attract other buyers to the area. With a gift of $40,000 from his uncle, Sterling purchased the lot and built a redwood house half a mile from town. In San Francisco, he complained, he had been "beat upon and semi-submerged by temptations to folly and luxury as an outling [*sic*] reef is harassed by the waves"—the life of business, he implied, had driven him to bohemian excesses like drunkenness and adultery. In Carmel, by contrast, "I will be able to live naturally and quietly, asking friends to visit me only as I want them," he said. "Already several 'literary gents' have signified a desire to come with me; but I wish to be a lone pioneer. . . ." Within months, however, the lone pioneer was joined by two other artists—the photographer Arnold Gethe and the novelist Mary Austin. Stimulated by his neighbors more than he expected to be, Sterling tried to convince his old friends Bierce and London to move to Carmel too: "I expect to stay here all my life," he wrote: "this is the only place I've ever seen that's fit to live in." London came often, leaving a record of the colony in his novel *The Valley of the Moon* (1913), but Bierce hung back. Carmel, he said, was full of "cranks and curios. . . . I'd not *live* there and be 'identified' with it, as the newspapers would say. I'm warned by Hawthorne and Brook Farm."9

Carmel's success was one part act of God, one part personal tragedy. First the San Francisco earthquake of April 18, 1906, displaced much of the city's bohemian element, which transferred its operations to the fledgling colony. Newcomers included Nora May French, a glamorously beautiful blonde poet; Jimmy Hopper, a journalist and story writer; Geraldine Bonner, another journalist and story writer; the poet Henry Laffler; the painter Xavier Martinez; Ray Stannard Baker, the muckraking journalist; and Harry Leon Wilson, the popular novelist. The next summer a reporter from the *New York Times Book Review* traveled to Carmel to do a story on the colony, suggesting that its fame now stretched across the country. Its permanent fame was secured in November of that year when Nora May French died by her own hand after trying first to poison Jimmy Hopper, whom she loved unrequitedly. She had prepared a cyanide-laced sandwich for Hopper in Sterling's kitchen, but in bringing it to him she stumbled and dropped it. Sterling's dog gobbled it and died almost immediately, in horrible spasms. Later the same night, before bed, French herself drank cyanide. Hopper never forgave himself: "She was playing tag with us tangle-footed blunderers, and suddenly with a dodge and a dart she eluded us—forever."10

In time suicide would claim several of the original Carmelites, including Sterling and London. Despite the lurid features of its story, though, Sterling's colony at Carmel was a serious attempt to create an ideal working environment for artists. William Rose Benét, who stayed only briefly, later described the Carmel life in *The Dust Which Is God* (1941): the men and women who lived there "talked about poetry/ and socialism and philosophy/ sang songs and quoted friends" and "moaned and groaned at writing. . . ."11 In *The Valley of the Moon*, London's two main characters, Billy and Saxon Roberts, come to Carmel to escape the city, looking for a place to settle. What they find instead is a running party—heavy eating, heavier lovemaking; drinking the heaviest of all.

> But it was not all play in Carmel. That portion of the community which Saxon and Billy came to know, 'the crowd,' was hard-working. Some worked regularly, in the morning or late at night. Others worked spasmodically, like the wild Irish playwright who would shut himself up for a week at a time, then emerge, pale and drawn, to play like a madman against the time of his next retirement.12

In her autobiography *Earth Horizon* (1932), Mary Austin says that the colonists "settled into a habit of morning work which it was anathema to interrupt." By early afternoon, though, worn out by the creative struggle and desperate for company, the writers and painters would emerge from their cabins "to sun themselves . . . and to make delightful impromptu disposals of the rest of the day."13 Such descriptions could be easily transplanted into a memoir of the Iowa Writers' Workshop. The colony at Carmel was an intense "hotbed" and "vortex" of creative work, not a utopian commune—despite the vague feelings of bohemian socialism that led some colonists to explain their motivations by saying that they had "spent their lives in a battle with the evil forces of Society; with poverty, sickness and despair. They have come out of the social pit" and yearned to be "free from landlords and steam-heat, and taxes."14 Politics was a staple of discussion, as in any gathering of artists and intellectuals, but the main topic was literature. Sterling complained that there was so much literary conversation on the beach at Carmel that he suffered from "book indigestion." And the talk was mere background to work. In one year—1907—Jimmy Hopper wrote a dozen stories and a novelistic exposé of prison conditions called *9009*. Nor was he an exception. According to Harry Leon Wilson, the Carmel post office handled more rejected manuscripts than any other post office of its size in the country.15

As in a writers' workshop so too at Carmel there was creative interaction between older and younger writers. Sinclair Lewis, still in his twenties and recently fired from an editorial job on the *San Francisco Bulletin* that Sterling had obtained for him, turned up in Carmel with a card file of plots—

well over a hundred plots, London was intrigued; he was the sort of writer who was better at working out stories than hatching them; he offered to buy some of Lewis's plots for five dollars apiece. Lewis sold him fourteen. One of these was *The Assassination Bureau*, which London left unfinished but was eventually made into a popular movie. There were the familiar sights and sidelights, too. In 1910 the colony established an outdoor theater and staged dramas that were written by the colonists. Before long the growing town of Carmel included a row of houses where some twenty professors from Berkeley and Stanford maintained summer residences, although the professors and the artists kept strictly apart like Jews and Arabs on the West Bank. Everyone in Carmel, living on the margins of civilized respectability, seemed to let himself go a little wild. In his *Los Angeles Times* article, W. H. Wright described the weird clothing and long hair of the colonists—"more hair per capita than in any town in America."[16]

Although it was a success in many ways, the Carmel colony was not without problems. And the biggest problem was implicit in the very idea of an artists' colony: it entailed a conflict between the yearning for a situation of ideal freedom in surroundings of natural beauty and the passionate seriousness, the almost pathetic earnestness, of the motives behind such yearning. On the one hand Carmel represented an escape from being a commuter and a good provider, from landlords and steam-heat and taxes. "It was a heady locale for free spirits," said one of Sterling's admirers, "for men and women who were at odds with the world and yearned to express this revolt, less with a challenge than with the portrayal of the Good Life."[17] On the other hand the colony was meant to be a hotbed of work—serious work. The conflict strained and warped many a personality. Ambrose Bierce was astutely insightful: Carmel replayed the theme of *The Blithedale Romance* with Nora May French in the role of Zenobia. No wonder Saxon Roberts in London's *Valley of the Moon* discovers that all is not well in the artists' colony. The colonists tend toward a pessimism that she attributes to the reading of too many books:

> The wild Irish playwright had terrible spells of depression. Shelley, who wrote vaudeville turns in the concrete cell, was a chronic pessimist. St. John, a young magazine writer, was an anarchic disciple of Nietzsche. Masson, a painter, held to a doctrine of eternal recurrence that was petrifying. And Hall [a poet who is modeled upon Sterling], usually so merry, could outfoot them all when he once got started on the cosmic pathos of religion and the gibbering anthropomorphisms of those who love not to die. At such times Saxon was oppressed by these sad children of art. It was inconceivable that they, of all people, should be so forlorn.[18]

The reason they were so forlorn was that they could not decide between the Good Life, flamboyantly expressing their contempt for the social pit, and a life of unremitting creative labor, which simply required making themselves unavailable to other people.[19]

The conflict was worsened by the beauty of Carmel itself. Harry Leon Wilson wrote to a friend that "It has the scenic beauty of Capri, more to my thinking, because it has more variety, and the climate is the perfection of the Italian climate. . . . I have never grown tired of the place, never got enough of its beauty."[20] Although Wilson himself worked hard and productively there, the climate and natural beauty of Carmel could be debilitating. Van Wyck Brooks, who first visited the colony in 1911, said that some writers

> who had come from the East to write novels in this paradise found themselves there becalmed and supine. They gave themselves over to day-dreams while their minds ran down like clocks, as if they had lost the keys to wind them up with, and they turned into beachcombers, listlessly reading books they had read ten times before and searching the rocks for abalones. For this Arcadia lay, one felt, outside the world in which thought evolves and which came to seem insubstantial in the bland sunny air.[21]

Whether it was the paradisal scenery or the book-induced pessimism, the merrymaking or the intrigues and suicide, life at the Carmel colony was forever threatening to become more absorbing than the work that was done there. It was also too closely associated with its founders to outlast them for very long. Diagnosed with breast cancer and told she had nine months to live, Mary Austin left Carmel in 1908; she wanted to die in Rome (she lived another sixteen years). George Sterling stayed on until 1914, when a divorce settlement cleaned him out; he returned to San Francisco, living in a room in the Bohemian Club on the generosity of an unnamed benefactor, until killing himself in 1926 with a dose of cyanide.[22] By the time Robinson Jeffers settled in Carmel in 1916, the colony had broken up. Jeffers came not as a free spirit but as a recluse: Carmel for him was not a scenic justification for breaking with society, but a courageous withdrawal into solitude. He built a house of granite there, and settled down to patient work. A few years later, in the short poem "People and a Heron," he recounted a day in his life at Carmel:

> A desert of weed and water-darkened stone under my western
>   windows
> The ebb lasted all afternoon,
> And many pieces of humanity, men, women, and children, gathering
>   shellfish,
> Swarmed with voices of gulls the sea-breach.
> At twilight they went off together, the verge was left vacant, an
>   evening heron
> Bent broad wings over the black ebb,
> And left me wondering why a lone bird was dearer to me than many
>   people.

Well· rare is dear: but also I suppose
Well reconciled with the world but not with our own natures we
    grudge to see them
Reflected on the world for a mirror.23

Critics describe this view as Jeffers's "inhumanism." Unlike many
Carmelites, he was not well reconciled with the world, let alone his nature,
and he begrudged the sight of other people—they reminded him that he was
more reconciled than he cared to admit. He preferred the company of granite, herons, sea-verge. He came to Carmel to find a Hillcrest, not a colony.

Other people preferred a colony, however, and soon the Carmel experiment was duplicated in other heady locales. What was sought was a compromise between a bohemian retreat and an academic program; what was
offered was a temporary accommodation—the summer conference. The
most famous was the Bread Loaf Writers' Conference, inaugurated in 1926,
which grew out of a summer school in English language and literature held
at a rambling three-story inn on the slopes of the Green Mountains about
twelve miles away from Middlebury College. The college had received the
inn and 30,000 acres of adjoining forest as a bequest in 1915, but within four
years it had decided to get out of the innkeeping business. The college faculty intervened to prevent the sale of the property, and in 1920 the first
school in English was held at the inn. "Investing it with this academic purpose," says Bread Loaf's historian, "justified its upkeep to the college
trustees and thus saved it from the melancholy fate of so many nineteenth-
century summer hotels."24 It was also saved from the fate of an artists'
colony like the one at Carmel. Summer conferences like Bread Loaf (or private summer retreats like the MacDowell Colony and Yaddo, the former
Trask estate in Saratoga Springs, New York, which opened in 1926) invested
the artist's yearning to live adagio—at leisure—with academic purpose, official status, a kind of social approval.25

Originally the summer school at Bread Loaf did not include the teaching of creative writing, although English composition was on the program.
In 1926, in order to keep the inn in use for another two weeks at the end of
summer, a "supplementary short course" was added, as the president of
Middlebury College put it, "purely for creative writing."26 The first session—calling itself the Bread Loaf Conferences on Creative Writing—was
held during the last two weeks of August. Organized by John Farrar, editor
of the *Bookman*, the conference announced in a leaflet that it would offer
"Expert guidance in literary problems for young people who are learning to
write. . . ." The leaflet went on:

> The program will consist of background lectures on the writing of short stories,
> novels, essays, plays and poems, with practical suggestions on developing a
> prose style and the preparation and placing of manuscripts. Informal discus-

sions on both the artistic and practical problems of creative writing, and group and individual conferences on manuscripts brought by the students, will furnish opportunity for professional criticism that should result in marketable writing.[27]

Clearly this was a striking idea—an attempt to realize Walter H. Page's dream of a professional school for writers, albeit in two short weeks. What the Bread Loaf program consisted of, though, was not really creative writing—it focused upon "practical problems" and "marketable writing." Creative writing per se is associated with the ideology of the aesthetic, which entails a rejection of the practical and marketable. Bread Loaf's historian says that although "inhabitants of the ivory tower" might find the practical emphasis "crass," the writers' conference succeeded in grafting "at least some of the academic community's standard of impartiality of education in promoting excellence in writing . . . onto the goal of demonstrating how to earn a living from it."[28] It would be more accurate to characterize Bread Loaf as one more in the long line of efforts to teach practical, professional writing (and a rather belated one at that), which I described in Chapter 3. It had little influence upon the development of creative writing per se. Bread Loaf's interest does not lie in its conception as a teaching institution, because it did not steady itself and begin to achieve success until the thirties when Theodore Morrison took over as its director. At the time, as he recalled, "The Conference was not well-known; its advertising and publicity were slight both in budget and in the spread of potential clients they reached."[29] Attendance during Morrison's first summer on the job (1932) was twenty-three. From the first, Bread Loaf was significant not in pioneering the teaching of creative writing—not many students were taught—but in conferring an academic structure and definition upon the rural artists' retreat. To go no further than 1932, the roster of writers who were given room and board and a little pay in return for lecturing on writing at Bread Loaf is impressive— Robert Frost, Sinclair Lewis, Stephen Vincent Benét, Archibald MacLeish, the Fugitive poet Donald Davidson, Gorham Munson, editor of *Secession*, Hervey Allen, author of *Anthony Adverse*, Margaret Widdemer, a Pulitzer Prize–winning poet, and Dorothy Canfield Fisher among others. It was not the teaching of creative writing, it was the recruitment of creative writers to teach, that made Bread Loaf important.

Bohemianism (as represented by the yearning for a retreat to a life adagio) is closer to academic traditions than might be expected. The sociologist Edward Shils, citing Helen Waddell's *Wandering Scholars*, points out that the ancestors of the Carmel colonists and the guest lecturers at Bread Loaf were the "restless scholars of the medieval universities and the homeless minstrels and minnesingers who lived from begging, thieving, and the hope of selling their artistic wares. . . ." The medieval scholars were footloose, Shils explains:

they were not incorporated into the routines and responsibilities which filled most of the medieval European social structure. They would not accept the burdens of family and vocation, and sought only to serve their own creative impulse and pleasure.30

Academic conferences and the visiting professorship are vestiges of the medieval tradition, but so too is the self-elected vagabondism and poverty of turn-of-the-century poets, who sought a position not in order to undertake a routine and accept responsibilities—they were awarded few permanent positions—but to seek a temporary relief from homelessness and beggary. Ezra Pound, for example, who would give it a try for one brief infamous year at Wabash College, showed that the academic life was imagined by at least one poet as a refuge from vagabondism. In 1907 (the year he earned his master's degree), in a poem written as a sort of valediction to being supported by his father (who had apparently ordered him to get a job), Pound asked his verse to tell

> To the bards in hell
> Who live on nothing a year
> That a Master of Arts
> And a man of parts
> Is trying the same thing here.

The poet's earthly life, he said, was an "ancient story"—illness, unpaid bills, and the desire for "glory" instead of a mortgage. And indeed the story is so ancient that its meaning has changed: poetic vagabondism, the insistence upon serving only one's creative impulse, has become a complaint against life, for which the vagabond feels contempt, envying the dead poets in their "good warm rooms below. . . ." And yet the burdens of family and a steady income are no longer a choice to be refused, but a condition to be mourned, and corrected if possible. Academe thus becomes the career for a poet who wants neither to have a career nor to renounce careerism altogether.31

Such an ad hoc, unplanned approach to life displayed itself in Pound's next few impulsive years. Shortly after becoming a Master of Arts and a man of parts, Pound was awarded a $500 postgraduate fellowship in romance languages at the University of Pennsylvania. He had no intention of undertaking a scholarly career, though. "The scholar," he said in an early magazine article, "is compelled to spend most of his time learning what his author ate and wore, and in endless pondering over some utterly unanswerable question of textual criticism. . . ." His decision not to go on to the Ph.D. seems to have been motivated by disdain for the routines and responsibilities of scholarship. Pound spoke with pride of being the only student to flunk Josiah Penniman's course in the history of literary criticism—and also the only student to take any interest in the subject. He boasted to a friend that he had "spatted with nearly everybody" at Penn. Yet despite his penchant for spatting with academic authorities, Pound took a position teaching French,

Spanish, and Italian at Wabash, a small Presbyterian school in Indiana. He rented a room in a lodging house frequented by roadshow actors and vaude-villians; he was seen around in town in black velvet jackets and flowing bow ties, wearing a floppy wide-brimmed hat and carrying a malacca cane; he spent much time in the art shop of a local painter who had studied in Paris and was considered "advanced" company. What happened in the sequel has often been told. One cold night in February 1908 he came upon a chorus girl (a "lady-gent impersonator," as Pound described her) who had been stranded when her show left town without her; he offered her a cup of warm tea and a place to stay. In one version of the story she slept in his bed while Pound slept on the floor, fully clothed, although a second version has it that she and Pound became involved. At all events, the college officials heard the story and the young poet-professor was sent packing.[32]

As J. V. Cunningham would later say, there was a conflict between the pedant and the creative soul.[33] And what is interesting is the question why the creative soul would even want to dwell in the precincts of the pedant. The answer, I think, is that for a poet like Pound the academic life was an *opportunity*—a way to be supported while doing something that was not entirely removed from scholarship. Thus the poet's complaint about scholarship often had little to do with scholarship as such; it was more likely to be concerned with the effort, the sheer amount of time, required for serious scholarship and other academic duties. What Pound wanted, evidently, was the benefits of the academic life with none of its costs—the pleasure without the commitment. If he and other early creative souls in the university were unclear why they were there the reason is that they had given little thought to the matter.

One such creative soul was the poet William Vaughn Moody (1869–1910). After Longfellow he was perhaps the first American poet to pre-pare himself explicitly for a career as a professor, choosing it (in the words of one student of his life) as "the least uncongenial" line of work open to him. Graduate training in English, though, nearly changed his mind. First the master's examination, then a thesis on the sources of Sir Philip Sidney's *Arcadia*: the whole ordeal, he wrote to Robert Morss Lovett, "left me limp as a rag, and [has] convinced me that, instead of an amiable divorce such as you suggest, Philology and Minerva"—learning and culture, that is, or pedantry and creativeness—"are destined to part with mutual scorn and vituperation, if indeed their feud does not result in pistols and pillow-chokings."[34]

Moody was born in Spencer, Indiana, the son of an ex–riverboat cap-tain and accountant.[35] After his father's death in 1886, Moody taught in a local school for a year and then left for Poughkeepsie, New York, to tutor his uncle's son for Yale. He himself entered Harvard in 1889, continuing to sup-port himself by tutoring college-bound men. It was this experience as a tutor that seems to have convinced Moody that he might make a not uncongenial professor. He soaked himself in the Harvard tradition, taking courses in Anglo-Saxon and Shakespeare from Francis J. Child, in the seventeenth century from Le Baron Briggs, and in the earlier nineteenth century from Adams Sherman Hill. But his fondest wish was to be a poet. And so he joined the literary circle around Barrett Wendell and the *Harvard Monthly*, publishing monologues in the manner of Browning. While still an undergraduate he tasted first success, landing a poem in *Scribner's*—"a professional magazine," as he apologetically described it to a girlfriend. Graduating second in his class in 1892, he stayed on at Harvard for what he hoped would be "an indefinite period," completing an M.A. in 1894 and then joining the English department the following year as an assistant in sophomore composition. He would not have taken the job, he told a friend, if he had not seen that out of Harvard composition emerged men of letters—"did I not have," as he phrased it, "such splendid examples before my eyes of gorgeous scholastic butterflies hatched from this dull cocoon."[36]

There is no telling whether he would ever have become a scholastic butterfly. All Moody was aware of was the dullness of the cocoon. Theme-correcting, he complained, demanded "early morning and midnight coping." He wrote little during his first year on the job—or he saved little—and throughout his career he found it difficult to write any poetry worth saving while also attending to his academic duties. He dreamed of release; he plotted escape. At first this assumed the form of looking for a better situation. In the spring of 1895, A. S. Hill offered him an instructorship and at about the same time his old friend Robert Herrick, now teaching at the University of Chicago, wrote to offer the same thing. Moody inclined toward Hill's offer, because it held out "a prospect, dim perhaps but cherishable, of pinching a fellowship at the end of it"—that is, of getting a year off, with pay, to study and write. Less than a month later he had reconsidered, though, and accepted the job at Chicago. The deciding factor seems to have been a higher salary. "I hope you will not think that I take an altogether mercenary view of the situation," Moody wrote to Robert Morss Lovett: "you must take the spiritual sub-intention for granted." Leaving Cambridge, he believed, would be good for him *and* his poetry. His biographer theorizes that Moody, who was detached and standoffish in personal relationships, was similarly detached from his experience at Harvard. "Harvard is a nourishing mother, but she keeps her children in leading strings until they reach an unseemly age," he wrote to Herrick. "I shall of course have to endure a pang or two at leaving Harvard but at bottom I shall feel a certain sense of liberation."[37]

Leaving Harvard for Chicago did not immediately liberate him from the early morning and midnight coping with student themes. Moody was assigned two sections of four-day-a-week English composition, one with forty students, the other with twenty. "Bah!" he reflected. Instead of struggling with the "hundred passionate powers and live hungers" that tingled through him, he found himself delivering "reptilian lectures on the structure of the paragraph." In his second quarter he was permitted to teach a little Keats and Shelley. And in the fall of his second year he handled his first course in advanced composition. Here at last Moody displayed the motives that first led him to seek the opportunity of combining poetry with teaching. The course, according to one student, was "artistic" in its emphasis. It was really a course in the daily theme, although Moody offered his students three options for lending their themes some coherence: the familiar journal, which was to be concerned with inner experience; the ordinary journal, which was to be founded upon observation and description of external reality; and the sketch book, in which (he told his students) the writer "should imagine himself an artist and his blank page, his canvas." He also accepted poetry, but urged students not to hand in poetry unless their aim was to write with power. "To have power in writing Poetry," he advised, "drench every word and line in suggestiveness." For one student the argument of the course was "Life and beauty for its own sake." Moody called this the Greek ideal, but it could be more accurately described as the liberal ideal restated by a creative soul.[38]

Despite a local reputation for bohemianism ("a Lovelace of the public parks," as he characterized himself, "a patient scavenger of the odds and ends of street adventure," he was often seen crossing campus early in the morning, hair disheveled after spending the night outdoors), Moody was held in esteem at Chicago. His third-year course assignments suggest as much. He was given courses in seventeenth-century poetry and the history and principles of versification, both of which he enjoyed; something rare for him. And his approach to the teaching of versification suggests that the esteem was not misplaced: Moody taught the principles of the French post-Symbolist poets, probably one of the first professors in America to do so. By the end his third year, though, Moody had exhausted himself; he begged his superiors to find someone to take his place; then he left for an extended stay in Europe. Six months later he was back in Chicago, unsure why he was depressed—unless it was teaching that depressed him. To a friend he described it as emasculating. No sooner had a new quarter begun than he was "heartily sick of theme work. . . . Every week I spend over it makes it more impossible for me to take my day-to-day existence seriously," he said: it made him feel "sheepish" in the face of "men who are doing the virile thing in a virile way." After meeting E. A. Robinson in February 1899, Moody was more conscious than ever of "not having sooner chosen the path of real courage," although his choice of teaching over the life of poverty—Robinson's choice—was "made tolerable by the increasing prospect of something like liberty in the future."[39]

The prospect improved the next year when Moody preceded Robert Lowell in writing an ode on Augustus St. Gaudens's monument in the Boston Common to Robert Gould Shaw and his black regiment in the Civil War. "An Ode in Time of Hesitation"—an openly anti-imperialist poem, one of the few works of American literature inspired by the Spanish-American War—appeared in the *Atlantic*. It created an immediate sensation and altered the course of Moody's career. Houghton Mifflin agreed to become his publisher; his verse began to appear regularly in national magazines like the *Atlantic* and *Scribner's*; his first book was released in 1901 to wide and exorbitant praise. (William Morton Payne, editor of the *Dial*, ranked him along with G. E. Woodberry as America's two greatest living poets.) Eager to maintain its connection with a celebrated poet, Chicago awarded him a promotion and a raise to $1600 for a two-quarter teaching load restricted to literature (no more composition).[40] Even so, after 1901 Moody rarely taught. Although his courses were announced, they were always withdrawn before the time arrived. He was offered the full salary of a professor if he would consent to lecture for only one quarter out of the year.[41] And still he avoided the Chicago campus, renting a studio in New York and traveling often to Europe. He did not want to burn his academic bridges, but he also did not want to commit himself to any academic duties. He explained:

> I am unwilling to bind myself just now by an agreement to teach any specified quarter. When the work which I have now in hand is done, I shall be very glad indeed to teach, but until then, I would rather keep myself entirely free.

There was always work in hand needing to be done. Coincidentally perhaps he turned from poetry to the drama at about the same time that he abandoned teaching, and his play *The Great Divide* (1906) ran on Broadway for over a year, earning him enough to win release from teaching forever. Thereafter he bristled when respectful critics referred to him as Professor Moody, and he resisted all inducements to return to the classroom.[42] "I cannot do it," he said; "I feel that at every lecture I slay a poet."[43]

Some poets may not have liked it, but academe was becoming established as a *pis-aller*. Joyce Kilmer, the young author of *Trees and Other Poems* who would be killed at the Marne in the First World War, thought it would lead to the abolition of poets. The business of poets was poetry, Kilmer declared, and the pursuit of a sideline (academic or otherwise) would spell the end for them. The process had already begun when poets began to become respectable. When they gave up looking like poets, he lamented, in "velvet jackets and sombreros," with hair to their shoulders,

> they took also to following prosaic occupations. Is there now living a man who does nothing but write verse? . . . Poets still write poetry, but the ancient art is no longer their chief excuse for existence. They come before the public in other and more commonplace guises. . . . All the poets have regular jobs.

For a time Alfred Noyes upheld the integrity of poetry and nothing else but poetry. "He alone, among book reviewing, story writing, magazine editing versifiers, was solely a poet," Kilmer said. "But now even he has taken up a side line. First he delivered the Lowell lectures; then he became a university professor. Over his laurel wreath he has put a mortar-board."[44]

Indeed the recruitment of poets to serve as university professors received its strongest boost when the most popular living poet—Alfred Noyes, author of "The Highwayman"—was recruited to teach at Princeton. Noyes taught at Princeton only briefly (from 1914 to 1916) and without particular distinction, but his appointment changed everything. The crucial fact was his immense popularity. If a poet like Noyes, self-supporting, in little need of money, could agree to teach at a university like Princeton it suggested that—except for those like Pound, Moody, and Kilmer still wedded to the medieval tradition of vagabondism—teaching was not a mere "prosaic occupation," but rather an honor. And, too, beginning with Moody and continuing with Noyes, universities saw the advantage to them of being associated with figures who were known outside the universities. The offer was tendered at Yale's graduation ceremony in 1913, where Noyes and Princeton president John Greer Hibben were both receiving honorary degrees. When the speechmaking and the pomp and circumstance were over, Hibben approached and asked Noyes if he would accept the Murray professorship of English literature—a chair named for Princeton's first English professor, the Rev. James O. Murray (see Chapter 1). Noyes understood that he was being honored, but he was not too flattered to bargain. "Though the invitation was tempting," he recalled, "I hesitated for some time, as I did not want anything to interfere with my writing; but on being told that I should have to lecture only twice a week for half the College year, and that the rest of my time would be at my own disposal, I accepted the offer. . . ."[45]

Noyes's method was to hold a "little weekly symposium, or preceptorial as it was called." Among his students were F. Scott Fitzgerald and Edmund Wilson. Neither was impressed with him. When a college friend's mother said that she had had lunch with "Alfred Noyes, the poet," Fitzgerald replied blandly, "Oh—is he a poet?" In later years Fitzgerald referred to his old teacher as "Alfred Noisy." Edmund Wilson found him to be of meagre inspiration to someone who was in training to become a modern writer, dismissing him as "prematurely middle-aged" and adding that "Noyes does not understand the modern world well enough to know what its romance consists of. . . ." Even so, he was of some help to both men. He printed five of Wilson's poems in his *Book of Princeton Verse* (1916), giving Wilson one of his first publications. The help he gave to Fitzgerald was less tangible but no less telling. As he recounted in his autobiography:

> Scott Fitzgerald once told me he thought he had it in his power to choose between writing books of permanent value, or writing for money. He asked me what I thought he should do, and I told him that if he wrote books of permanent value I believed he would have more satisfaction in the long run. He looked doubtful about this, and told me a little later that he had decided to "take the cash and let the credit go." But that was only expressing a mood of

the moment; and I think he was right in supposing he had the power to make the choice.

Noyes may have been a popular poet, and popularity may have been at odds with the modern image of the poet, but he was loyal to his academic em-ployer and its standard of impartiality—he was faithful to the aesthetic dis-avowal of the cash motive—and he believed the choice between them was within a writer's power. In this way he was an important founder of the American clan of poet-professors, turning it from a nostalgia for vagabond-ism toward a modern calling of some dignity.[46]

Although the poets did not linger in the academic groves—keening constantly for liberty and not wanting anything to interfere with their writ-ing—the appointments of Pound, Moody, and Noyes were intended to be permanent. Even Pound thought that tenure was worth waiting for—at least at first.[47] Perhaps as a concession to their restless and vagabond spirit, per-haps as a second best to permanent appointments, the idea evolved of hav-ing poets "in residence" on college campuses. The first two poets in resi-dence were Robert Frost, who taught at Amherst from 1917 to 1920, and Witter Bynner, who taught at Berkeley for one semester in 1919.

Frost almost single-handedly created the role of poet in residence, al-though somewhat by default. His appointment too was initially expected to be long-term: Amherst named him to the rank of full professor. Two things were different about Frost's academic experience. First, he never stayed for long in any one position, but unlike Pound, Moody, and Noyes he never en-tirely gave up teaching either. He taught at Amherst for two-and-a-half years before departing for a three-year stint as Fellow in the Creative Arts at the University of Michigan, and then he returned to Amherst to teach and lec-ture on several other occasions after 1920. Second, Frost was something of a theorist—or perhaps apologist—for the idea of hiring poets to teach. At the time of his initial appointment he was forty-three years old and had three books behind him: *A Boy's Will* (1913), *North of Boston* (1914), and *Mountain Interval* (1916). He had tried chicken farming—"so to speak," he said,

> but less as a farmer than as a fugitive from the world that seemed to 'disallow' me. It was all instinctive, but I can see now that I went away to save myself and fix myself before I measured my strength against all creation.[48]

After a chicken farm what better place for a fugitive from the world than a small liberal-arts college? Not merely a hideout, it would also be a place to try out ideas. Two years before coming to Amherst, Frost had written to a friend saying he coveted "a quiet job in a small college where I should be al-lowed to teach something a little new on the technique of writing."[49]

Frost's appointment—as was generally recognized at the time—was an experiment, and it points to the intimate connection between academic ex-perimentalism and the development of creative writing. The man who hired

Frost, Amherst president Alexander Meiklejohn, was one of the leading academic experimenters of the early century. A former philosophy professor at Brown who had been named to preside over Amherst in 1912 (and who went on after his resignation in 1920 to head up the experimental college of the University of Wisconsin), Meiklejohn believed—as he said in his inaugural address at Amherst—that "The college is the one agency specifically set apart by society for the training of the intellect." Above all else, then, the college should be a teaching institution. And yet teaching was being neglected in favor of scholarship. "Our future professors are rigorously prepared for the activities of scholarship," he observed. "We demand and require that they 'know their subjects.' But we do not demand that they understand or master the teaching process, that they know what students need and how their needs can be supplied." Behind the hiring of Frost was the hope that a poet, a man who had withdrawn to fix himself before measuring his strength against all creation (a man, moreover, who had taught previously at a preparatory school and a state teachers' college for women), might have some notion what students needed.[50]

"The general impression," said a professor at an eastern university, was that having a poet on campus "is an experiment which cannot succeed." Marion Hawthorne Hedges, a young Beloit professor and (future) novelist who favored the experiment, countered that "it is an event which ought to rock the educational world." What was so revolutionary about it? It was not that Frost heralded the coming of a new generation of college-trained poets. "[N]o advocate of creative teaching will for a moment pretend that colleges can, at will, or should undertake to produce gifted writers," Hedges said. Instead, the moral was that creative teachers "keep alive the creative principle in college" so that "students not gifted with the divine flame" will come "to understand and appreciate one who is" and will therefore populate "the great audiences who are inevitably the prerequisite to great writers." This was not far removed from the argument Frost himself advanced to justify his being on campus. He propounded what he called "education by presence," explaining that

> Students get most from professors who have marked wide horizons. If a teacher is a power outside as well as inside the college, one of whom you can hear along other highways, then that teacher is of deep potential value to the students. If the student suddenly finds that the teacher he has perchance listened to with indifferent attention or not at all, is known all over the country for something not too bad, suddenly his communication takes on luster.

Frost is arguing for a broadening of the traditional definition of liberalism in higher education. There is something else of importance in addition to learning for its own sake; there is also the value of studying under someone who has been heard of "along other highways." The argument is not as self-serving as it sounds; nor is it as radical. It had belonged among the tenets of writing instruction at least since Wendell (see Chapter 2). Frost is a little misleading in emphasizing celebrity, but the idea of education by presence is worth pondering: a man or woman should not merely *impart* a portion of the human heritage but should also *embody* it. Frost embodied "the creative principle." He made this patent in a letter written only a few days prior to taking up his duties at Amherst. In academic life, he said, "You get more credit for thinking if you restate formulae or cite cases that fall in easily under formulae, but all the fun is outside saying things that suggest formulae that won't formulate—that almost but don't quite formulate." This comes very close to defining the creative principle in education, which (following Emerson's lead in "The American Scholar") is insistently antiauthoritarian, individualistic, and extrainstitutional.[51]

The first true poet in residence was Witter Bynner, because his appointment at Berkeley was intended from the start to be a short-term one. The idea originated with Charles Mills Gayley, dean of undergraduate studies, who had already endorsed the proposal of accepting creative work for graduate credit in English (see Chapter 3). Now he took a bolder step toward installing the creative principle on an American campus. He hired Bynner to teach what would now be called a poetry workshop—a limited-enrollment "class for poetic experiment," as Bynner described it, to which students made application and were admitted on the basis of samples of their work. By the time he arrived in Berkeley the thirty-eight-year-old Bynner (1881-1968) had already published four books of verse and had a fifth in press. A homosexual who once proposed marriage to Edna St. Vincent Millay, he had nearly become an instructor in English at Harvard upon graduation in 1902, but after a grand tour of Europe he went to work for *McClure's* magazine instead. Once settled in at *McClure's* it never occurred to him to return to Harvard to teach. In 1906 he quit to devote himself full time to writing. Within a few years he was reduced to lecturing in order to earn money, and so Gayley's offer was welcome.[52]

Bynner taught only one semester at Berkeley. The reasons for his leaving may have been political, although Bynner said nothing publicly.[53] "Only once that 'first fine careless rapture' " was all he would say. And yet his one class in poetic experiment was remarkable for the number of students who later went on to make names for themselves—Hildegarde Flanner, Genevieve Taggard, David Greenhood, Stanton A. Coblentz, Idella Purnell, and Eda Lou Walton, who expanded the ripple by encouraging Henry Roth, the future author of *Call It Sleep*, while teaching at the City College of New York in the twenties. Bynner did not claim to have made them into poets: "they were poets when I met them," he said. He was not their teacher but "their friend and fellow worker." Unlike Frost, he had no plans for teaching something a little new on the technique of writing; he had no special teaching method at all. The important thing was for the members of the class to enjoy one another. They smoked together; they met outdoors under a eucalyptus tree; they discussed their favorite poets; they traded poems anonymously and criticized them without malice; they laughed and made friends. "Little by little, the lessons developed," Bynner said. "The whole class taught and the whole class learned." Poetry *can* be taught, he concluded—but only to poets, not to anyone else.[54]

Two other poets followed in residence at Berkeley—W. W. Lyman and Leonard Bacon—but by the time Bynner came to write of his teaching experience in the *New Republic* in 1923 none of them was connected with the university. The rap against them was their lack of a Ph.D. and the scholarly preparation it signified. "Doubtless," Bynner replied, "each of us regards the young lives we have touched with our own lives as a composite thesis more valuable to himself and to the world than any paper in which we might have been solemnly guilty of wrapping old bones for the university." He wished there was some system under which more poets "might ardently and profitably share a year of their development with the young at our universities."[55]

Two years later Leonard Bacon wrote a little book called *Ph.D.s* containing two narrative poems—one comic, one tragic—about the training of young literary scholars, a training that enmeshed them

> in a spiritual intrigue
> Where plodding pedantry replaced affection
> And humor and all things that are in league
> With natural youth.

In slapdash ottava rima Bacon satirized philological scholarship (the "reverse precisely of imagination"), which takes the rotten poems and feeble semi-epic blunders of early English literature "painfully to pieces" and issues in something like "a barren thesis, reference-piled,/ On the Final E in Middle-English Rhymes." The attack was, by this time, noddingly familiar. But *Ph.D.s* was not distinguished by its attack. It was significant—if at all—because it suggested that despite six decades of mutual hostility, despite the suspicion of Bynner and Bacon and other poets in the classroom, literature and scholarship were being drawn uncomfortably together in intellectual as well as institutional forms, even if the *content* of their exchanges continued to be the hashed-over commonplaces of alienation and distrust. Bacon's very choice of a subject for poetry suggested as much. Although he was not exactly happy about it, the poet turned to an academic career to fill his stomach while his soul burned after literature. But he refused to take a mercenary view of the situation; he had a spiritual sub-intention too. He had a reason for wanting to teach:

> he chose to be interpreter
> To others, lecturer, tutor, what you will,
> Of all that beauty mere discoverer,

> That in himself it had hurt so to kill.
> He would make straight the pathway as it were
> For youth with the authentic lyric thrill. . . .56

These lines were written in imitation of Horace in the *Ars Poetica*: "I'll play the role of whetstone, which is good enough to put an edge on iron but is out of luck when it comes to cutting. While I write nothing myself, I'll teach the gift, the business of the poet. . . ."57 By the 1920s, having failed to come up with some way to live at leisure in a world of work, poets had found a reason for taking jobs in the university: they had rediscovered the ancient truth that they had something to teach. "I go for myself," Frost said on the eve of departing for the University of Michigan, "but I wouldn't go if I wasn't interested in education."58 What the poets had to teach might not be itself the writing of poems, but it was not worthless: it was a way of sharing their development with the young. All that remained was for someone to give it a name, a method, and a base of operations.

Chapter 5

❧ The Sudden Adoption of Creative Work

Creative writing was first taught under its own name in the 1920s. It began in a junior high school where it was originally conducted as an experiment to replace traditional English—grammar, spelling, penmanship, even literature classes—with something more appealing to young people. As such it was part of a broader movement to reform American education in the first half of the twentieth century. The cry was that *subjects* should not be taught, *students* should; the reform movement called itself progressive education. Creative writing was invented to transport progressive methods and materials into a junior-high-school English classroom. The man who invented it was a progressive educator—once well known, now largely forgotten—named Hughes Mearns.[1]

In *Pictures from an Institution*, Randall Jarrell's comic novel of academic life, Gertrude Batterson is hired to teach creative writing at Benton College before progressivism rolls over the school like thunder. This is how it may have seemed to writers returning from the Second World War, who found jobs waiting for them on campus and did not question their good fortune. But it is the reverse of the order in which creative writing had actually got its start a quarter century earlier. The image is exact: when creative writing dawned, it dawned like thunder. "With characteristic hustle," Hughes Mearns marveled at the end of the twenties, "America has suddenly adopted 'creative work.' " And yet the sudden adoption of the new subject at schools across the country came about only because creative writing made league with progressive education. Creative writing was perhaps the most widely adopted of the curricular reforms instituted by progressive education; in many ways it was the model progressive subject. In *The Child-Centered School*, the 1928 book that served a generation of teachers as a primer in progressive methods, Harold Rugg and Ann Shumaker explained that the teaching of "creative self-expression" was an "article of faith" among progressive educators. It was an attempt to depose "the copybook régime in art." Already by 1928 it was perhaps the reform movement's biggest success. "The success of the new school has been startling," they said, "in eliciting self-expression in all of the arts, in discovering a marvelously creative youth." The very phrase "creative youth" belonged to Mearns. Along with Satis N. Coleman, who pioneered the teaching of music, Mearns was the most visible of the progressive educators to introduce creative expression into the schools. Rugg and Shumaker unambiguously named him the leader of the movement behind creative writing.2

William Hughes Mearns (1875–1965) was a dramatist manqué and self-styled "writing man." Like Barrett Wendell, he published unsuccessful novels—*Richard Richard* (1916), *The Vinegar Saint* (1919), *Lions in the Way* (1927), *I Ride in My Coach* (1923), *Hounds of the Moon* (1934)—and came to be known primarily for his writings on the teaching of writing. His single most famous piece, though, may be a quatrain that is usually printed anonymously, because of Mearns's disappearance into oblivion:

> As I was walking down the stair,
> I met a man who wasn't there.
> He wasn't there again today.
> I wish, I wish he'd stay away!

Originally these lines were part of a play entitled *The Psycho-Ed*, in which a student sings them while a professor ponderously analyzes them. Born in Philadelphia, Mearns (pronounced *murns*) attended the city's famous Central High School, where he was a pupil of Albert H. Smyth, an early champion of the teaching of American literature and a fierce opponent of philology.3 He entered Harvard late, graduating at the age of twenty-seven. There he fell under the influence of Wendell, George Pierce Baker, and William James. Wendell encouraged him in his writing, Baker inspired him with the ambition to become a playwright, and—once Mearns had woken to the fact that he needed some means of support while trying to write for the stage—James urged him to become a teacher, although he made Mearns promise not to get a Ph.D. Mearns was as good as his word. He studied in the graduate school of the University of Pennsylvania for the next six years but never took an advanced degree.

For eighteen years he taught English at the Philadelphia School of Pedagogy, eventually rising to head the department, but his more profitable affiliation was with the Shady Hill Day School. While director of the school from 1914 to 1917, Mearns began to experiment with the creative processes of children three to eight. His work came to the attention of Abraham Flexner, the educational reformer who was serving as assistant secretary of the General Education Board of the Rockefeller Foundation, and Flexner recruited him to take charge of the secondary English curriculum at the Lincoln School, a progressive laboratory school run by Teachers College, Columbia University. With the Foundation providing his $1000 salary, Mearns joined the Lincoln staff in 1920. From then until his resignation to accept a position at New York University in 1925, Mearns conducted the "deliberate experiment" of replacing English with creative writing. But again like Wendell, Mearns was something more than a mere teacher of creative writing; he was also a publicist for a wholesale "creativist" reformation of literary study. In two widely read books of the twenties, *Creative Youth* (1925) and *Creative Power* (1929), Mearns reported the findings of his experiment at Lincoln and issued a challenge to other teachers to follow his lead. In the earlier book the phrase "creative writing" was used for the first time to refer to a course of study. It was not called creative writing until Mearns called it creative writing. And then it was rarely called anything else.

Creative writing first came to public attention in 1922 when William Stanley Braithwaite selected a poem by Katharine Kosmak, one of Mearns's junior-high-school students, for inclusion in his annual *Anthology of Magazine Verse and Yearbook of American Poetry*.[4] The next year, buoyed by success, Mearns gathered three years of his students' best work and published it as *Lincoln Verse, Story, and Essay*. In a preface to the book, Lincoln headmaster Otis Caldwell said that while it may not be a "full answer" to the complaint that classes in English composition produce results that "are not good enough," creative writing might yet develop into the answer. Mearns himself said that his reason for publishing the little anthology was to supply "a text for the teaching of the making of verse and prose."[5] The response was greater than he could have anticipated. Readers saw in *Lincoln Verse* something more than a textbook; they treated it like a manifesto. Doubleday, Page and Company immediately commissioned Mearns to write an account of his experience in teaching creative writing, publishing it two years later as *Creative Youth*. (A historical irony, that the late Walter H. Page's company should have been the one to publish creative writing's Declaration of Independence.) Mearns was invited to schools around the country where he promoted his ideas and urged teachers to send along examples of their students' writing, which he printed in his books and articles as corroboration of his methods. He addressed meetings and conventions devoted to the teaching of creative work, adopting the motivational rhetoric of an after-dinner speaker rather than the unenthusiastic tones of an academic investigator. And he contributed the opening, definitive essay to the Progressive Education Association's famous 1932 volume *Creative Expression*, which ratified the place of creative work in American schools. After the publication of *Creative Youth*, in which Robert Frost and Witter Bynner were named as the models for teaching creative writing, schools began to form Robert Frost clubs to replace literature classes and the *Scholastic* magazine instituted a Witter Bynner poetry prize for student writers.[6] So popular were Mearns's books and ideas among teachers and parents—Robert Frost touted *Creative Power* as "the best story of a feat of teaching ever written"—and so rapidly were his materials swung into place in schools across the country that, little more than a decade after the first news of Mearns's experiment, creative writing had become one of the most popular subjects in the curriculum, receiving the official sanction of the National Council of Teachers of English.[7]

It is doubtful whether creative writing could have captured the public imagination if progressive ideas of education had not already begun to win a following. By the twenties they had begun their long march through the schools; by the mid-forties progressive education had become the ruling philosophy of American education.[8] Although the Progressive Education Association was founded in 1919 (with Charles W. Eliot as honorary president), the movement from which it took its name was at least a quarter century older. Its beginnings can be dated from the appointment of John Dewey in 1894 to chair the department of philosophy, psychology, and education at the University of Chicago, for in many ways progressive education can be defined as an organized, national movement to put Dewey's ideas into effect.

But Dewey's importance to progressive education is not to be explained solely by his ideas. In the 1920s he began to complain that he was being misunderstood and twisted out of shape by a good many progressive educators. Perhaps even more important than his thinking as such was Dewey's place in the history of educational ideas. By 1894 educational theory in America had broken into open warfare between humanism and developmentalism. On one side stood the advocates of education as a disciplining of the mind, who emphasized the intellectual challenge of the great monuments of human civilization. The humanists were led by William Torrey Harris, superintendent of schools in St. Louis from 1868 to 1880 and then U.S. commissioner of education until 1906, who believed that knowledge is a rational activity under command of the will; his term for it was *self-activity*. Although they agreed in part with the fashionable slogan "learn to do by doing"—a slogan that Harris was the first to place in the context of historical thinking about education—the humanists argued that doing only issued in learning where it enabled persons to make use, for themselves, of the human heritage. On the opposite side were the advocates of education as an unfolding of a child's *interest*, who embraced the Rousseauistic conviction that the "human heritage" had too often meant a bridling of the child's true nature. The developmentalists were led by G. Stanley Hall, professor of psychology at Johns Hopkins from 1880 to 1889 and then president of Clark University until 1893, who held that knowledge grew by natural stages, in the life history of the individual and the race as a whole. And the question of what to teach could only be answered, then, by paying attention to children's natural impulses; classroom materials ought to correspond to the child's stage of development.[9]

Dewey's role in the history of education was to wage a peace between humanism and developmentalism. And, likewise, his theory of education in large part was an attempt to combine *self-activity* with *interest*. He did so by invoking the principle of self-expression. Underlying most educational errors was the assumption that knowledge was a body of materials lying outside the student, which either had to be made interesting by artificial methods or had to be mastered by jaw-tightening activity. In plain truth, knowledge is a way of expressing, of bringing out, the self. The self can only be felt with any confidence to exist in as far as it is brought into the open and differentiated from other selves (not to do so is autism). And thus self-expression is of vital necessity to the human being; except in mental illness it cannot be suppressed. If the school does not recognize this fact, Dewey said, it will not make full use of the child's abilities:

> If the external conditions are such that the child cannot put his spontaneous activity into the work to be done, if he finds that he cannot express himself in that, he learns in a most miraculous way the exact amount of attention that has to be given to this external material to satisfy the requirements of the teacher, while saving up the rest of his mental powers for following out lines of imagery that appeal to him.[10]

Dewey's concepts of interest and self-activity became the dogmas of progressive education. In the name of "interest," content was provided: what was taught was determined by children's own experience rather than hand-me-down knowledge. In the name of "self-activity" the new education borrowed its form: lessons and recitations were replaced by what would come to be known as the "workshop method." Now the turn to experience and activities of learning is at least as old as the ideas of the eighteenth-century Swiss educational reformer Johann Heinrich Pestalozzi. Progressive education was significant not so much because its beliefs were new but because its influence upon the disciplines brought about deep and permanent changes. In English study its subordination of materials to the student led inevitably to a reconception of literature: no longer a record of what has been said, it became a means of saying something; no longer a subject of historical and linguistic examination, it was now a form of self-expression.

A good example of how these ideas were put into effect was the Lincoln School. It had been founded in 1917 in response to Abraham Flexner's call for a "modern" or "realistic" school. What is needed, Flexner had said in a widely read essay, is a school in which the curriculum is not "determined by tradition" but "by a fresh and untrammeled consideration of present needs." Take the humanities, for instance. "The extent to which the history and literature of the past are utilized [in the modern school]," he said, "depends not on what we call the historic value of this or that performance or classic, but on its actual pertinancy to genuine need, interest, or capacity." Thus curricular decisions based on "actual pertinancy" entail a correction of the mistaken emphasis upon books. A student's "intellectual and aesthetic capacities ought to develop . . . on the basis of first-hand experience." Books must be assigned in school "solely in order that [the student's]

real interest in books may be carried as far and as high as is for him possible," not in order "tó ñiäkè uf lüm a makø-believe literary scholar." In a
modern school like Lincoln, in short,

> we hope to train persons, not to write poems or to discuss their historic place,
> but to care vitally for poetry—though not perhaps without a suspicion that this
> is the surest way of liberating creative talent.11

The Lincoln School provided an institutional warrant and setting for
his mission of liberating creative talent, but more importantly Mearns was a
self-acknowledged follower of Dewey. He dedicated *Creative Youth* to him
and echoed Dewey's thinking—sometimes his exact phrasing—in everything he wrote. According to one of his colleagues, Mearns's system of education (which he described either as "creative education" or simply "creativism") and progressive education were "parallel movements, both
stemming from the philosophy and psychology of John Dewey."12 It is not
clear, though, why Mearns's system cannot be embraced by the term *progressive*. Lionel Trilling once quipped that progressive education "means to think
in the progressive pieties rather than in the conservative pieties. . . ."
Perhaps nowhere is this clearer than in the attitude, pietistic or not, that
Dewey and Mearns shared toward the humanistic ideal of culture. Dewey
believed it was undemocratic and in decay. To speak of someone as cultured,
he said, indicates "possession of a certain kind of knowledge and ability
which marks off the person . . . as having had superior educational advan-
tages, together with a certain social ease and grace of speech that enables the
person to display this knowledge to good special effect. . . ." On this showing culture means "familiarity with literary and historic allusions"; so it can
either be a "genuine refinement" or merely an "external veneer." Mearns
shared Dewey's contempt. Suggest to someone who is still teaching an out-
moded curriculum in English that "a boy may write a better composition by
avoiding topics like 'The Knocking at the Gate in *Macbeth*' or 'An Analysis of
the Tone Values in *The Vision of Sir Launfal*,' " he says, "and you are met with:
'Ah!—but what about culture?' " Mearns knew what culture meant:

> Culture is an incommunicable communion with Nature; it is clean hands and
> a pure collar; it is the possession of great-grandparents—white, Christian pre-
> ferred; it is the achievement of tolerance; it is the proper use of "shall" and
> "will"; it is a knowledge of Hegelian philosophy; it is Greek; it is Latin; it is a
> five-foot shelf of books; it is twenty thousand a year; it is a sight of truth and a
> draught of wisdom; it is a frock coat and pearl gloves. . . . No one ever saw it;
> it cannot be measured or chemically analyzed; the fellow that claims it loudest
> never has had it; the chap that really has it never mentions the matter; and it
> can be obtained only by a studious cultivation of one kind of education—my
> kind!13

If progressive education is seen as nonhumanistic and anticultural it
may be clearer why English composition was one of the first subjects the
movement set out to reform. As the headmaster at Lincoln had said, classes

in composition produced results that were not good enough. By the 1920s (as I argued in Chapter 3), English composition had been converted into a course in basic proficiency, abandoning any concern with creative self-expression. On one view this may be described as a democratic change founded on the sensible observation that any course required of all students ought to provide instruction in what all students require. And in this light creative self-expression looks elitist, ignoring the many for the sake of the few. From the standpoint of Dewey's progressivism, though, what looks elitist is the assumption that only a few are capable of creative self-expression. According to Dewey, this assumption reflects the corrupt dualism between labor and leisure (the Greeks' word for school). Some such dualism had opened the way to "a permanent division of human beings into those capable of a life of reason and hence having their own ends, and those capable only of desire and work, and needing to have their ends provided by others." And so too the ancient distinction between art and craft, which could now be seen as a vertical one: the crafts were those activities defined as "useful" because they produced usable results, while the arts were elevated to a separate realm. For Dewey the true distinction was a horizontal one: art is merely any form of work that is "unusually conscious of its own meaning."[14] The only real difference between an art and a craft is in the extent of a person's awareness of what he or she is doing. In other words, any education that seeks the goal of training students for useful ends, as determined by people other than the students—and "proficiency" seems such an end—is a form of ideological conditioning, preparing the many for lives as mere functionaries.

In *The Child-Centered School*, Rugg and Shumaker attacked the way English was taught for encouraging conformity, adaptation, and adjustment to the social order. Under the prevailing system, they pointed out,

> instead of writing because they had something to say, children wrote for the future. They practiced the mechanics of penmanship, correct usage of grammatical forms, punctuation, sentence structure, and paragraphing against the day when later life would demand of them the ability to write.

In a course of basic proficiency, writing was reduced to an external set of standards to which students were expected to conform. It became, as Fred Newton Scott called it, a mode of behavior—a mode of *correct* behavior. Under such a conception English composition might even become an agent of repression. Scott, a Michigan professor who was a pioneer in the teaching of both composition and journalism, said there was a "clash between, on one hand, the instinctive, inherited impulse to communication, and, on the other hand, the scholastic system of abstract symbolism which, under the name of language studies, grammar, and rhetoric, we now use in the schools and regard as indispensable as a medium of culture." And it was not so much that the demands of culture and communication were incompatible; it was rather that they were treated as an either/or. By the twenties the prevailing approach to the teaching of writing was to repress communication for the sake of culture. Or, to say it otherwise, as Scott did: "upon this seething caldron of communicative impulses, the school, as ordinarily conducted, clamps the lid of linguistic ritual."[15]

Creative writing was offered as a way to unclamp the lid of culture from the seething caldron of communicative impulses. "Children seem to be driven by an inner necessity of putting forth something," Mearns said, and they are not particularly worried about cultural evaluations such as the correctness or even the beauty of what they do:

> Their impulse at its best is to place something in the outside world that is already (or almost already) in their inside world of perceiving, thinking, feeling; they measure their success or failure by the final resemblance of the thing done to the thing imagined.[16]

If this is true it follows that the teaching of writing ought to be governed not by external, cultural standards but intrinsic, expressive ones. "In a creative-writing class," as a later devotee said, "almost any writing is better than no writing at all."[17] Nothing must be assigned or even required; Rugg and Shumaker said Mearns was prepared to wait an entire year for a student to write anything at all. The teaching of writing must seek to remove the cultural impediments to creative expression. And so it is founded upon what Mearns characterized as a "theory of permittings." Writing, which he characterized as

> an outward expression of instinctive insight, must be summoned from the vasty deep of our mysterious selves. Therefore, it cannot be taught; indeed, it cannot even be summoned; it can only be permitted.[18]

Perhaps the best way to demonstrate the distinctiveness of Mearns's plan of creative writing is by distinguishing it from other plans that went by the same name. Not long after Mearns began to make his ideas public, especially after the appearance of *Creative Youth* in 1925, several other books came out with similar titles. Bernard L. Jefferson and Harry Houston Peckham, two professors at Ohio University, published *Creative Prose Writing* in 1926; Adele Bildersee, a professor at Hunter College, published *Imaginative Writing* in 1927; and in 1929 William Webster Ellsworth, a publisher, grabbed the honor of being the first to adopt the straightforward title *Creative Writing*. Despite their use of the name, though, none of these books understood creative writing as a new bearing in education. Only the name was new; the conception of writing instruction was the same as it ever was. Ellsworth was not even sure that a writer should submit to instruction. "Could Walt Whitman have spent four years at Harvard and then written *Leaves of Grass*?" he asked.[19] He assumed the answer was a self-evident No, suggesting that he was basically out of sympathy with creative writing. He borrowed the name because it was on many lips in the twenties, not because he agreed with others who were speaking it.

For their part, Jefferson, Peckham, and Bildersee thought of creative or imaginative writing as a narrow division of English composition dealing with description and narration.[20] They were unhappy with the way composition was being taught, however. In their preface, Jefferson and Peckham said that, although they were not indifferent to "the purely utilitarian forms of writing," they were convinced that

> early in the course in English a well-directed effort should be made to give the student an intelligent interest in literature and a desire to do creative work, to the end that English composition may cease to be purely formal and may evade the charge of producing only that which has no counterpart in real literature.

The goal, in a word, was appreciation. The student of creative writing learns to become "a discriminating critic . . . and gains acquaintance with the exacting requirements" of literary art. Bildersee was less parochial (or less focused), thinking about life and the future in addition to literary appreciation. The goals, she said, were three: "To go through life with senses alert and mind interested, to be able to get from books what the writer intended one to get, to be equipped to write when the call to write comes." The organization of her course was somewhat daring too: instead of separate assignments, students were to turn in seven successive chapters of an autobiographical novel. If we write these, she said, "we shall not have the feeling that what we write is in the nature of an exercise only, a discipline—it is, in its way, literature. . . ." And yet it was also in its way an exercise only, a discipline. After seven chapters the novel was abandoned.[21]

These plans can be seen as an attempt to return English composition to its original intent. But the problems implicit within them reflected a conflict that, pretty much from the start, had plagued every effort to come up with something better—something more like literature—than philology. "Should Power to Create or Capacity to Appreciate Be the Aim in the Study of English?" asked the title of an 1894 essay in the journal *Education*. Although "the development of creative power" was offered as a way out of the impasse, it was not clear what this meant. The aim, it was said, is not to foster "an ambition for literary distinction" or to outfit students to earn "a livelihood with the pen," but sheerly to give them a "sense of joy and life."[22] A decade later, writing in the same magazine, Professor Clara F. Stevens of Mt. Holyoke College tried to be more precise, arguing that although literature should first be studied as life and then analyzed as art, to these ought to be added

> such further study of literature as art as will enable the student to discover, make his own, and use the fundamental principles of art; for it is constructive work which more than any other gives power. In college some, if not all, may legitimately study the construction of novel and drama, and may plan a novel or dramatize one for the college stage or write an original play. It does not mat-

ter that they are not going to spend their lives writing blank verse and sonnets, drama and novels; it does matter that they have gained a certain mastery over one form of art.23

Stevens's use of the adjective *constructive* rather than *creative* implied a fundamental difference. Writing was subordinated to appreciation, but resorted to. And why? So that instead of studying the principles of literary construction in the abstract students would be led to a self-discovery of them through the concrete need to use them. The emphasis was on the subject, not the students. "Constructive work" was a means to an end, and the end was literary understanding.

From this angle creativism appears related to constructivism, but distinct from it. As a believer in the new curriculum pointed out, the old idea of "appreciation" connoted the teaching of literature for the sake of interpretation and analysis. "To teach the poem meant probing for its thought, making sure that the children understood every word, so that they might appreciate it," John Hooper said. "It is possible that they would have enjoyed presenting the poem simply for its sound or its images, but the belief that no poem could be appreciated unless it was fully comprehended turned a possible pleasure into an uninteresting problem." Similarly, in the first instructors' manual drawn up on Mearnsian lines—a book sponsored by the Progressive Education Association—Lawrence H. Conrad said that creative writing must

> be pursued for its own sake, and for its own distinctive values. There must be no secret intention on the part of the teacher to trap the students into an increased fervor for grammar or rhetoric or literature. These other phases of English require scholarship. Scholarship is an excellent discipline. But creative endeavor is also an excellent discipline not provided by any other part of the English program. And the full benefit of the creative discipline cannot be had when writing is pursued as a means of improving scholarship.

Except for the word *discipline*, which he would never have used—it smacks of the humanism he rejected—this is an excellent summary of Mearns's ideas. It makes the central distinction clear. To qualify for the name, creative writing must not be simply a means of improving an understanding of literature. It must be pursued for its own sake.24

And writing for its own sake meant writing for some other reason than to perform an exercise for an English class. The whole point of introducing progressive methods into the teaching of writing was to participate in what Mearns called the "vigorous struggle to eliminate from school studies the great mass of functionless school information"—the distinction between metonymy and synecdoche, for example. In the new teaching the emphasis was upon "child growth rather than on purveying a set of facts." Writing for its own sake, then, meant writing for the sake of personal development; English was to be studied only as it was genuinely pertinent to this end.

Mearns was not interested in training writers; he was not even particularly interested in the literary education of the young. "In classroom and in groups outside the classroom," he explained, "my interest had never been primarily in subjects of study or in anything taught or studied, but rather in the swirl of wild and often incoherent imaginings that roared continuously in the conscious undercurrent of the mind." In other words, he gave more thought to the activity of expression than to knowledge of the already expressed. Even though he had been an English teacher his entire working life, he claimed not to be defined by teaching at all. "I am a writing man," he protested, "and not a teacher of the subject of writing." What aroused his loyalty first and foremost was the creative process. At least at first, then, creative writing was not an active ingredient in his classroom instruction. "[T]he writing of poetry has never been with us a classroom exercise but really a by-product that had no regular place in the school program," he said. "Our poetry, we always felt, was something we did for its own sake, and that naturally we should use our time for it." Although the phrase "poetry for its own sake" is not used here in the same sense in which Cardinal Newman would have used it, Mearns's view is a liberal one nevertheless. It is not so much utilitarianism that is being repudiated, though, as the study of English itself. For Mearns the traditional study of English, whether philological ("the proper use of 'shall' and 'will' ") or humanistic ("a sight of truth and a draught of wisdom"), comes to the same thing. It places culture in the way of personal growth.25

The underlying complaint is a profound one. On neither the philological nor the humanistic conceptions does the study of English have any real *use* in human life. It is merely "bookish lectures and bookish pother among the bibliographies." Rightly conceived, Mearns said, English ought to be "not a branch of study, an isolated and obvious exercise at certain hours of the day, but rather something that comes out of the everyday activities of our children, something called forth by the actual needs of everyday expression." And yet English study was not given a merely instrumental function in Mearns's thinking. It would be more accurate to say that, in his plan, writing was the efficient cause of an education in which the final cause was personal growth. Mearns insisted that in his statements on writing instruction the discussion was "always of self-expression as a means of growth, and not of poetry [as such]. . . . The business of making professional poets is still another matter—with which this writer has never had the least interest." Now personal growth as an educational ideal is a Deweyan concept. In Dewey it is conceived "intrinsically" rather than by comparison with adult standards; growth is "the *power* to grow"; it is not something that is done to children, "it is something they do." Mearns took this principle and applied it to the teaching of creative writing. The aim was "to touch some of the secret sources of [students'] lives, to discover and to bring out the power that they possessed but, through timidity or ignorance, could not use; to develop personality, in short."26

From this view the educational value of literature is that it is perhaps the best means that humans have devised to touch the secret sources of their lives. But if it is to do so it must be studied from within. It is not to be learned *about*, but experienced firsthand—from the creative, not the scholarly point of view. "The creative life is spun from within," Mearns said; "the scholar's life is built of outside materials." The student of literature, then, must be "a literary person, a maker of literature." The theoretical premise seems to be that the only way to "become possessed of that culture whose spirit is poetry" (as William Stanley Braithwaite put it in a letter to Mearns) is to *write* poetry: the sole access to poetry runs through poetry. In creative study the emphasis is "not upon the teaching of the laws and principles of art as something to be learned outside of experience, but upon knowing them sensitively through continuous experience." The doctrine is learn to do by doing, but under Dewey's influence it has been reinterpreted to mean that students of literature and writing learn best "by self-activity self-approved and, if possible, self-initiated." In short, students learn to write neither directly from a teacher nor by the humanistic method of exactness of study and multiplicity of reading. They learn by the continuous experience of developing themselves as literary persons, as makers of literature.27

What is the role of teachers? Mearns's "theory of permittings" would seem to imply that students of writing have small need of them. The theory was rapidly becoming creative writing's stutter of self-doubt. Adele Bildersee said that, after twenty years in the classroom, she had concluded "the art of writing cannot be taught; it can only be learned." William Webster Ellsworth was only a little more encouraging, saying that "writing can not be taught, but a would-be writer may perhaps be helped and inspired." So fixed a part of creative writing's structure did this idea become that half a century later the Iowa Writers' Workshop would still be introducing itself to prospective students by reassuring them that "Though we agree in part with the popular insistence that writing cannot be taught, we exist and proceed on the assumption that talent can be developed. . . ." This is a compromise doctrine, neither too close nor too far away from the late classical and essentialist dogma that poets are born, not made.28

The problem was one that baffled progressive educators. Mearns's colleague at the Lincoln School, third-grade teacher Martha Peck Porter, believed the "greatest influence" upon the development of a child's creativity was the encouragement of teachers; it was far more influential than books, at home or school. The teacher was on the lookout for opportunities of creative expression and when something occurred she was quick to suggest a poem to the child. Critics pointed out that under these conditions it was really the teacher who was coming up with the ideas for poems and students were being intensively trained in one specific and restricted field of poetic subjects. Percival C. Chubb, author of what had been the standard guide to English teaching until the rise of progressive education, drew attention to "the strained falsetto notes" in the "up-to-date and often modish work" produced in Lincoln's "intensive and . . . hot-house culture." To avoid the appearance of undue influence—or to solve the problem by not thinking about it—many teachers of the creative arts simply refused to give their students any guidance at all, even though Dewey whistled that "There is no spontaneous germination in the mental life."[29]

Mearns was self-divided on the question of teaching. On the one hand he argued that

> the modern discovery of the child as artist—a very ancient bit of knowledge, of course—is coincident with the realization of the beauty of primitive art generally. The child is a genuine primitive. He needs little or no instruction.[30]

On the other hand he swore that he and others like him who were conducting classes in creative writing were not "gaily giving up [their] function as teachers." Some teaching is required in learning how to write; trusting to natural growth—the intrinsic power all students possess—is necessary but not sufficient. "If growth under pleasantly free surroundings were all of the new education," he blinked, "then my occupation is gone; for I conceive of my professional skill as something imperatively needed to keep that growth nourished." How are these two positions to be squared with each other? If Mearns truly believed that students of writing need little or no instruction then the claim that teaching is imperatively needed is mere special pleading. As John Barth said many years later, if it is true that writing cannot be taught 'twere fraud to teach it.[31]

Let's take the two positions one at a time. The disdain of instruction, as Mearns made clear, was dependent upon an enthusiasm for primitive art. The ideology of the primitive, as originating with Montesquieu and Rousseau, was a celebration of natural "freedom" from civilization's "restraints." Writing at about the same time as Mearns, the literary scholar Lois Whitney traced the contemporary vogue of primitivism to eighteenth-century critics like Hugh Blair, Joseph Addison, Thomas Warton, Adam Ferguson, Thomas Percy, and Richard Hurd. Primitive poetry was said to be more direct and impassioned, distinguished by its freedom from restraint and what Blair called its "glowing style." It was said to be more emotional, more sincere, more metaphorical, marked by simplicity and what Warton described as "fantastic imagery." To a man the primitivists agreed with Bishop Hurd that primitive poetry belonged to "the simple ages of learning, when, as yet, composition was not turned into an art, but every writer, especially of vehement and impetuous genius, contented to put down his first thoughts."³²

Thus primitivism was of a piece with educational developmentalism, which held that the growing child recapitulated the cultural epochs of human history. Gertrude Buck demonstrated how the ideas were brought together, for example, in arguing that metaphor is not a sophisticated and highly stylized use of language—neither an "extraneous adornment" nor an "artificial perversion"—but rather an early stage in language development: "the necessary stage through which speech must pass on its way to literalism." It is more characteristic of primitive peoples and children than civilized peoples and adults:

> Those savage tribes who have no words for 'round,' 'hard,' and such abstract qualities, but must say 'like the moon,' 'like a stone,' etc., are still in the midst of the process, as are those children who instead of calling a silver dollar large and a dime small, call the one 'mamma' and the other 'baby.' It is only through the metaphor-process that abstract ideas come into existence.³³

From this view it was a short step to the conclusion that rhetoric is an advanced subject of the curriculum while poetic—to revert to the now discredited term for writing in metaphor—is a more appropriate subject for children. When he declared that young poets need little or no instruction, then, Mearns was defending creative writing on developmental grounds. The teaching of creative writing belonged in the lower and middle grades because the urge to poetry was developmentally prior to penmanship, grammar, rhetoric, and literary study.

When he turned from the defense of creative writing to the criticism of it, he changed his tune. Mearns complained that he was forever receiving

> sheaves of bad poetry from all over the country. "See what my children have done without any instruction whatever!" is the tenor of the accompanying letters. My pity goes out to the children; so obviously have they needed someone to be by to point out the way.

Acceptance and approval are crucial stages in a person's development as a writer, but the process does not stop there; or if it does the person will never become a great writer. The first two stages must be followed by three more: criticism, indirect teaching of principles, and "finally, that miracle of artistic superiority which you might call something approaching the work of genius." The full flowering of artistic genius occurs only *after* criticism and the learning of principles.³⁴

This provides a role and function for the teacher. He or she points out the way, which means giving students "immediate experience with something better than they have hitherto known." In other words, the teacher suggests reading. Not the classics, or what Mearns scorned as "the reiterated dead giants of the past." Since the students were struggling with the problem of writing they were most likely to find answers in contemporary writers—John Masefield, Carl Sandburg, William Rose Benét, Alfred Noyes, Edna St. Vincent Millay, Amy Lowell, James Oppenheim, Vachel Lindsay, Adelaide Crapsey, Frost, and "the type of poets who [were] found mainly in the *Dial*," including T. S. Eliot, although Mearns's students "were not particularly interested in Eliot." It may appear as if creative writing were a precursor of demands to open up the literary canon, but it would be more accurate to say that under creative writing a principle of usefulness—a twist on the ancient principle of decorum—replaced that of canonicity. Students read the writers they found useful to their own work. Writing came first, reading after: "the interest in literature has followed rather than preceded the writing of literature," Mearns said. Although he sometimes recommended poets from among his favorite Elizabethans and pre-Raphaelites, Mearns said that he thought of these recommendations as a variety of criticism. He would offer them only to students who felt balked by a lack of technique and only when they had put a piece of writing behind them.[35]

"The main result" of literary study, Mearns said, must always be

> to uncheck the flow of expression; for if my answers depend solely upon my own experience I speak out freely and without fear, but if I am held wholly to thinking based upon another's experience, or to an alien and unfamiliar form of speech, I am robbed at the start of the very instruments of independent judgment.

The phrase "independent judgment" is a little bothersome. Mearns intended it as a synonym for originality. Authentic poetic language, he said, is "unlike any other in the world"; "[e]ven the verse form" is more impressive when it is "not a standard pattern"; authentic poetry is denoted by a "unique quality of individual freshness." But as the literary critic W. C. Brownell observed a few years earlier, Matthew Arnold had suggested that something else may be behind the thirst for independence and originality:

> Thinking for oneself meant . . . that neglect of the thinking of others which produces less the thinker than the thinkist—to adopt a useful distinction; a result that [Arnold's] prescription of culture, which he defined as the knowledge of others' thinking, was particularly designed to prevent.

On this showing it could appear as if Mearns had prescribed the neglect of literary culture; as if his teaching were designed to produce less the literary creator than (to use his own word) the literary creativist.[36]

On the contrary, Mearns wanted to rework both the teaching of writing *and* the teaching of literature in the light of the creative principle. He called his plan of literary study "creative reading, a new term for a very old art." The term of course was not exactly new, although he may not have known that Emerson had coined it. Mearns's use of it was probably derived from

J. E. Spingarn, whose 1917 book *Creative Criticism* also contained a seven-year-old essay that was the first to refer to a new movement in literary thought as the new criticism. A disciple of the Italian expressionist philosopher Benedetto Croce, Spingarn defined the new term for the old art by asserting that criticism and creativity at bottom were the same activity:

> That is to say, taste must reproduce the work of art within itself in order to understand and judge it; and at that moment aesthetic judgment becomes nothing more nor less than creative art itself. The identity of genius and taste is the final achievement of modern thought on the subject of art, and it means that, in one of their most significant moments, the creative and the critical instincts are one and the same.

Mearns too believed that the critic and the writer were the same person, but he did not found an account of literary knowledge upon the fact of this identity. For him, rather, criticism and literary knowledge were dependent variables: their value depended upon (and were subordinate to) the writer's need of them, which need of them varied from writer to writer.37

Thus the teacher of creative writing made suggestions but never demands. Even when suggesting something—reading, revisions—he or she spoke unimperatively, in the voice of a fellow writer who had acquired perhaps a wider experience. "With these pupils," Mearns said, "we have taken the attitude of writing persons who meet to discuss values and effects in our chosen art." This, it will be recognized, is a restatement of a cardinal tenet of antiformalism in education that had belonged among the ideas of writing instruction since the time of Wendell; it is also an adaptation of Frost's education by presence. Progressive education freshened up the ideas by contending that instruction ought to be based on a teacher's practical experience. "If he is a teacher of school biology," as Mearns put it, he must be "also a practicing biologist." The principle was that a teacher should be *representative* of a subject—the principle that Roman Jakobson would later mock as appointing elephants to teach zoology. But others did not think it was ridiculous to propose that writing is not an abstract body of knowledge but a concrete activity best taught by someone fully committed to it. "The teacher should be himself a writer," Lawrence Conrad said. "He need not have attained fame, or even have published his work. But his knowledge of the problems of writers, and his sympathy with them, will proceed out of his own continued endeavor to write." A teacher of creative writing, in short, was to be (as Witter Bynner had tried to be at Berkeley) his students' friend and fellow worker.38

What would come to be known as the "workshop method" grew out of progressive ideas about teaching. In the new curriculum, said John Hooper, teachers sought to encourage "the communal making of poetry." And Martha Peck Porter showed how such communal making worked. In Porter's third-grade class, a girl named Carol read her poem aloud:

I like to see the flower cart
Come skipping down the street.
It has such pretty colors,
Red, white, blue and yellow.
It brightens up the city streets.

Porter suggested that "one of the ideas in her poem was perhaps not quite true to the thing she had seen." Before Carol could reply, another child in the class cited the second line of the poem. Immediately Carol proposed a change: "Come slowly down the street." Mearns's classes operated upon a similar principle. Students mimeographed their writings and these were "given to the class, then criticized, rewritten by the author and criticized many times." In the creative writing classroom, said Lawrence Conrad, the "central activity" is the discussion of student writing. And the purpose was to give courage to criticism—"to develop in each student the power of objective criticism of his own writing and of himself in relation to it," and to school the students as a body "to regard the criticisms that are made in class as a kind of 'voice of the people' speaking about their work," which "should be taken to heart only when the critic puts his finger upon a sore spot." What Walter H. Page had once called "helpful criticism" became a method of communal criticism in creative writing classes.39

The workshop method, or the communal making of poetry, was an effort to apply the principle of manual arts training to the study of English. The manual arts training movement, which had emerged in the 1870s around the figure of Calvin M. Woodward of Washington University, influenced progressive education through Dewey's reinterpretation of it. Its first principle was the education of artisans through their work. Generalizing from this, Dewey said that an art's "customs, methods, and *working* standards" constitute its artistic tradition. And though it is true (as humanists argued) that initiation into the tradition is necessary before anyone can become an artist, mere initiation does not suffice. For the tradition to be "a factor in his personal growth," the young artist must feel the urgent need "to join in an undertaking. . . ." This is why the manual arts workshop held up such a good model for what Dewey hoped the school would become—"a miniature community, an embryonic society." In a workshop everyone is engaged in a similar project and "common needs and aims demand a growing interchange of thought and growing unity of sympathetic feeling." The problem with schools run on humanistic principles is that "just this element of common and productive activity is absent." In its place the humanistic school substitutes a competition to see who can get ahead of others in gathering information. "Where active work is going on, all this is changed," Dewey said. "A spirit of free communication, of interchange of ideas, suggestions, results, both successes and failures of previous experiences, becomes the dominating note, . . ." The method of communal making and communal criticism *is* the workshop method.40

The theory of knowledge its own end was dislodged by a theory of knowledge as the means to productive activity. *Work* replaced *leisure* as the prerequisite of education. Schools were "discovering the blessedness of work and its great value as an educational motive," Mearns said. To illustrate how work could motivate a student, he explained that when a student was assigned a task in the workshop of a modern school he was not performing "mere work"; the task was also "an excuse for the most intense sort of instruction." The reason for this was that his teachers "have caught the child doing something he would rather do than eat. Therefore he wants to know—he is on fire for knowledge." Where knowledge was missing, though—where the workshop method was adapted to the teaching of the liberal as well as the manual arts—*productive* activity was sometimes replaced by *creative* activity. Creativity was conceived as a way of filling in the gaps; it was a stand-in for scholarship and research, skills that would presumably be developed later. In her third-grade class, for example, Martha Peck Porter assigned a class project: the children would study Holland and compile a book for future classes that were interested in the subject. Toward the end of the project, Porter said to the students: "You didn't find many stories which children in Holland probably have read. Why not make up some like those you think they must read?" In a progressive classroom empirical methods were supplanted by the communal, workshop method (or what progressive educators liked to call the "project method") and inquiry gave way to creativity.41

Creativity was not exactly the same thing as productivity. It involved a shift from *product* to *process*. And in literary terms, this meant the poem carried little weight next to poem-producing. "[F]rankly we do not care much about the product itself," Mearns said; "our interest goes out to the value in growth of personality that comes from genuine self-expression." An anecdote in *Creative Youth* reveals much about Mearns's poetic theory. A mother told Mearns about her daughter, who was distressed at having her poetry discussed in class. "She has been writing poems all her life," the mother said,

> but I have learned not to talk about them to her, although she knows I have saved all of them. When one is finished she drops it on my dressing table. After that she never cares about it but begins another.

This was also Mearns's view of poetry: it was a continuous activity. The poem as something *made* or *said*, as something that has finality, was foreign to him; and thus to his conception of creative writing too. Even the term *creative writing* implies something in progress, imperfect, not yet complete. Better this, however, than something finished and possibly flawed. "There can be no failure, so we teach," he said, "when one continually produces."42

The ideal of creativity was founded upon the assumption that no special means or preparation was necessary for creative expression. "To say that the poet speaks a special language is to give credence to an unfortunate conception of what constitutes poetic expression," John Hooper wrote in *Poetry in the New Curriculum.* "There is no class distinction among words, nor is it any word's particular privilege to be called 'poetic.' " On the level of theory, this was little more than a reassertion of the romantic repudiation of poetic diction. On the level of classroom practice, however, it was something more. It was very nearly a social and political demystification of poetry. There was no longer any "class distinction" between poetry and other modes of speech; poetry was to be understood merely as the opportunity to express oneself. It is easy to see how this would have encouraged the abandonment of poetic artifice—meter, rhyme, set stanzaic patterns, traditional forms and kinds, anything that suggests that poetry is not ordinary language. The first classroom poetry—what was named "children's poetry"—was invariably written in free verse, although it may perhaps more exactly be characterized as a daily theme (that is, observations of life) put into what J. V. Cunningham calls "parsing meter": nondiscursive prose divided into lines at punctuation marks and just ahead of prepositions. Because there is no *formal* difference between poetry and other modes of speech, the difference had to be located in poetry's *content*. The difference between prose and verse, John Hooper declared, is "one of substance and attitude." Poetry was not a special means of saying something; there was nothing special about it at all. "Do you ever talk to yourself?" Mearns would ask his classes. And when a student replied that everyone talks to himself, Mearns would say: "Poetry is when you talk to yourself." The despecializing of poetry was the logical consequence of the progressivist shift from subject matter to student. The objective was to make poetry available for the actual needs of everyday expression—to make it less daunting to beginners—but one consequence was to shift attention from poetry as form to poetry as experience. The doctrine of creativity supplied the theory behind this shift.[43]

Talk about creativity was something of a commonplace in the first decades of the twentieth century. "Creative work" or "creative expression" are good (it was promised) not because of what is *made* or *said* but because of what creativity does for a person. This belief was not confined to the English departments of progressive schools. In the twenties, as Diana Trilling recalls in her autobiography, many people spoke honorifically of the "creative impulse."[44]

Now the word *creative* originally found its way into English in the 1670s and by the third decade of the eighteenth century it had become a common epithet in literary criticism, customarily attached to "power," "imagination," or "genius."[45] By the twentieth century the epithet had outgrown literary criticism and began to hook up with strange new partners, as implied by titles like Helen Marot's *Creative Impulse in Industry* (1918) and

May Plowman's *War and the Creative Impulse* (1919). Many writers closer to our own era have snickered over its promiscuous use—creative selling, creative circuit design, creative ways to transform your garden—but in doing so they merely exhibit a romantic nostalgia for a time when the epithet was reserved for genius. The widening distribution of the word dates from the period around 1920 when the idea of creativity was being democratized.

The doctrine of creativity entailed a rejection of the essentialism inherent in the belief that artistic talent is "born" or "hereditary" (see Chapter 2). For one thing, such thinking seemed undemocratic; for another, unmodern. In *The Creative Spirit* (1925), Rollo Walter Brown objected that modern psychology had established the contrary principle that "the power to create varies [among individuals] only in degree."[46] Even more recent psychology, in arguing that a capacity for creative work is a sign of psychological health, has merely confirmed what many in the 1920s had already guessed. *Everyone* is capable of creativity.[47] For many like Brown, "creative-mindedness" was linked to the democratic reform of institutions, because it was distinguished from the "conservative," "average," "repressed," "businesslike," "overfed," "respectable," and "colorless."[48] In cultural thought it was distinguished from what Brown called the museum habit of mind, the tendency to huddle together works of art and passively admire them. Such a mental habit "influences institutions of higher learning," Brown said, "so that most of them do not attempt to offer courses that unfold the creative spirit and make art vital by making it a matter of participation, but, instead, courses in the appreciation of museums."[49]

The system of ideas that might be called "creativism" took nineteenth-century cultural nationalism and restated it in politically progressive terms. It started from Emerson's principle that American culture must not be meekly accepted from another people, but created anew; and then it reinterpreted creativity as democratic participation. The message of 1920s creativism was that the conditions for cultural renewal were political and educational: first creative ability had to be democratized, then education had to find a way to set it free. Left unanswered, though, were two questions. To create anything at all (including a new culture) did it suffice merely to liberate creative talent? And even if it did—even if creative talent were just as democratically distributed as the creativists said—did not a culture also depend upon undemocratic distinctions between greater and lesser creative achievements? Wasn't *criticism*—not helpful criticism, not communal criticism, but unsparingly evaluative criticism—also necessary? Democratic participation may have been a first condition of cultural renewal, but the appreciation of the achievement of an elite seemed the inevitable result. By shifting attention from the aesthetic object to the aesthetic experience, creativism tried to sidestep this problem.[50] The distinction between participation and appreciation was inescapable, but creativists made the best of it by emphasizing the benefits upon art. Wider participation would lead to wider appreciation, even if the ones chosen for the latter were fewer than those called to the former. "[W]hile the number of poets cannot be increased by education," Mearns quoted the poet James Oppenheim as saying of his efforts at the Lincoln School, "what we can hope for is that 'audience interminable' which Walt Whitman prophesied; an America where art is a living thing."[51]

By the early 1920s most universities had not yet begun to make the literary art a matter of participation rather than appreciation, but the schools had—and with remarkable suddenness too. By the end of the decade, creative writing even began to percolate upward into the universities. The publication of *Creative Youth* in 1925 marks the dividing line. Before then the teaching of literary composition was restricted either to practical, how-to courses in the short story and the drama or to courses in versification (Brander Matthews's "metrical rhetoric") for the purpose of appreciation. After Mearns, what was taught was creative writing. It was a course in personal development by means of self-expression for its own sake, not for the sake of demonstrating mastery of concepts in English language and literature. Yet something was missing. Schoolchildren everywhere were invited to try their hands at poetry, but the business of making professional poets— something with which Hughes Mearns had never had the least interest— was left to take care of itself. Other people were more interested, but they did not believe it sufficient merely to liberate the talent of young poets. They also believed in the necessity of criticism. And so they started the business of making professional poets by drawing up a partnership between criticism and creative writing. Although the partnership was short-lived, it led to the establishment of a new literary and academic institution—the graduate writers' workshop. We now turn to it.

Chapter 6

Criticism Takes Command

By 1925—the year of *Creative Youth*'s publication—the teaching of writing as literature (or literature as writing) was divided between practical courses in the short story and Hughes Mearns's experiment in English, which had pioneered the name *creative writing*. The one was for those more excited by literary commerce than literature, the other forsook all interest in the literary training of writers. Addressing the Modern Language Association that year, the novelist William McFee denounced every attempt to teach people to make literature, bemoaning "the present-day infatuation for 'courses' in the practice of fiction-writing," usually taught by correspondence, which were devoted to "the study of rules and fetishes in order to make your product marketable. . . ." Literature is a fine art, McFee thumped. He rejected the tendency on one side to organize it according to rational business methods and the belief on the other that the number of Americans capable of it could be increased by democratizing it:

> Literature is not a democracy where numbers rule. It is an aristocracy where brains and originality are paramount. . . . [It] is not a trade to be learned by every earnest young person who can read an advertisement, but a holy mystery, demanding a special equipment of heredity and experience.

This is a good modern example of the way in which, in the Renaissance, Castelvetro said the theory of inspiration operated: to keep outsiders from inquiring too closely into the poets' methods. McFee demonstrates how the privileged essentialism that sniffed "writing cannot be taught" was joined to the vagabond antiprofessionalism of late nineteenth- and early twentieth-century writers from George E. Woodberry to Ezra Pound. This *Anschluss* was one of the distinguishing features of the genteel tradition in American literary thought. What is interesting, though, is that by the mid-twenties the genteel aestheticism invoked here by McFee seems to have grown defensive, sensing itself to be under attack from all sides. The old verdict that literature-making could not be taught, that no one *should* be trained for the making of literature, was about to be overturned.1

In the pages of *School and Society* an English professor at the American University in Washington, D.C., took it upon himself to file a challenge. "Here and there, in the classrooms of the past and of the present," said Paul Kaufman, "college teachers have quietly ignored this verdict and their students have called them blessed." Kaufman urged the colleges to make a home for creative writing—he used the term indifferently to refer to a course of study and a specific kind of writing, just as the term *history* might be used in much the same way. Already, he said, good writers were coming out of the Harvard composition program, especially out of Le Baron Briggs's classes. What then was behind the "contention that conditions in American colleges are positively hostile to creative writing?" Kaufman named two things: a lack of teachers qualified to teach creative writing and a lack of belief in literature. The latter was underscored by the way English was taught. On one hand there was composition, the singular and obsessive aim of which was "training in the rudiments of clear and correct English. . . . [W]hat can [students] salvage out of the most ardent creative desire after being ground through this factory routine?" On the other hand there was scholarship: "by persistent and well-nigh universal overemphasis upon the investigation and appreciation of existing literature," Kaufman said, "we have deprived American youth of the priceless opportunity of making a literature of their own." The answer, he concluded, was to hire professional authors—"established, respectable authors"—to teach writing. All other professional schools "draw heavily upon the prominent exponents of these arts and professions in their course of teaching. Creative literature alone is not so represented in our scheme of higher education."2

As Kaufman suggests, before 1930 no program of creative writing had been formally installed on any university campus in America. An *English Journal* survey found that forty-one colleges and universities had adopted "some form of creative writing as part of the curriculum." But college creative writing at this time was a vague and aimless pursuit, one-half composition, one-half creative self-expression. Its *form* was Barrett Wendell's gift to the course, while its *content* was Hughes Mearns's. At the University of Pennsylvania, for example, what could perhaps have been called "creative writing" was not called by that name. The subject consisted of courses in advanced composition with a portion of the time yielded up to "creative experiments." Composition teachers at Penn were "primarily interested," one of them said, "not in art but in a process of mental and spiritual development taking place in the [student], in connection with art." Even at Iowa, where creative writing would come into its inheritance, a professor of story writing insisted that "the making or training of professional writers is not the business of creative composition. . . . The real objective is the development of a pupil's capacity for creative experience."3

These were significant precedents, but they were not the beginnings of creative writing in the university. Although it was taught here and there, haphazardly, creative writing as a university discipline was not instituted as the unforeseen consequence of a dozen haphazard experiments—or even three dozen—operating under nearly as many aliases. It was a deliberate effort carried out for an articulate purpose in a single place. As such it was founded by Norman Foerster (1887–1972). A critic and historian of criticism, Foerster was hired in 1930 to assume control of the newly established School of Letters at the University of Iowa; this became creative writing's first business address. Not the Iowa Writers' Workshop: originally, creative writing on the university level was merely one track of a more extensive graduate program in English organized around the study and practice of criticism. It was one *part* of a plan, and the larger plan was to take command of literary study for the purpose of revolutionizing it.

Foerster (pronounced *firster*) was born in Pittsburgh, the son of a minor composer who was active in the city's musical life. In high school he studied under Willa Cather. "She recognized my talent," he said many years later, "and advised me to submit one of the first papers I wrote to the *High School Journal*. From there on, I went on my own."[4] (He later dedicated his book *Toward Standards* to her.) Going on his own carried him first to Harvard, where he came under the influence of Irving Babbitt; and then, after graduation in 1910, to the University of Wisconsin, where he was hired as an instructor in English literature. He earned a master's degree at Wisconsin in 1912. His interests were those of an advanced student of literature but in those days, he said, such a person was forced to "choose the investigator's Ph.D. or nothing."[5] Foerster chose nothing: he wanted to be a writer, not a scholar. In 1914 he was named associate professor at the University of North Carolina and in 1919 he was promoted to full professor. His history of *American Criticism* appeared in 1928; his attack on literary scholarship, *The American Scholar* (1929), and a collection of essays, *Toward Standards* (1930), followed in rapid succession. Because of his contempt for conventional literary scholarship, Foerster was treated like an "academic red" at Chapel Hill (in electoral politics he was a conservative). It was not difficult for Iowa to hire him away in 1930. Although local detractors protested that he came to Iowa City "[l]ike a wolf onto the fold," saying it was impossible to think of him "in any sense except as Irving Babbitt's errand-boy, with the arrogance one associates with the Toady-Come-Into-Power," Foerster himself called the Iowa years the high point of his career.[6] He published *The American State University* in 1937 and *The Future of the Liberal College* the next year. In 1941 he edited *Literary Scholarship: Its Aims and Methods* including his own views on "The Study of Letters" plus essays by Iowa colleagues John C. McGalliard (on the study of language), René Wellek (on literary history), Austin Warren (on criticism), and Wilbur L. Schramm (on creative writing)—a volume that might be described as the floor plan of the School of Letters. After resigning in 1944, he returned briefly to North Carolina before accepting an appointment at Duke, where he retired in the early fifties.

Foerster was recognized for his achievement at Iowa—in a 1941 volume of critical essays he was credited with originating "one of the most important experiments in this nation toward making creative as well as critical activity a part of our system of higher learning"—but he was better known as a new humanist.[7] A disciple of Babbitt and Paul Elmer More, he edited the movement's collective manifesto *Humanism and America* (1930) and his polemical labors on behalf of the new humanism earned him the abuse of Allen Tate, Yvor Winters, and T. S. Eliot among others—all of whom ought to have been favorably disposed toward his labors as a founder of creative writing. The new humanism's historian describes him as "the most consistent and enduring exponent of Babbitt's ideas and the major Humanist voice after the deaths of Babbitt and More in the middle 1930s."[8] And yet the most consistent and enduring product of his thought has been the Iowa Writers' Workshop. Stephen Wilbers, its historian, asks whether the workshop would have been established without Foerster's "contribution and influence." Barely pausing to contemplate the matter, he concludes that it "would have been established, although perhaps not for some time."[9] Aside from the rather obvious question how he could possibly know this—history is knowledge of what happened, not a revery about what might have happened if only things had been different—this conclusion ignores the place of creative writing in Foerster's original scheme of literary education. Ignore it, however, and the original idea behind creative writing at Iowa—to say nothing of how idea became reality—is left unspecified. Yet creative writing was not this unspecified but (somehow) historically inevitable force, a restless dybbuk in search of an unsuspecting college administrator through which to work its will. It exists at Iowa (and, consequently, at other American universities) only because originally it was a vital element in Norman Foerster's thinking. It was one piece of a broader scheme to reconstruct graduate training in English. And it was subordinate to that scheme.

The scheme was set forth in his manifesto-sized book *The American Scholar* and put into operation when Foerster became director of the School of Letters the next year. He was clear about his objective: "We must set about restoring the traditional alliance of scholarship and criticism, the divorce of which has worked injury to both and played havoc with education." The time was ripe for a restoration: "the age of philology and minute historical research," he declared, "is drawing to a close." An age of criticism was dawning. And creative writing (as one of his assistants phrased it) would be criticism's natural ally. Foerster wanted the School of Letters to be a school of criticism—an intention that he made clear in advance, at least to his friends. As Austin Warren said in writing in April 1930 to congratulate him on his new appointment at Iowa, "You are to create, I take it, the sort of graduate school of criticism you plead for so eloquently in *The American Scholar*." Warren was right. Although his salary was doubled to $9000, Foerster said later that that was not the inducement. "If I attempted it," he said, "it would be because of the chance to make a humanistic experiment in a good place."[10]

The idea behind the School of Letters was to create a centralized unit (in the words of Iowa dean of liberal arts George F. Kay) to foster and develop the common areas of literary study. Edwin Greenlaw, the disputatious champion of *The Province of Literary History* (1931), was the first choice to direct the new school, but he had no desire to leave his teaching position at Johns Hopkins. He recommended Foerster, though—or so at least Foerster always believed. "You shouldn't go back [to Iowa] without seeing Foerster," he was supposed to have told Iowa's recruiters. Having already interviewed one controversial figure, they probably saw little reason not to consider another. And indeed the controversial fact of Foerster's connections with the new humanism was seen—at least by Iowa president Walter A. Jessup—as a real strength. So too was Foerster's plan to include creative writing among the literary curricula. Announcing the appointment, Jessup told the press that Foerster was expected to strengthen "the whole art side of the University through his emphasis on creative work and the new humanism." The emphasis on creative work, as Foerster told Dean Kay in a 1937 progress report, would come in time to seem "our widest departure from convention." But as he cautioned the *Daily Iowan* at the time of his appointment, the School of Letters was not intended as "a vocational school for authors and critics"; the true purpose of "this departure in graduate study," he said, was "to give all types of literary students a rigorous and appropriate discipline."[11]

The stress fell on the word *appropriate*. Literary study in the twenties and thirties was still in the grip of what Babbitt sneeringly called "the philological syndicate." Although it may have been thoroughly discredited in some eyes, it remained institutionally powerful. When Douglas Bush enrolled at Harvard for graduate study in 1921, for example, he was pained to discover that all but two of the sixteen courses he was required to take "consisted of medieval languages and philology (including not only Anglo-Saxon, and the various dialects of Middle English and Middle Scots, but also Old French, Gothic, and other recondite tongues)."[12] Fifteen years later, for someone who was serious about literature, philology remained the only avenue to an academic career—unless one could find fulfillment in the teaching of English composition. When she graduated with a B.A. and an M.A. from the University of Colorado in 1936, Jean Stafford accepted a fellowship to the University of Heidelberg. She planned to become a philologist, despite having been a star at the university's summer writers' conference—she was praised and encouraged by Martha Foley of *Story* magazine—and despite having a shaky knowledge of German. Toward the end of her year abroad, Stafford wrote to her former teacher Irene McKeehan, asking to be recommended for a graduate fellowship at Harvard. McKeehan flatly refused, snapping that Stafford was not cut out to be a scholar. "For thirty years now," Stafford said in 1976, "I have been earning my living as a writer, largely because of Miss McKeehan's blunt demolition of an impossibly silly daydream." Longing also to be a novelist—"I wanta be a novelist," she whined to a friend—but having nowhere to turn for a rigorous and appropriate training, Stafford was reduced to taking a job teaching composition at a junior college in Missouri.[13]

Stafford's impossibly silly daydream was a rarity among wanta-be writers. Philology had scared off many from academic careers: "a generation of creative youth," said *Saturday Review* editor Henry Seidel Canby in 1929, echoing Hughes Mearns's famous phrase, "has been driven from scholarship by disillusionment more bitter than economic necessity." What was needed was a rethinking of the assumption that only a fact-stuffed scholarship contributes to knowledge. "Knowledge of what?" Canby demanded. "Not life, for then poetry, fiction, even the literary essay or criticism of contemporary literature would be legal tender," counting toward academic advancement. The trouble, as Foerster had rued the same year in *The American Scholar*, was that literary scholars had fallen out of touch with literary creation; as a result, poets (and poets' point of view) had been excluded from academic literary study. "The poets should be inside the universities," Canby said, "for scholars in literature should be poets even if they never write a line of verse."[14]

By the twenties, graduate study in English had come to mean the acquisition of a research method—the *wissenschaftliche Methode*, as it was called with nostalgia for the days of Germanic scholarship—and the investigation of the history behind literature. Even after linguistics began to develop into a separate discipline, as I argued in Chapter 1, the name *philology* was retained to designate this activity of historical research. George Lyman Kittredge of Harvard, author of books on Chaucer (1915), Shakespeare (1916), and *Gawain and the Green Knight* (1916), was the leading light of historical and philological scholarship. In the twenties, as a Vanderbilt professor said, "Kittredge dominated practically every English department in the country."[15] Sometimes the name of Kittredge was substituted for the name of philology, but whatever it was called such scholarship was not—in the eyes of its enemies it was not—an appropriate preparation for a literary career. "We study literature today," Allen Tate said,

> as if nobody ever again intended to write any more of it. The official academic point of view is that all the literature has been written, and is now a branch of history. If a poem is only an instance of its history, the young writer is not going to find out how to study the poem; he will only know how to study its historical background.

Its motives might be different, but historical literary scholarship had much the same effect as the essentialist view that literary creation was a "holy mystery," not to be taught: it closed the door to the literary study of literature. At its heart was a confusion. Literary scholars, Foerster said, "proclaimed that literature must be studied laboriously, but were never very clear as to why it should be studied at all." Their scientific bias—what Basil Gildersleeve called their botanists' conception of literature as opposed to a florist's conception—had led them to prefer historical facts to literary values. They had confined themselves to an investigation of literature from a standpoint independent of it, because this (to their minds) was the lesson of science. According to Foerster, the triumph of science should have taught them instead to adjust their method to their subject matter—"this, indeed, is the prime lesson which the humanities should have learned from science." What was wanted were intrinsically literary methods of study. The overriding need, he said, was for "a scholarship more closely affiliated with the creative and critical interests of letters."[16]

Creative and critical interests banded together to oppose the philological syndicate. From the late 1920s to the early 1940s the battle between these two sides was as pitched (and dubious) as the canon wars. Most English departments were split between a right wing that stood for philology and a left wing that stood for anything but. "[I]t is sufficiently obvious," Brander Matthews had observed four decades earlier, "that the philologist and the literary critic are little likely to be found in the same man." It was more likely that the critic and the writer would be found in the same skin, because both were dedicated to what Henry Seidel Canby called literature-in-the-making. Canby said that

> there should be a Professor of Modern English in every great department, who is fitted by training, experience, and temperament to teach and understand the literature-in-the-making of his own day. No department of English is well-organized without at least one scholar who is critic and perhaps creator also, and in closest touch with our own imaginative literary thought.

This was a daring proposal, and it was what such opponents of the philologists as Matthews and Babbitt had been calling for since the turn of the century. Earlier efforts failed because (as W. C. Brownell pointed out in 1914) "the art of criticism is so largely the business of reviewing as to make the two, in popular estimation at least, interconvertible terms." American criticism had not then succeeded in distancing itself from book promotion. By the thirties, however, a new criticism, no longer commercial in its obligations, had emerged. The partisans of criticism were a strangely mixed band—ranging from turn-back-the-clock Southerners like John Crowe Ransom and Donald Davidson to New York Jewish–style Marxists like Philip Rahv and William Phillips, from university-trained scholars like R. S.

Crane and Joseph Warren Beach to self-taught polymaths like Kenneth Burke and R. P. Blackmur, from the genial Mark Van Doren to the pugnacious Yvor Winters, plus the remnant of the new humanists, primarily Foerster—an alliance of normally hostile parties that shared little else besides the conviction that criticism provided a sounder basis for literary education than did philology and historical literary research. For a time at least their differences were submerged in a mutual effort to gain academic accreditation for criticism. Prior to 1930, as Diana Trilling recalls, "Criticism was not an approved activity in the academy; when the young Mark Van Doren came up for promotion at Columbia, he had to be forgiven the fact that he published book reviews." By the end of the twenties, said Duke professor Jay B. Hubbell, "methods of research" were "no longer a part" of criticism, although they once had been "[c]losely allied." Criticism and research had gone their separate ways. They had become sworn enemies.17

The critical movement gained strength throughout the thirties. John Crowe Ransom was appointed to the rank of full professor at Vanderbilt in 1927, by which time most of his poetry was behind him and he had turned to criticism. Yvor Winters joined the faculty at Stanford the same year and in 1928 he converted from free verse to meter, beginning to insist upon a rational element in poetry and writing many essays to drive home his point. R. P. Blackmur took over editorship of *Hound and Horn* in 1929 and moved its offices to New York soon after, severing its connections with Harvard. The agrarian and new humanist manifestos *I'll Take My Stand* and *Humanism and America* came out in 1930; Robert Penn Warren took his first teaching job at Southwestern in Memphis. Kenneth Burke published *Counter-Statement*, his first book of criticism, in 1931. Philip Rahv and William Phillips founded the *Partisan Review* in New York in 1934 and Robert Penn Warren and Cleanth Brooks followed suit with the *Southern Review* at Louisiana State University the next year. R. S. Crane's "History versus Criticism in the University Study of Literature," perhaps the central statement of the case, appeared in the *English Journal* in 1935. *Understanding Poetry*, the syllabus of the new critical movement, was issued in 1938. Cleanth Brooks published *Modern Poetry and the Tradition*—sometimes cited as the best introduction to the new criticism— in 1939. Two years later the victory of the movement was complete: George Lyman Kittredge died just as John Crowe Ransom was preparing to release the book that would give the movement the name by which it would be known forever after—*The New Criticism*.18

Originally the name referred not to any special method of criticism but to the academic condition of the subject prior to 1941. The emphasis was not upon *new* but upon *criticism*. What was new was the argument that criticism was the best means for studying literature, not the kind of criticism itself— just as, about half a century later, a similar argument was heard: not that a new style of historicism was needed, but that the study of literature simply must return to history from "the cult of autonomy," the delusory faith in "an independent aesthetic sphere."[19] The new critics did more than anyone to advance the cult of autonomy, but their conception of autonomy—to say nothing of their special method—has been badly misinterpreted. It was set forth in the Letter to the Teacher attached to *Understanding Poetry*: "though one may consider a poem as an instance of historical and ethical documentation," Brooks and Warren said, "the poem in itself, if literature is to be studied as literature, remains finally the object for study."[20] *If literature is to be studied as literature*: right there was the major premise of the new criticism. The blunder of most commentators has been to treat this as the minor premise, assuming the new critics set to work by stipulating that literature is virginally isolated from the social and historical context in which it is created.

Literature was not so much *defined* in this way as *studied* in this way. The new criticism was first of all a pedagogy. "In historical terms," says Monroe K. Spears, "the New Criticism is related to larger cultural developments: to the increase of literacy and the spread of education in general, and specifically to the rise of English literature as a university subject and the consequent need to devise effective ways of teaching it." Hence the search for a method that would rival the analytical rigor of science while escaping "the stigma that attaches to the romantic view," as Ransom called it—treating literature as "at best a heroic but childish affirmation in defiance of the most conscientious revelations of science. . . ." What was sought was an approach to literature that treated it as subject to conventions, principles, standards, criteria, rules, and rule-like propositions of its own. The attempt was to purify literature, not by remanding it to an independent aesthetic sphere, but by devising a technical vocabulary "in which the terms," as Ransom said of any purely scientific vocabulary, "are entirely functional." Those who belonged to the cult of autonomy were those who set about to study literature in the terms of a functional critical discourse—"those who purify the world they study by isolating it," as Ransom said of academic investigators in general. The isolation of an object of study is a practical necessity, a methodological expedient, which falls to those who would study something instead of everything.[21]

The new critics turned their scrutiny onto the internal structure of poems. What all of the critics had in common, Blackmur said, was "a tendency to make the analyzable features of the forms and techniques of poetry both the only means of access to poetry and somehow the equivalent of its content." The technical bias came to them honestly: the other thing they had in common was that most were practicing poets. Ransom, Davidson, Van Doren, Burke, Winters, Blackmur, Warren, Babette Deutsch, Louise Bogan, Malcolm Cowley, Horace Gregory, Allen Tate, Rolfe Humphries, Theodore Spencer, Louis Zukofsky, Howard Baker—the number of poets who actively wrote criticism (or vice versa) was not small. Even some publishers like Alan

Swallow and James Laughlin doubled as poets. When an important new critic like Cleanth Brooks appeared on the scene it was a bit unsettling if he was *not* a poet. It is an open question whether some of these might not have been better critics than poets, but the key point is that their criticism grew out of their practical interest in writing poetry. The method that came to be known as "practical criticism" or "close reading" was founded upon the sort of technical discussion of poetic problems that would occur among a group of poets. One such group—the central group—was the Fugitives, who initially came together when Ransom and Davidson returned to Vanderbilt from the First World War in 1919 and 1920. Davidson explains how the meetings went:

> First we gave strict attention, from the beginning, to the *form* of poetry. The very nature of our meetings facilitated and intensified such attention. . . . Every poem was read aloud by the poet himself, while the members of the group had before them typed copies of the poem. . . . Then discussion began, and it was likely to be ruthless in its exposure of any technical weakness as to rhyme, meter, imagery, metaphor and was often minute in analysis of details. . . . It was understood that our examination would be skeptical. A poem had to prove its strength, if possible its perfection, in all its parts. The better the poem, the greater the need for a perfect finish.

To examine a poem was to examine its construction—with the ruthless skepticism of someone who might have constructed it differently. The poet-critics did not feign a scientific detachment; nor a genteel disregard for the professional problems of poets; but this did not render their judgments any less pure. Purity was a *function* of their intense loyalty to the perfection of poems. "Their original approach to poetry was therefore pure," Tate said—"that of craftsmen. I hesitate to describe this approach as esthetic," he went on, "for the term is debased. The chief emphasis was laid, or, more strictly, was discovered to have been laid, upon form and style."[22]

The campaign to win a place for critics on the faculty of English in American universities proved so successful that, a quarter century later, Alfred Kazin could say as if it were self-evident that critics "seem to belong there. . . ."[23] It was not so obvious that writers belonged there too. The critics believed so, and not merely because most of them were also writers. More significant was their belief that criticism and writing were two aspects of the same activity, just as eating and conversation are two aspects of having dinner with someone. Starting with J. E. Spingarn, who first uttered the magic name in 1910, the new criticism was distinguished by its confidence in the identity of criticism and literary creation (see Chapter 5). Even R. S. Crane, the least craft-conscious of the new university critics, argued that criticism must be grounded upon a practical experience of writing.[24] This was perhaps the central doctrine of the new constructivist approach to literature.

And as early as the mid-twenties it had become orthodoxy in which school-teachers were trained. In a college textbook, a professor at the Western State Normal School in Kalamazoo (now Western Michigan University) said the good student of poetry

> must be able to enter into and share the experience of the poet if he would pass judgment on the poet's work. He must realize in himself the mood from which the poem was born and all the poem might have been. . . . This the critic will be able to do only in proportion as he has mastered the form of expression in which the artist has moulded his ideas.[25]

By the end of the thirties the distinction between critical and creative was becoming blurred in the official thinking of college English. "Sharp lines between mental activities called *creative*, and mental activities not decorated with that high-flown title, are falsely drawn," said an English professor at Hamline, reporting on the "creative life" there. "Especially false and vicious are distinctions between *creative* and *non-creative* forms of writing."[26] This was closer to Mearnsian creativism than to constructivist ideas. The new critics did not mean that criticism and creative writing were exactly the same thing. To write a poem, on their understanding, was to decide critically among the many creative directions it might take; to read it was to reenact these decisions. And to write criticism, then, was to duplicate the poet's experience—in a different medium. Blackmur said that "the composition of a great poem is a labor of unrelenting criticism, and the full reading of it only less so; . . . the critical act is what is called a 'creative' act, and whether by poet, critic, or serious reader, since there is an alteration, a stretching, of the sensibility as the act is done."[27]

The lines between criticism and creative writing *were* being erased. Irving Babbitt had warned that "a sharp line is now drawn between critics and creators with a view to disparaging the former." He and the critics who followed him wished to erase the line with a view to extolling the former; criticism, they believed, could be as creative an act as the writing of poetry and fiction. At the Iowa School of Letters, then, Foerster was raising a graduate school on the common ground between the new humanism and the new criticism. He agreed that "creation and criticism are one," but he meant something specific by this. Since both have their source in personality, both criticism and creation are the expression of one person; "and in this respect," he said, "creation and criticism are one." Thus criticism could be the agent of integrating the various and distinct kinds of literary activity in one person. The aim of education at the Iowa School of Letters would be the development of the whole literary mind. A thorough training in literature, he said, means

> the development of a whole set of powers that should be active in the study of literature. It means the development not only of a [philological] sense of fact and a [historical] sense of time . . . but it means also the development of aesthetic responsiveness, of the ability to handle ideas, of taste and judgment or

the critical sense, and the power of writing and speaking in the sensitive language appropriate to literary discussion.[28]

For examples of thoroughly integrated literary personalities Foerster turned to the Renaissance humanists—Petrarch, Poliziano, Erasmus—who took "all of literary scholarship as their province." The divergence of the humanists from "the typical scholar of the present day" was captured, he said, in the term used by the great historian Jacob Burckhardt to describe them in *The Civilization of the Renaissance in Italy* (1878): they were "poet-scholars." They were not only concerned with close scholarship but were "equally concerned with the creation of poetry." Even the editors and scholiasts attached to the Museum of ancient Alexandria—men like Callimachus and Rhianus, normally a parable for the decadence of scholarship—"presented much of their learning in the form of 'creative writing.' " The moral was clear: the modern critic "needs a type of mind akin to that of the creative writer." And by conversion the writer needs the mind of a critic.[29]

Criticism and creative writing went hand in hand at the Iowa School of Letters. As Foerster explained in his inaugural address, literature would be studied there from both the creative and critical points of view. Approaching it creatively means "[w]e are to study it from the inside, we are to see it, so far as possible, with the eyes of the creative artist." The ultimate aim, as he had put it in *The American Scholar*, was "to assist in an inner comprehension of art." But the aim was comprehension: creative writing was an effort of critical understanding conducted from within the conditions of literary practice. It was the acquisition of a certain type of knowledge entailed in a certain type of practice. It was *not* a merely professional grounding in a current manner of living, a glib and superficial training in what Foerster scorned as "practical shortcuts and trade tricks." Quoting the *Cambridge History of American Literature*, Foerster noted that one of the fundamental doctrines of the new humanism was its rejection of "the naturalistic 'education of the senses' "—the sort of thing a daily theme or a creative composition was good exercise for—in preference for the study of the "human tradition." Someone who is serious about literature, whether he would teach it, criticize it, investigate it, or merely write it, "needs a preliminary discipline in books of every kind and especially an intimate acquaintance with the traditions of his art." Foerster agreed with what Rollo Walter Brown had said in *The Creative Spirit*: no art should be taught only in "a workshop for the initiated." Creative writing at Iowa was never intended to become a free-standing apparatus of courses, an autonomously constituted "workshop," leading to a separate degree. It was to be only one branch of study in the literary tradition designated for *all* types of students—teachers, critics, scholars, *and* writers.[30]

Writers needed a more thorough literary education. According to Henry Seidel Canby, many of the "tragedies and mishaps of American literature" could be attributed to the fact that very few American writers had received the right education. Poe and Whitman in particular might have been less tawdry, more detached, if they had only been trained in the literary art. Even in recent years, Canby said,

> it is easy to cite many American authors . . . who did not know enough to get the best from their talents, did not know how to control their thinking, or handle their facts. The American novelist and short story writer has displayed a frequent lack of education. . . . Many well-known writers do not know their own trade. They do not know literature one-quarter as well as a lawyer must know law.

Foerster said much the same thing in *The American Scholar*, describing contemporary writers as "lamentably uneducated." Universities ought to make it their business to correct this lamentable situation, because the whole purpose of a university was to ensure "the establishment of a sounder culture than has yet appeared in this country." And yet, as he observed in an address delivered at the first Iowa Writers' Conference in October 1931, "[t]here is little indication that our institutions of higher learning are concerned with providing a program of study and an intellectual and emotional atmosphere suitable for 'mere' writers," even though they "plainly need a university education." The writers would never educate themselves. They were perfectly satisfied to be knowledgeable about the literary currents of the day—or, as Foerster put it, they were "elate in their contemporaneity." Justly scornful of philological scholars who were "unhappily indifferent to the letters of the present," they were themselves "unhappily indifferent to the letters of the past." In consequence they had become "largely content with problems of technique," little interested in their work to present "a compelling picture of human excellence."[31]

Foerster did not accept the essentialist dogma that writing could not be taught, though he also rejected the practical vocational alternative to it. In an unpublished lecture on "The Education of a Writer" delivered after he had left Iowa, he identified two popular fallacies: (1) "that a writer can be trained—that if he is promising, and takes enough courses in various types of writing, he will be started on his career and thereafter advance by a natural process of growth"; and (2) "that formal education has *nothing* to offer the writer, that he develops from within as he grows in experience of actual life, especially life in the raw." Although seemingly antagonistic, the two ideas were really two sides of the same sentimental naturalism. They merely expressed an unwillingness to undertake the responsibility of educating writers. Foerster sought a mean between these two extremes: "I would have the writer go to college," he declared, "but I would not have him become what we call an 'academic.' "[32]

Writers plainly needed a college education, but what they plainly did *not* need was undisciplined practice in creative self-expression. "Expression is a type of solipsism," Foerster scolded, "based on the view that the self can know and depict only its own states." And the literary counterpart of the philosophical fallacy of solipsism was this: "While representing a private perception or experience, [the self] communicates doubtfully at best, unless the artist in some way explains." This was why he looked to bind creative writing tightly to the activity of criticism. Foerster's scheme of literary education drew down a critique of creativism. "Each student has, it seems," he said, characterizing the theory, "what Walt Whitman called a 'precious idiocracy'—precious to that student if not precious to the world—and he should therefore have a chance to be 'creative.' " He agreed that each student should have a chance to be creative; each graduate student in English at least. But in order to come truly into possession of creative power, he was convinced, a writer must ally his or her "precious idiocy" to a discipline of ideas—that is, to a critical power. As Paul Elmer More had written, framing the humanist view, "A manifest condition is that education should embrace the means of discipline, for without discipline the mind will remain inefficient just as surely as the muscles of the body, without exercise, will be left flaccid."[33]

As a humanist Foerster believed that writers required a humanistic education that would give them a permanent sense of literary tradition, or what his cohort repeatedly huzzahed as "standards." The larger purpose—the motive behind Foerster's whole plan of literary education—was to rediscover critical standards and put American literature on a new footing. The humanists said America was suffering from what W. C. Brownell called a "crisis of suspension of standards." "America suffers not only from a lack of standards," Babbitt elaborated, "but also not infrequently from a confusion or an inversion of standards." The confusion or inversion was particularly acute in education, he said—"above all in our higher education." By talking about standards the humanists were openly picking a fight with the creativists. Progressive education, it will be recalled, had argued that where learning to write entails legalistic conformity to an external set of standards, students are robbed at the start of the very instruments of independent judgment (see Chapter 5). Or, as Babbitt rephrased the argument, the ethos of creative self-expression sought "emancipation of the imagination from any allegiance to standards, from any central control"; and in so doing the creativists "merely fell from legalism into anarchy." Also into the same dull round of habit. As Foerster pointed out, "a natural, spontaneous action is rare, since, even when it is only once repeated, it is already in danger of moving toward a convention or social habit." The real alternative to convention or habit, if creativists were serious about finding one, was standards internally selected in reference to external models. Thus the humanist demand for a working out of new standards was not the neoclassical error of "legalism"; it was not, that is, a literal-minded reliance upon externally imposed rules. It was merely the assumption that a writer needs something more than a conviction of his or her own creative power. To be engrossed in self-expression is to shut oneself up, Foerster said, "in new creation rather than in criticism of what has already been created." And this is a distemper of learning because it means the student turns away from the effort to understand other minds in order to absorb himself "in the only uniqueness that he deems within his reach, namely, his own." This was why—to the humanists' way of thinking—the writing instruction of the day was defective: from English composition on up it was riddled with the notion of the absolute importance of the creative impulse. "The undergraduate," Babbitt was sad to say, "often has a considerable conceit of his own genius in writing his daily theme." Discipline and standards and *not* creative expression—this was what the writer required if he or she was ever going to amount to anything more than a precocious and untutored child.34

As conceived by Foerster, then, creative writing was very different from the subject conceived by Hughes Mearns. Learning to write on the humanist view was not learning merely to express oneself; it was also learning to assimilate and make use of the cultural values implicit in the forms of writing. The drawback of the creativist approach, Babbitt said, "is that it leads to a loss of the representative quality." It yields writing, in other words, that is *merely* expressive, of no interest to anyone outside the writer himself, perhaps his parents and teachers, possibly his classmates. Creative self-expression seemed to Foerster precisely the wrong way to conceive of creative writing. "Freedom and power and happiness cannot be won," he said, "by those who practice the modern philosophy of what is loosely termed 'self-expression.' " No system of education that excluded everything but his or her own creative impulse could ever equip a writer to obtain the artistic freedom that comes from being able to express something more than oneself.35

Lewis Mumford and Van Wyck Brooks said that writers had been wrecked by material values—they held "society responsible for the creative impotence of artists and critics," Foerster said—but they had no "definite programme" to repair the damage. *He* had a definite program: "an experiment toward a more inclusive literary training," as he described it—"more inclusive in the sense that it adds to the old disciplines, linguistic and historical, which are still almost exclusively dispensed at other institutions, the two new disciplines, critical and creative." The school's curriculum was to be not merely a two-year hitch of writing seminars (as it is now in the Iowa Writers' Workshop) but a sequence of courses in noncontemporary texts and authors, criticism, literary history, and even the history and structure of the English language. Creative writers would do scholarship; scholars would creatively write. In a university press release announcing the acceptance of creative and critical work toward advanced degrees, Foerster was paraphrased as saying that "an excellent means of insight into the creative process of literature is the attempt to do what literary artists do, that is, write poems, stories, or plays. 'For the literary scholar,' " he was then quoted, "'perhaps the best laboratory is pen, paper, and waste basket.' " The plan was similar to one put in effect at the University of Chicago by R. S. Crane. In lieu of creative writing, the Chicago plan (as Crane told Foerster in a letter) preferred "the interpretation of prose works of a nonimaginative type." Left unanswered, however, was the question whether this interpretation was to be philological, historical, practical, aesthetic, or whatnot; the distinction was made on the basis of *materials*, not *methods*. Foerster's scheme was the more radical and the more coherent. Creative writing, like criticism, was conceived as a self-contained *discipline* of literary work. The radicalism of the plan is that either one was conceived as a discipline at all. To Foerster's mind the advantage of any such conception was that, lacking a precedent and tradition in the higher learning, criticism and creative writing were departures from "the unwritten law of the university that every subject that has worth . . . should be studied by specialists in a scientific manner." Criticism and creative writing, in other words, were fields that had not yet been trampled by the research specialists.[36]

Foerster's definite program covered three main points. (1) It would be a *graduate* program. (2) For master's candidates the "heart" of the program would be a seminar—"a sort of literary club presided over by a professor keenly interested in writers' problems." (3) There would be a Ph.D. option, culminating in a dissertation that is a "piece of imaginative writing" (or what has since become known as a creative thesis). The only demands put on the creative dissertation would be that it demonstrate the writer's command of literary technique and reveal him or her to be a writer possessed by "creative energy." For the master's candidates, though, perhaps it would be well to demand no thesis at all. Instead, at the end of the program there would be a "searching general examination," after which anyone who wished to proceed on to a Ph.D. should be encouraged to do so—in any one of the "four disciplines," including creative writing.[37]

It was by means of criticism and creative writing—the "new disciplines" or, alternately, "lost provinces"—that graduate study in English would be revolutionized. Although he never said so outright, Foerster seems to have envisioned an English department made up, not of scholars of different periods of English literature, but of practitioners of the various literary disciplines—philologists, literary historians, critics, and writers. For him literature was divided not into historical periods but into something like the "faculties" of medieval scholastic psychology. Foerster's comment on faculty psychology, in fact, sheds light on his thinking about the practical organization of literary study:

> Any terminology dividing human nature is, of course, more or less forced, and open to criticism. The criticism that has been levelled against the rigid "faculties" . . . is justified. But it is noteworthy that modern psychologies that have

cast out the faculties have not succeeded in establishing anything in their place. Somewhat like "periods" in history, they are a practical necessity for fruitful thinking.

The dividing lines between creative writing and criticism, or creative writing and the study of language, were not intended to be rigid. Creative writing was self-contained, but it did not stand apart—any more than (in faculty psychology) there can be judgment without common sense or either without memory. It *was* a discipline, however; "an honorable discipline," insisted Wilbur L. Schramm, Foerster's choice to be the first director of creative writing at Iowa; and so it deserved "a place beside the honorable disciplines of language, literary history, and literary criticism in the graduate school."[38]

The literary education mapped out by Foerster was *both* an academic revolution *and* what Babbitt called a humanist reaction. The goal was to achieve a careful balance of liberalism and professionalism—writers and critics with a solid foundation of humane learning, teachers and scholars with a firsthand awareness, from the inside, of the technical problems of the subject they expected to study and teach. Each would be prepared for a professional career, but liberally rather than vocationally—with a view to the enduring standards embodied in any great literary performance rather than the tricks and shortcuts entailed in a merely current manner of living.

As Foerster confided in a report to the upper administration at Iowa, the School of Letters was "attempting to lead a national reform of the study of letters. . . ."[39] The widow of Edwin Ford Piper—a writing professor at Iowa from before Foerster's time—used an even stronger word: the school was a "takeover." What was involved, she said, was nothing short of a modernist grab for power. The School of Letters belonged to an organized national effort to redirect literature toward new ends. The losers in the campaign were a "middle generation" of writers including James Oppenheim and Randolph Bourne, who shared—the phrases are Mrs. Piper's—a craze for psychoanalysis and an enthusiasm for socialism, humanitarian movements, the naturalistic novel, impressionistic criticism, and lyricism of passionate adolescence.[40] Now if by the modernists Mrs. Piper meant the second generation of modernist writers, including the new university critics, she was on to something. In the thirties they took control of the institutions of American literary life, starting with the English departments of many universities. At the beginning of the decade, Newton Arvin had complained that "the literary life in America is the scene of a sweeping separatism: the typical American writer is as tightly shut up in his own domain, and as jealous of his prerogatives, as one of the Free Cities of the late Middle Ages." To Mrs. Piper's "middle generation" he attributed the discovery that it is not possible for a writer to develop his or her individual talent without "organizing it with reference to a significant purpose."[41] Although Arvin called for a proletarian literature, writers like Ransom, Davidson, Van Doren, Tate, Winters, Blackmur, Warren, Brooks—and Foerster—found significant purpose in education instead. Their intent was to break out of the purely literary domain and carry literature, *studied purely as literature*, into a social and cultural institution—the university. Like proletarian literature, creative writing and the new criticism were attempts to end the separatism in American literary life—not by socializing literature, but by making the social institution of literary study more purely literary.

By the end of the decade they had begun to achieve their aims. The onset of the Depression slowed their progress temporarily. Several professors left Iowa, including John T. Frederick, a story writer and editor of a little magazine called the *Midland*, who had been teaching there since 1921; and only one new addition to the staff—the linguist John C. McGalliard—was made between the years 1930 and 1936. Elsewhere, though, the effort was joined. The University of Michigan, which in 1928 had taken a $320,000 bequest from the playwright Avery Hopwood to fund a student writing prize rather than a program in creative writing, announced that beginning in 1938 it would go ahead and offer "a proseminar in English Composition leading to a master's degree in English" in order to "create a place in our University for young writers to do the work they come here to do."[42] At Harvard, after succeeding Robert Hillyer as director of freshman composition in 1939, the novelist Theodore Morrison—who doubled as head of the Bread Loaf Writers' Conference—began the practice of hiring talented young writers like Delmore Schwartz, Wallace Stegner, Howard Baker, and John Berryman to teach sections of the course. Princeton started up its Creative Arts Program with a grant from the Carnegie Foundation, recruiting Tate in 1939 and then making Blackmur his assistant the next year. The flood of American writers into the university would not occur until after the Second World War, but the thaw before the flood had begun. Although Foerster resigned his post at Iowa in 1944 in a dispute with the administration, his School of Letters was not dismantled when he left. He had expected creative writing to be the first thing to go. "[Y]et it is thriving," he marveled in the sixties, "and is . . . used probably too much today."[43]

Foerster and the new university critics sought to devise a literary education that was more inclusive, and in one important respect they were successful. Prior to the rise of creative writing, women had largely been excluded from the literary profession by being excluded from the institutions of literary education. Creative writing put an end to all that, and in two ways. (1) The shift from philology to criticism in literary study also entailed a shift from the past to the present—from a dead to a living literature—and this presented women with an opening. Although they had been squeezed from the traditional canon of literary study, the turn to constructivism—to what Canby called literature-in-the-making—gave them a fresh go at it. (2) The emergence of practical criticism desexed literature by inverting the categories and values of the older literary and educational establishments. Although literary women continued to associate aestheticism with men—the "arty bone," one woman writer called it—the emergence of a formal and technical criticism transformed literature from a genteel male preserve into an impersonal constructive technique that anyone—even they—could learn. They embraced the stereotypes of the older male critics (genius could not be taught, women were idle and gossipy creatures) and wrote books in which they offered to teach women practical techniques for turning their sexual handicaps to literary advantage.

The enormously popular novelist and story writer Margaret Deland— who had rung the bell in 1888 with *John Ward, Preacher*—wondered "whether a certain kind of education does not stimulate a little too much the critical faculty, and if the mind is always critical the creative faculty is bound down and spontaneity is lost. I can not at this moment think of a teacher of literature," Deland concluded, "who has produced great literature." The commonplace split between critical and creative "faculties" in literary education was—as we have seen—in the process of being healed by the 1930s. What Deland was pointing to may have had less to do with an antagonism between criticism and creativity than with an antagonism between literary men and women. Even if they belonged to opposing parties, after all, men had long controlled criticism and the institutions of literary education. Writers like Deland were denied access by one group, who confined them to the spheres of domesticity and religion, and then were excluded from serious consideration by the other group, who declared that novels of domesticity and religion were beneath criticism. As Amy Kaplan has argued in regard to Edith Wharton, literary professionalism in the early years of the twentieth century was a means for women writers to distinguish themselves from the tradition of domestic fiction. But it was also a means for male critics to exclude women from the literary profession of which they were the custodians. Despite many other changes in culture and higher education, little had changed for women who wrote. As Elaine Showalter has observed in *Sister's Choice*, "For the literary women who came of age in the 1920s, the post-war hostility to women's aspirations, the shift from the feminist to the flapper as the womanly ideal, and especially the reaction against the feminine voice in American literature in the colleges and professional associations made this decade extraordinarily and perhaps uniquely difficult."[44]

In the thirties, however, as one party of men gained power over both criticism and literary education, women were able to assert their own claim at last. A remarkable run of books on learning how to write was published by women during this period: Adele Bildersee's *Imaginative Writing* (1927), Dorothea Brande's *Becoming a Writer* (1934), Esther L. Schwartz's *So You*

Want to Write! (1936), Margaret Widdemer's *Do You Want to Write?* (1937), and Brenda Ueland's *Help from the Nine Muses* (1938). Women also contributed significantly to the streams of criticism that were undermining the authority of the genteel tradition and the old philological guard. Marguerite Wilkinson studied poetry from the point of view of the poets' own creative impulse in *The Way of the Makers* (1925), and Elizabeth Nitchie, who had been teaching criticism at Goucher College since the early twenties, published a textbook in *The Criticism of Literature* (1928) that was intended to afford students a training in criticism—just as they get in the other arts, Nitchie said. These books suggest the degree to which creative writing assisted the feminization of American literature: first by giving women access to the institutions of literary education and then by breaking down the barrier of official criticism. It is revealing that the first thesis in creative writing to be accepted at the University of Iowa—in 1931—was written by a woman.[45]

Adele Bildersee's *Imaginative Writing*, which I glanced at in Chapter 5, indicates how the move toward contemporary literature—the move involved in teaching creative writing—was influential in opening the literary profession to women. Bildersee's honor roll—the list of models she recommends to student writers—is saturated with gender: Rebecca West, Amy Lowell, Constance I. Smith, Anne Parrish, Anne Douglas Sedgwick, Willa Cather, Winifred Sanford, Mary E. Wilkins Freeman, Alice Brown, Zona Gale, Katharine Fullerton Gerould, May Stanley, Fannie Hurst, Alma Burnham Hovey, Sandra Alexander, Helen Dore Boylston, Sara Haardt, Thyra Samter Winslow, Mrs. Henry Dudeney, Dorothy Canfield Fisher, Margaret Lynn, Edna Ferber, Katherine Mansfield, Edith Wharton, Inez Haynes Gilmore, Josephine Dodge Daskam Bacon, Elizabeth Jordan, Mary Stewart Cutting, Kathleen Norris, and Virginia Taylor McCormick. It might be argued that Bildersee is recovering a lost women's tradition, and in some ways she is. And her act of recovery may also be attributed to the fact that Bildersee was teaching at Hunter, at the time a women's college. These are only partial explanations, though, because there is no reason that she could not have confined herself, as would have been traditional and expected, to a male-dominated list of readings. Instead she offers models who are women to students who are women. But what is more, they are contemporary models for contemporary women. The contemporaneity is as important as the feminism, at least as an explicit principle. For she also offers a specimen passage from Hemingway's *In Our Time*, published just two years earlier; her book was among the first to quote Hemingway, helping him take his first steps toward canonization. More explicitly, she urges that the student—and the pronoun is hers—

> keep to books written in his own generation or in a generation not too remote from his own, because writing changes in fashion, as everything else does; and he will have difficulties enough in learning how to write, without the gratu-

itous difficulty of unlearning a manner of writing that will sound bookish and insincere in him, because it was called for, not by the conditions of his own day, but by those of a day now past.

Although not explicitly feminist, this call for contemporaneity could not help but be feminist in implication, because it had the consequence of calling into question (at least as a set of models) the traditional canon of male writers. As if to underscore the point, she cites with approval Mary E. Wilkins Freeman's story "The Revolt of Mother" in which (as she phrases it) "after all these years of meek submission, Mother's will clashes with Father's. . . ." It may be significant that as a Jew—she also wrote a biographical history of postbiblical Judaism—Bildersee probably felt alienated from the English tradition in at least one other way as well. In one place, for instance, she urges writers to retain "surnames that reflect race," for in her experience these often "gave the story the foundation it needed." At all events, her students responded to Bildersee's summons to give a contemporary account of women's experience, writing—in illustrative passages that she quoted from them—writing of sewing, making jelly, going to the delicatessen to buy whitefish.[46]

Schwartz's *So You Want to Write!*, Widdemer's *Do You Want to Write?*, Brande's *Becoming a Writer*, and Ueland's *Help from the Nine Muses* were not college texts but what would now be shelved among the self-help books. Then as now such books were primarily women's books. Brenda Ueland explicitly enunciates the principle behind the genre: "the lives of most women," she says, are "vaguely unsatisfactory." And why?

> They sense that if you are always doing something for *others*, like a servant or a nurse, and never anything for yourself, you cannot do *others* any good. You make them physically more comfortable. But you cannot affect them spiritually in any way at all. For to teach, encourage, cheer up, console, amuse, stimulate or advise a husband or children or friends, you have to be something yourself. And how to be something yourself? Only by working hard and with gumption at something you love and care for and think is important.

In the thirties writing appeared suddenly to be a way for women to become something themselves. Though Ueland's book is largely a restatement of Mearns's testament to "creative power," it is striking in its call to readers to shun duty—one chapter is entitled "Why Women Who Do Too Much Housework Should Neglect It for Their Writing"—and to cultivate idleness. The book is not addressed to women only, and yet its message is quite similar to the interpretation that Sandra M. Gilbert would later put on the old canard about "woman's 'inconstancy'—her refusal, that is, to be fixed and 'killed'" by men's representations, "her stubborn insistence on her own way." Ueland takes the time-honored misogynistic accusation of woman's idleness and inverts and revalues it, laying it down as a necessary condition of all creative work.[47]

All the authors of women's how-to-write books pursue some such strategy of inversion. In *Becoming a Writer* Dorothea Brande argues for example that anyone can learn to be a creative genius. The wife of Seward Collins—who as editor of the *Bookman* was an eager supporter of Babbitt, More, and the new humanism—Brande starts off with a dislike for the very category of "genius." Where her husband and the other humanists associated it with romanticism, though, she associates it with "the brotherhood of authors," which closes ranks around the solemn oath "genius cannot be taught." In arguing instead that it *can* be taught Brande seeks to break the brotherhood's stranglehold over literature. *Becoming a Writer* is an act of cultural demystification. The "holy mystery" behind writing amounts to little more than this: what a beginning writer must do is learn how (in her words) to induce the "artistic coma," the state of semiconsciousness—the state confused with genius—in which the true artist works. And women in particular have techniques available to them for inducing the coma: long baths, lying down in a darkened room, even housework: " 'I'd be all right if I had a floor to scrub,' one of my pupils said to me, a professor's wife who had written in the intervals of bringing up a large family, and had found that her stories fell into line best when she was at work on the kitchen floor."[48]

In *Do You Want to Write?*—a book whose very title expresses impatience for the male counsel of self-doubt, hesitation, and deferral—Margaret Widdemer attacks the standards of the genteel tradition head on. Despite winning the Pulitzer Prize for poetry in 1919 for *Old Road to Paradise*, she had been ignored by the critics, who considered her beneath notice. In response, Widdemer dumps the critics' values on the floor. Much like the recent linguist Deborah Tannen, she argues that literary standards and values are a matter of cultural difference: men and women have different storytelling styles, and a preference for a certain type of story is merely an unknowing preference for one's own sexual difference. Most critics are men and men tend to insist doggedly upon the reasons-why. It is no surprise, then, that the

> writers and critics who dominate fashions in writing far more than they used to, the reading public being far meeker than it was fifty or a hundred years ago, naturally prefer the introvert, or inward-turned mind, because that's the kind of mind they have themselves. So, in the past twenty years the writers and critics have made the introvert, why-it-happened, story more critically admired than the extrovert, how-it-happened, story.

Dividing the magazine market into "the slicks, the highbrows, and the pulps," Widdemer urges her readers to aim at the first and last, avoiding "the scholarly, together with the more radically-minded." She scorns the homogeneity of taste in the so-called little magazines with their almost universal preference for introverted writing. The cost of this scorn may be critical admiration, but there is a payoff: the more extroverted writer enjoys "a wider audience," she laughs. "For the general reading public is extrovert-minded." And the general reading public tended to be women: an economic survey of the book trade found not only that "women read a little more, on the average, and more of them are book readers," but also that women "read faster because they 'get' the meaning of words more quickly, not 'resisting' the meaning of the image or stopping to reason about it"; and for this reason "women allow themselves to be 'carried away' more by what they read. . . ."49

With a career as a serious literary artist out of the question for most Depression-era women, Esther L. Schwartz's fifty-two-page instruction book makes a positive virtue out of the practical (and artistically unserious) alternative. *So You Want to Write!* is a housewife's book. Its cover acknowledges that the book's audience—the author herself—are outsiders to the established insitutions of literary education and patronage, but suggests there is something that may yet be done by women who want to write:

> The author of this book has been able to earn $50 a week writing during her spare time, while taking care of her children and household. This book tells you how you can do the same.

Accordingly, Schwartz addresses her reader in the unpretentious tones of a practical economist—someone for whom literature is a commodity that can contribute to the household income. Her own stories take two hours to write, she says, and earn between fifteen and a hundred dollars apiece. "I do not know of any other occupation at which a woman can earn as much as that in her own home, at her own convenience," she adds. Then she goes on:

> Of course if you want to be the sort of writer who lands in *Story*, *Harper's*, *Scribner's* and the like, the group we call quality magazines, you must be wary of advice and help from people like me. I haven't an arty bone in my body. . . .

The tones of practicality and candor are refreshing. But something more is going on. The cheerful repudiation of "quality" and "artiness" may be a defense against exclusion, a means of self-accreditation by repulsing the "arty bone" of the literary and educational establishments. Schwartz describes herself as forty-five years old, a first novelist with a book of verse also to her credit, who has been writing for eight years. By the time she came to tackle *So You Want to Write!* she had finished, by her own estimate, some fifteen hundred stories. Of which she'd sold 300. By the criteria of the critics she may be an unimportant, even trivial writer. But it is clear that, by her own standards, she is a complete success.50

By the mid-thirties women had less and less need to adopt a strategy of inversion. The critical and institutional turn to literature-in-the-making permitted writers like Schwartz to be self-making, even where they continued (through no fault of their own) to stand outside criticism and the institutions. In a magazine article Schwartz rued that she had never taken a college course in writing. "You don't need to take college courses, lady," an

admirer wrote to say. "You need to *give* one!"[51] Women like Elizabeth
Nitchie, Adele Bildersee, Brenda Ueland, Dorothea Brande, Margaret
Widdemer, Katharine Fullerton Gerould (who taught at Bryn Mawr), and
others *were* giving courses by the mid-thirties; where they were not giving
them they were taking them; and in this way—giving and taking courses in
writing and criticism—they helped to correct what they saw as a false view
of literature being disseminated in the universities. Literature was neither a
holy mystery nor a body of historical data on which to conduct minute
scholarly investigations. It was a craft that could be taught, but it was not
merely a craft. It was also a means of self-definition, a way to snatch critical
standards away from the old men of literary culture and education and—
whether the writer agreed with the new humanists, the new critics, or the
new literary women—to replace them with new, more appropriate standards.

Around 1934, in New York, Lionel Trilling taught a course in creative
writing to women in the Junior League and a decade later he wrote about the
experience in a story called "The Lesson and the Secret." The "lesson" in the
title refers to a session of the class (the story is told in the frame of one fifty-
minute hour), but it also refers to the argument that Trilling's alter ego, the
class instructor, subtly weaves about writing—it is founded upon experience,
it requires a familiarity with literature, it demands discipline, its value is determined by its effect upon the mind. In short it involves everything that is
implied by the word *criticism*. The "secret" refers to something else: the
women in the class believe there is a secret to writing and they want to know
what it is. They are "divided between those who believed that the secret lay
in learning to sell and those who believed that it lay in learning to write."[52]
The women might be forgiven their beliefs; men had concealed the secret of
writing from them for too long. The lesson, though, was that writing was
more than a secret; becoming a writer entailed more than learning to write. If
in the subsequent history of creative writing this lesson was forgotten—if its
alliance with criticism lasted only long enough for creative writing to get on
its feet—this too might be forgiven. Whatever direction pursued by the academic study of it, after the critics and writers took command in the 1930s literature would never again be treated as if everything had already been written,
as if nobody could hope to write any more of it ever again. From then on, the
knowledge of how literature is made would no longer be a secret.

Chapter 7

The Elephant Machine

Outside of Iowa the first graduate programs in creative writing were set going in the first few years after the defeat of Hitler and Japan. Elliott Coleman founded the writing seminars at Johns Hopkins in 1946; Stanford began its fellowship program in writing in 1947, the same year that Alan Swallow started the program at the University of Denver; Baxter Hathaway set up the program at Cornell in 1948. The purpose was to fashion a separate master's degree for teachers of creative writing, courses in which were becoming a fad on the postwar campus, according to Wallace Stegner. "If candidates are properly screened and trained," said Stegner, who assembled the program at Stanford, "they are competent to teach writing in any college better than it has customarily been taught in most, and more competent to teach it than teachers who have been thoroughly trained in the Ph.D. system."[1]

For two decades the first five programs performed the bulk of the work. Under the poet Paul Engle, who had been appointed its director in 1942, creative writing at Iowa filled up like an auditorium, reaching a peak enrollment of 250 in 1965. Engle, who was said to have been carefully groomed for the job, was the right man to oversee Iowa's expansion: he was an academic entrepreneur who had to cultivate his talents as a press agent and fund raiser, because until the mid-sixties the Iowa Writers' Workshop subsisted on gifts and contributions. The real growth in creative writing programs came after this date, and was symbolized by the turn at Iowa to state funding. By 1970 the number of programs had climbed to forty-four and by 1980 to over a hundred. The history of creative writing since the Second World War has been the history of its development into what American industry calls an "elephant machine"—a machine for making other machines. Creative writing programs became a machine for creating more creative writing programs. As early as 1964, Allen Tate warned that "the academically certified Creative Writer goes out to teach Creative Writing, and produces other Creative Writers who are not writers, but who produce still other Creative Writers who are not writers."2

The development came in two stages. First there was an age of criticism, a period during which men like Stegner, Coleman, Swallow, Hathaway, and Engle—all of whom were critics in their way, even if none was in the front rank—consolidated the gains of the earlier generation of university critics; and then, once creative writing was set firmly on its feet, it was swept up into a period of expansion within the university as a whole. In both stages creative writing might be described as going through an interval of "professionalization," although I would prefer to say that in the first stage creative writing settled into a *discipline* while only in the second stage did the teachers of this discipline make themselves bodily into a *profession*.

In the first stage creative writing was the perfection of one tendency in the history of criticism. It was an effort to handle a single order of human discourse in a way that would yield a unified body of theory. It was the movement of criticism toward constructive knowledge—knowledge *how* conceived as both the only means of access to and somehow the equivalent of knowledge *that*. This view of the matter led the first generation of full-time teacher-writers (as one of his students said about Tate) to consider "teaching to be an integral and consistent part of the creative work of a professional man of letters." To think of oneself as a professional writer in the years immediately following the Second World War was to perform all the duties of a man or woman of letters, including what Horace had called "the role of whetstone." It was to seek to integrate and make consistent the knowledge and creative practice of literature. Literary professionalization was a way of taking oneself seriously; it was not a campaign for prerogative and authority. In some other professions by contrast—business, education, the military—attempts to standardize professional training predated the existence of any special knowledge in which to train anyone. And in this regard postwar writers in the university were closer to engineers and commercial artists, who have to master a growing body of knowledge or techniques without a comparable degree of control over the conditions of their employment. At the same time writers *were* becoming professionalized in the more usual sense of the term: they were less worried about the opinion of outsiders, including common readers, and more concerned with the judgment of their fellow writers. Even here, though, the insistence upon autonomy might be put in disciplinary rather than professional terms, as when Stegner tries to cheer up a writer who has (he says) "the uncommon touch" and who will find readers (he assures her) "vertically through many years rather than horizontally in any one publishing season"; or when Saul Bellow differentiates the "great-public novel" from the "art-novel," in which "a reduction in human scope must be compensated or justified by brilliant workmanship—by art." In the first stage of its postwar growth creative writing might be described as an effort to systematize and transmit the knowledge required to enjoy the vertical compensations of art rather than satisfying the horizontal demands of a great public.3

In the second stage creative writing became one of the primary engines driving the postwar expansion of the American university. The boom of creative writing coincided with an unprecedented growth in higher education, but it did not merely coincide with it. Creative writing was a means—a justification—for expanding the university's very role in society. During the period from the late forties to the early seventies the university began to reach beyond its traditional function as a site of teaching and research to provide institutional sanctuary for the arts, including literature. Ezra Pound had said in 1950 that

> this much is certain, if America has any desire to be a center of artistic activity she must learn her one lesson from the Ptolemies. Art was lifted in to Alexandria by subsidy, and by no other means will it be established in the United States.

Only a decade later Pound's challenge seemed well on its way to being met. In 1961, Engle observed that "It is conceivable that by the end of the twentieth century the American university will have proved a more understanding and helpful aid to literature than ever the old families of Europe." He could have said "the not so very old families of America," because the university began to assume a role that had previously been left to families like the Guggenheims, Rockefellers, and Fords, who endowed philanthropic foundations, and the MacDowells, Trasks, and the owner of the Bread Loaf Inn, who turned their homes into artists' retreats. As I argued in Chapter 4, summer conferences like Bread Loaf and summer colonies like MacDowell and Yaddo were attempts to subsidize and give sanction to the life of art, but at best they were temporary accommodations. After the Second World War the university stepped forward to become the permanent center of artistic activity in America, and this aggrandizement of its historical mission seemed to be abundantly justified by the expansion of its size.4

The poet Theodore Weiss shows how the two stages of creative writing's postwar progress are brought together, although in reverse order. In explaining how he had benefitted from a university career, Weiss says that

> it has provided some official status for what I do, a kind of societal approval. The workshop also has obliged me to sharpen and to justify my own attitudes toward writing, to rationalize and articulate them. Thus it has ripened my awareness of what I am—or ought to be attempting to do.

But what exactly is it that Weiss does or attempts to do at his job in the university? Does he write poetry? Teach other people to write poetry? Some combination of the two? This points to a confusion at the heart of postwar creative writing. It is a confusion that materializes every time the question is asked *Can writing be taught?* According to the novelist Walter Van Tilburg Clark, there is only one answer to the question. "[T]he teaching of writing can have but one purpose, the production of writers," he said in 1950. "That must be its central purpose, just as surely as the central purpose of teaching law, engineering or medicine, is to produce lawyers, engineers or physicians." And by writers Clark meant those who are devoted to " 'serious poetry and fiction,' as distinguished, presumably, from commercial or formula writing. . . ." To seek anything else from creative writing than to produce serious writers is to fall back upon "secondary values." Indeed, no other account of their "central purpose" would suffice to rationalize and articulate the many graduate programs in writing that were founded after the war.5

And yet the purpose of a *program* would appear to be different from a *course*. By the early eighties, for instance, undergraduate enrollment in creative writing courses at Western Michigan University was running above 100 per semester. This was advanced as a good reason for founding a master's program there—the students in these courses were described as the "clients" for such a program—but it is a little difficult to believe that many of these students were being "produced" as writers.6 When conceived as a mere course instead of a full-scale program, creative writing was defended in terms of its older "secondary value" as constructive knowledge, a way of seeing literature from its makers' point of view.7 The divergence in aims between the program and the course suggests the real nature of creative writing's professionalization, which did not occur until the late sixties and early seventies. It was not until then that creative writers—graduates of creative writing programs—gained the nearly exclusive right to teach a course whose presence in the curriculum was argued for on different grounds. When it finally occurred, professionalization as such had little to do with literature as such: writers were not professionalized as writers but as writing teachers. If their aims as writers diverged from their aims as teachers, if they were hired and promoted on the basis of criteria that were established by their colleagues and not their "clients," this made them very little different from professors in other walks of university life who also experienced (as Le Baron Briggs had put it many years earlier) a difficulty in adjusting their academic specialties to the needs of general education. This is the true meaning of academic professionalization. Creative writing reached its full growth as a university discipline when the purpose of its graduate programs (to produce serious writers) was uncoupled from the purpose of its undergraduate courses (to examine writing seriously from within).

Despite a steady immigration of critics, poets, and novelists into university teaching positions, the American writer's problem of how to get a living had not been solved for good. By the end of the Second World War, as one historian of authorship has said, five different categories of writers could be made out:

the independent, free-lance writer stood at the top of his profession; another group of writers supplemented their free-lance earnings with occasional stints of salaried work; a third group relied exclusively on service writing to pay their bills; a fourth group relied on another occupation for their main financial support while occasionally selling a story, novel, or poem; finally, a vast pool of amateur writers rarely if ever sold their work.

When the critic and editor Malcolm Cowley addressed the Iowa Writers' Workshop during the 1949–1950 academic year, he warned students that only five or six writers of serious fiction were able to make a go of it, chasing at least one of the students into law school. "Writing novels is not a career, or a profession, or even a trade," agreed Vincent McHugh in a 1950 *Primer of the Novel*. "It is a gambling game. The player's chances are somewhat less favorable than if he were betting on the horses, though the stakes are sometimes larger."8

Although the nation's gross domestic product averaged 2 percent growth per worker per year from 1950 to 1973—although it was a period that stood witness to what the historian John Brooks has described as "one of the most dramatic redistributions of income that any nation ever went through in so short a time"—American writers did not immediately share in the prosperity. In the five years from 1953 to 1957, for example, it was found by one investigator that

> The average professional author earns insufficient income to live on from his chosen profession. . . . There are many thousands of men and women who are free-lance writers, or are trying to be. Probably no more than a dozen really make a good living at it.

The average income of a full-time freelancer was $3400—this during an era when, while the population rose by 11 percent, the number of Americans who earned less than $5000 a year declined by 23 percent. Meanwhile, writers who supplemented their income with occasional stints of salaried work made nearly five times as much money from their employment as from their writing: annual literary earnings of not quite $1500 compared to almost $7000 a year from working for someone else. While one American in twenty held down a second job, for writers—counting their writing as a "job"—the number was one in three.9

One cynic speculated that, as writing declined in profitability, writers turned to teaching instead. It was not quite as simple as that. Long before the rise of the movies and the slow collapse of the pulp fiction market that once made it possible to earn a living at writing stories—long before the Depression and the Second World War—as I argued in Chapter 4, teaching was an option that was available to writers; but unless they were writers like William Vaughn Moody, Alfred Noyes, or Robert Frost—one of those about whom (in Frost's words) "you can hear along other highways," who were "known all over the country for something not too bad"—a teaching post was not likely to be a sinecure. After earning his Ph.D. at Iowa but before going to Stanford, Wallace Stegner taught at several other colleges. "It is possible," he wrote from the University of Utah in 1937,

> to conform to the mores of the pedagogical profession, grind over comma faults and agreement errors and faulty parallelism during working hours, and yet keep close and inviolate a certain artistic integrity which labors to learn the craft of writing. . . . [N]o matter how hard the apprenticeship in pedagogy for the average man, it can be withstood, and it cannot ruin him as an artist. It can perhaps retard him, but it can also pay his board bill while he struggles with his fundamentals—and it is notable that with the first success or two writers consistently abandon the classroom.

Two decades later, though, the attitude toward teaching had begun to change. In a 1958 study of the poet in American society, the Harvard sociologist Robert N. Wilson found that opinion among poets was still divided on the question of what else besides poetry they should do to earn a living. At that time, apparently, teaching was still merely one option among several, including the professions of law and medicine, the business world, manual labor. And yet teaching increasingly struck poets as a "job close to poetry," because it called upon them "to double up on the one outstanding skill they possess—facility with language. . . ." Many poets taught college English, Wilson found, "and despite the traditional horror of mixing pedagogy and creativity they appear to be happy and productive." What was the cause of their happiness and productivity? According to him,

> Teacher-poets report that many university appointments are better suited to the poet's needs today than has been true in the past, since some administrators have come to realize that writers require leisure and are not overloading them with class hours.

It is just as likely that teacher-poets had convinced administrators that grinding over comma faults and agreement errors and faulty parallelism was not what most needed doing.[10]

The improvement of writers' lot—both economically and pedagogically—depended on upholding the distinction between "serious" and "commercial or formula" writers; a distinction, for that matter, which is related by marriage to the one between creative writing and practical composition. These distinctions, as I argued in Chapter 3, date from the earliest years of the century and are central to the development of creative writing as both an institution and a system of ideas. Creative writing is at least partly an effort to solve the problem that has always faced serious writing in America: a lack of economic viability. It does not follow, however, that the distinctions between serious and commercial, creative and practical, are wholly ideological. The economic neglect is merely the end result of a habit of disregard that starts at a much more basic, much less conscious, level. As Howard Nemerov once said, "A primary pleasure in poetry is surely something low enough to be beneath the notice of teacher or critic"—or consumer, he might have added—"the pleasure of saying something over for its own sweet sake and because it sounds just right." And yet the distance between "pleasure" and "seriousness," between saying something because it sounds just right and expecting to receive something for it, is the distance between a logical distinction and an ideological claim. In a 1959 letter of advice to a young writer, Stegner demonstrates how one shades over into the other. "To go on writing" with integrity, he says—in a way that is not calculated to win popular success, "slowly, carefully, with long pauses for thinking and revising"—a writer needs "some sort of subsidy. . . . Of the possible jobs," he goes on, "teaching probably offers most, because its hours are flexible and because it entails a three-month summer vacation." Anyone can write with care but not everyone can expect a subsidy and a three-month vacation. What is going on here is the identification of a certain kind of writing with a certain class of writers. The historian Barbara Tuchman objected to something similar: the narrowing of the word *literature*. In an article published in 1966 she said, "I see no reason why the word should always be confined to writers of fiction and poetry while the rest of us are lumped together under that despicable term 'Nonfiction'—as if we were some sort of remainder." The reason of course is that the hiring of fiction writers and poets to teach in the university had narrowed the scope of "serious writing" and "literature" to what the writers wanted to teach. For the writers themselves this was not experienced as a narrowing at all. On the contrary, they believed passionately in literature, viewing it as the most important of the humanities, even if they confined it to fiction and poetry. "I come of a generation, now largely vanished," Saul Bellow said recently, looking back upon his generation's heyday, "that was passionate about literature, believing it to be an indispensable source of illumination of the present, of reflective power."[11]

The first generation of full-time teacher-writers neither ground over comma faults and agreement errors and faulty parallelism nor produced serious writers; they taught literature. The poet and critic Randall Jarrell was on staff at the University of North Carolina at Greensboro when the school founded its master's program in creative writing, but as Fred Chappell recalls, "Randall made it clear that he had no interest in teaching writing on the graduate level." Not all teacher-writers shared Jarrell's clear lack of interest, but most of them felt the need to teach literature. As the critic Ray B. West reported in 1950,

> Most 'writing' instructors also offer more or less standard 'literature' courses. It is true that they often confine themselves to fields (such as recent criticism and literature, foreign literature, or the study of contemporary forms) not adequately supplied by the traditional English program, quite often not because this represents their preference, but because these courses fulfill a need which the literary scholar does not feel.

The writers taught literature because it—or at least as they conceived i
continued to be neglected by the scholars. As more and more of them bro
into the university after the war, literature came more and more to be iden
tified with them and what they did or attempted to do.[12]

Certainly they broke into the university in numbers. The generation of
poets born after 1910 was almost exclusively a generation of teacher-poets.
John Berryman taught off and on at Wayne State, Harvard, and Princeton
from 1939 to 1955 and then full time at Minnesota from 1955 until his suicide
in 1972; Josephine Miles taught at Berkeley from 1940 until her death in 1985;
John Malcolm Brinnin taught at Vassar for five years during the war, then at
Connecticut for nearly one decade and Boston University for two; J. V.
Cunningham began his postgraduate career at Hawaii in 1945 and then
taught at Chicago and Virginia before settling in at Brandeis from 1953 until
his death in 1985; Nemerov began teaching in 1946 at Hamilton and put in a
long tenure at Bennington and a shorter one at Brandeis before serving on
the faculty of Washington University from 1969 until his death in 1991;
Robert Hayden taught at Fisk from 1946 to 1969 and at Michigan from 1969
to 1980; John Ciardi taught from 1946 to 1961 at Harvard and Rutgers;
William Meredith taught at Princeton for four years after the war, 1946 to
1950, and then at Connecticut College from 1955 to 1983; Jarrell taught at
Greensboro from 1947 until his death in 1965; Joseph Langland taught from
1948 to 1979 first at Wyoming and then at the University of Massachusetts at
Amherst; Anthony Hecht taught at a string of colleges beginning at Kenyon
in 1947 and ending at Rochester four-and-a-half decades later; Theodore
Weiss taught at Bard from 1947 until moving on in 1966 to become professor
of creative arts at Princeton, where he was made emeritus in 1977; Edwin
Honig taught from 1947 to 1982 at New Mexico, Harvard, and Brown; Karl
Shapiro taught first at Johns Hopkins from 1948 to 1950 and then from 1956
until his retirement in 1985 at Nebraska, the University of Illinois at Chicago,
and the University of California at Davis; Philip Booth taught from 1949 to
1986 at Bowdoin, Wellesley, and Syracuse; Richard Wilbur taught from 1950
to 1986 at Harvard, Wesleyan, and Smith; Edgar Bowers started at Duke in
1952 and finished at the University of California at Santa Barbara in 1991;
Donald Justice began teaching in 1953 and worked at five different universities, including Iowa twice, before retiring at Florida in 1992; William H.
Matchett taught at the University of Washington from 1954 to 1982; Louis
Simpson taught at Columbia from 1955 to 1959 while working on his Ph.D.
and then joined the staff at Berkeley where he stayed for eight years before
winding up at SUNY Stony Brook, becoming distinguished professor in
1991. The list could be extended much farther. The thing to notice about it is
the clustering of starting dates around the end of the war. I shall return to
this point, but for now there is something else to notice: while most of these
poets held at least an M.A. and several held a Ph.D., none earned a master's

creative writing, although two of them (Langland and Justice) did study the subject at Iowa and a third (Bowers) accepted a creative writing fellowship at Stanford starting in 1948.

What did the teacher-poets do or attempt to do? As Nemerov said, "Our betters constantly admonished us, in our earlier years, that we must teach literature As Literature, not as an adjunct to history, psychology, philosophy, or (beneath all) the sociable sciences. . . ." Even if no one was quite sure what this meant, it was the first commandment for an entire generation of teacher-writers. The new criticism had become the established church nearly everywhere writers were hired to teach after the war. When Robert Lowell lived and taught there in 1950, the new criticism (he said) was one of the marks of Iowa City—the others were stray dogs, highbrow movies, and a local murder trial. The age came to be known by Jarrell's name for it: it was an age of criticism. Between 1950 and 1970 new volumes of literary criticism went from being 42.1 percent of the total number of new titles in fiction to 67.5 percent. Criticism became one of the major genres of contemporary literature: ambitious young writers like Richard Chase, Alfred Kazin, Irving Howe, or Hugh Kenner could make names for themselves almost exclusively by writing literary criticism. What is more, for a time it became perhaps the most influential form of learning in the American university. As the critic and *Commentary* editor Norman Podhoretz recalled, after having studied under Chase, Lionel Trilling, and F. W. Dupee in the late forties,

> In the classroom as on paper, the critics were not only our guides to the secret riches of literature, they were our guides to philosophy, theology, and politics as well. As explicators of difficult texts, they taught us a method of reading and gave us a veritably gnostic sense of power; as theoreticians of literature, they introduced us to the thrilling metaphysical categories which, banished from the philosophy department by the triumph of logical positivism, found a new home in criticism.

Indeed the exorbitant claims that are still made sometimes for literary criticism—such as Fredric Jameson's "literary criticism is the one discipline that passes judgment on contemporary society from a utopian point-of-view"—are far more indebted to the new criticism and its passionate belief in the importance of literature than they care to admit.[13]

The teacher-writers were second-generation new critics. They equated the writing of fiction and poetry with the explication of difficult texts. This held true even for a novelist like Bellow: "rescued . . . from freshman comp papers" when Robert Penn Warren persuaded Joseph Warren Beach to make him an assistant professor in 1946 at the University of Minnesota, he spent the rest of his career teaching literature on the university level and writing fiction as a way of dealing with critical ideas. Stegner too: although he held out against his Stanford colleague Yvor Winters that literature "is neither conceptual nor propositional," he insisted nevertheless that it is "a means to truth" and that its truths have "an enduring ability to satisfy or at least allay human questioning"; no one who reads his fiction, with its concern for human questioning, can doubt that Stegner was passed through the humanism of Norman Foerster's School of Letters. The other program founders were lesser figures—minor critics, minor writers—but they were literary figures: critics and writers. In addition to two dozen volumes of poetry, Elliott Coleman wrote several books on modern French criticism. While a student at Michigan, Baxter Hathaway won a Hopwood Award for the novel later published as *The Stubborn Way* and then, teaching at Cornell, wrote another novel and two studies of Renaissance criticism. Besides being the publisher of Winters and J. V. Cunningham and thus one of the leading promoters of the view that literature is both conceptual and propositional, Alan Swallow saved enough of his own poems to fill a small volume. One of them was a reflection upon (as the subtitle called it) "a writers' workshop in the Rockies":

> These faces warm and smile, but laughter lies
> Uneasy in the throat. For what can be
> More serious than incubus of pen?
> Here brims the sun, water, the mountain tree—
>
> But how indifferent, how marvelous!
> There moves one hand we cannot know or tell.
> And we are serious—visited by words
> Whose quarrel drives the brain within its shell.
>
> Grandeur is not ours, indeed. It lies
> Upon that slope where water finds the lichen.
> When we forget our dreamed idolatries
> The ironical word shall find us fit, less stricken.

Against the intense seriousness of the writers' workshop Swallow pits "the ironical word," which word of course—at least according to the most influential of the new critics—was simply another word for modern poetry. In 1949, Cleanth Brooks admitted that "*ironical* is in danger of becoming a catchword of our period"—the new critics had tended to overuse it to characterize the structure of modern poetry—but the reason was that the possibility of a modern poem's being ironical arises any time its unverifiable "truth" is at issue. Irony was thus a stance toward experience for the new critics and the writers who were influenced by them. What Swallow recommends is that creative writing follow a new critical ideal—a way to keep itself from being narrowed and confined by its seriousness—pointing out that, despite its name, creative writing cannot create the world. And thus he comes to pretty much the same conclusion about it that Allen Tate would come to a little later: "the name for this activity, as well as the activity itself, is here to stay, however disconcerting it may be for the student or the instructor to pretend to be the surrogate of God."[14]

Surveying the postwar literary generation, Judson Jerome detected a "domination of good sense in current poetry—both in the work and in the poets' careers. . . ." The teacher-poets' good sense came forth as an example of how to write and conduct literary careers, and remained so for creative writing. "A man who has course assignments to fill is likely, I think," said Helen C. White, a historical novelist and Renaissance scholar who also taught creative writing, "to waste less time and energy on the rituals of the literary life, to regard his main undertaking in a more workmanlike spirit, and to be less sentimental about his craft and himself, to say nothing of his fellow-practitioners." The good sense, the lack of sentimentality, could be defined in other less flattering ways. A recent literary historian says the new criticism "tranquilized" poems in the fifties and Reed Whittemore ironically compared the work of a contemporary poet to assembly-line production:

> Lines off his line became smoother
> And smoother as more and more
> Know-how came in the window
> And verses rolled out the door.
>
> Now everyone in the market
> Knows his new works are sure
> To be just as the country wants them:
> Uniform, safe and pure.[15]

"Know-how" may not be a perfectly accurate description of the technical discipline exhibited in much fifties poetry—the sense (to flip a phrase from Wordsworth's Preface) that nothing of much difficulty was being overcome—but Whittemore was exaggerating to make a point. The point was well-made: Stegner felt that he must defend contemporary literature from the similar charge of "semantic positivism," the temptation "to write or read by the rules of the quantitative method. . . ." The second-generation new critics—the teacher-writers—were not semantic positivists, but they did tend to tighten criticism to an instrumentalist or even vocationalist function, assisting the practice of contemporary writing. This tendency displayed itself in everything from a disparagement of the irrational sources of literary inspiration to a confidence that the effect of a poem could be reduced to a rational account. In *Reading Modern Poetry*, a 1955 school anthology he coedited with Warren Carrier, Paul Engle declared that the theory of inspiration is

> dead wrong, for it assumes that the writing of poetry is not a conscious activity. The strange truth about poetry, the source of all that makes it a live and

human art, is this: it comes both out of the remotest depths of the mind, for no reason that can surely be found, and out of the reason itself, openly and by the conscious use of the brain. Always it is this combination of the "subconscious," bubbling up into the poet's hands, and the conscious intelligence working on these materials. . . .

In its extreme forms such a rational discipline could overbalance into an almost compulsive attention to details. During a summer writers' conference at the University of Utah in 1959, for example, John Berryman examined the first sentence of Stephen Crane's story "The Open Boat." He spent an entire morning on the sentence, pointing out that it was written in iambic pentameter and then repeating it over and over with varying stress:

None of them knew the color of the sky.
None of *them* knew the color of the sky.
None of them *knew* the color of the sky.
None of them knew the *color* of the sky.
None of them knew the color of the *sky*.

What finally was the point of the lesson? The poet John Matthias (who was there) is not sure, but "it was a marvelous display of pedagogical virtuosity and critical ingeniousness," he testifies. Another observer might have been struck by the deliberation, the sheer effortfulness, with which Berryman carried out the exercise. It was almost as if he believed that, by fixing his attention microscopically upon one element, he could *will* Crane's style to yield up its secret. Although the lesson was a variation on the new criticism's practice of "close reading," it had begun to drift away. Close reading was originally designed as a method for limiting the context of meaning to the text itself. There could be, it was argued, no knowledge of a text's subject matter that was prior to a close reading of it; the text was the *whole* context of understanding. In Berryman's hands the context shrank to the scope of a sentence; there was no larger whole. And meaning was not at issue at all. The critic's entire attention was absorbed by a technical detail.[16]

The absorption in detail may have been the unavoidable concomitant of literature's being treated as an end in itself. Instead of being studied for the sake of a "secondary value"—its moral effect—literature was studied for the knowledge of how *literary* effects are attained. The shift, as the poet Karl Shapiro urged, was toward vocationalism:

Let us give up the old pedagogical idea that the effect of poetry on the world is salutary. To believe that men are bettered by poetry is as narrow as to believe that they are worsened by it. Let us think of it another way. Let us think of creation in art as the vocation, and only the vocation of a certain kind of man. Let us then give it the honor of any vocation for knowledge.

At all events, the vocation for literary knowledge remained the first justification for a program in creative writing, and the name for this special knowledge continued to be *criticism*, although it was beginning to be defined in a new way. Three decades later the story writer Donald Bartholme would give the definition most clearly. He agreed that a writing program probably cannot make students into serious writers. "But you can teach the notion of what's dead or alive," said Barthelme, who taught at the University of Houston. "You can teach them how to be critics of their own work." Even in the fifties this idea of vocational criticism was becoming fixed. Ray B. West, who taught at Iowa starting in 1949, doubled back on Foerster's idea of the writing program as a school of criticism. Because "every writer must learn as best he can," West said, "to distinguish exactly what it is in his work which succeeds from that which fails," and because this ability to distinguish success from failure—this critical sense—"operates . . . at all points in the creative process," it follows that "[i]t is in the cultivation of this sense that the writing program can achieve most." If the emphasis was vocational, though, it was not yet fully professionalized. "The problems of recognition and publication will always be secondary," West said, "and they will arise as a result of the writing"—that is, as a consequence of having written—"not as a professional aim in the sense that the student would be encouraged to 'slant' his unfinished writing toward any particular publisher or publication."[17]

Over and over writing teachers said that writing itself cannot be taught, but a discipline of criticism that is associated with it can be. Jean Stafford, for example, suggested there was more to be learned in a writing class than how to write, saying that

> the student who, in class, learns to analyze a story or a novel, to separate its components, and then to see how the author has united them into an infrangible integer may never himself write a publishable piece of fiction, but he will know better what writing is, and his enjoyment of reading—and therefore, of life—will be greatly enriched. It is more fun to watch a tennis match if you know how to play; but even if you don't know how, if you learn the rules, then you can differentiate among the idiosyncratic styles of individual players and be a judicious spectator.

Not everyone was as blunt as James Whitehead of the University of Arkansas. "I teach reading," he said, "and I teach reading the way writers read." *Reading as a writer*—it became the unexpected bonus of creative writing. Dorothea Brande had coined the term in the mid-thirties in *Becoming a Writer*, but it fell to R. V. Cassill, in *Writing Fiction* (1962), to develop the term into a concept. A novelist and Iowa professor who went on to found the writing program at Brown in 1966, Cassill defined "reading as a writer" as the kind of literary study that distinguishes creative writing from the on-the-job training of journalism on the one hand and from literary scholarship on the other. Good writers are interested in something more than the application of commercial formulas, and so they must study texts in addition to principles. Unlike scholars, though, they are not particularly interested in determining the sources of literary texts. Above all they are interested in how texts are *made*—how the parts are united into an infrangible integer—which means they are committed to the view that a text might have been made otherwise than it is. "A writer reading must be aware," Cassill says, underlining every word, "that the story exists as it does because the author chose his form from among other possibilities." Again, this is clearly a vocational concept of knowledge, embedded in a highly organized discipline of work. But, again, it is not truly a *professionalized* concept, because it does not depend upon a literature or a set of problems accessible only to specialists. "You know," an undergraduate student of creative writing told his professor, James K. Folsom, in the early sixties. "This is the best course in criticism given in Yale College." Pondering what he had meant, Folsom decided that the course

> had given him an insight into the techniques of literary analysis by making him aware of how other writers had succeeded where he himself had failed. It taught him by example rather than by precept that the proper question to ask in the interpretation of literature is not "What does the story mean?" but rather "How does the story work?"

Creative writing remained a discipline of criticism, but the criticism was neither "know-how" nor an absorption in technical detail; perhaps even "vocationalism" is too hidebound. Creative writing was the knowledge of how literary texts are made, how they work; it was a discipline of constructive knowledge.[18]

Howard Nemerov explained how he happened to become a college teacher. He was twenty-six, and though he had got a Harvard education, he held no advanced degree. He was just back from the war in Europe where he had served as a pilot in the Army Air Corps, flying combat missions against German shipping in the North Sea. He was also newly married; he had to start earning a living. "[I]n 1946," he said,

> by the exemplary generosity of our government in establishing the G.I. Bill and so inducing colleges and universities to find warm bodies to put up against the veterans (twenty of them, and still in combat boots), I became a teacher, or anyhow a kind of dogsbody responsible for The Bible and Shakespeare and The Modern Novel and Modern Poetry (with my first book [*The Image and the Law*] coming out, I was presumed to know something of that) and whatever else needed doing.

The need to find warm bodies to put up against the veterans explains much about the postwar influx of poets and fiction writers into the university. Under the G.I. Bill—officially, the Servicemen's Readjustment Act of 1944— veterans were allotted forty-eight months of free education at the college or university of their choice. Although the administrator of Veterans Affairs predicted that only 700,000 of them would do so, under the provisions of the bill 2,232,000 veterans crowded into American universities and colleges after the war, with more than a million of them enrolled during the single academic year 1947–1948, An army of warm bodies was needed to put up against them—and quickly. Small wonder so many poets and fiction writers began their academic careers about this time. Accounts of its effect upon the curriculum tend to be overstated—creative writing, to name one subject, had already begun to grow prior to the war—but the G.I. Bill left its mark on the university in other ways. "The uncritical acceptance of largeness became a major legacy of the G.I. Bill," says the historian Keith W. Olson. "This legacy, in turn, served as perhaps the most important intellectual foundation for bigness that characterized higher education during the 1960s and 1970s." Another legacy, tied to the first, was the uncritical acceptance of the practice of hiring writers—who, with books coming out, were presumed to know something about it—to teach modern writing. As the postwar university expanded so did the need for writers.[19]

The mass expansion of American higher education received political backing when the President's Commission on Higher Education, consisting of twenty-eight members appointed in July 1946 and chaired by George F. Zook, president of the American Council on Education, linked physical enlargement to an enlargement of the university's public role. "American colleges and universities must envision a much larger role for higher education in the national life," said the Commission's report, *Higher Education for American Democracy*:

> They can no longer consider themselves merely the instrument for producing an intellectual elite. They must become the means by which every citizen, youth and adult, is enabled and encouraged to carry his education, formal and informal, as far as his native capacities permit.

The colleges and universities did their best, although the first thing that was noticeable was their growth in sheer physical size. From 1930 to 1957 college enrollments more than doubled, going from 1,101,000 to 2,637,000. Then between 1960 and 1969 they doubled again, rising to over seven million.[20]

Although the enlargement of the university was seen politically as a democratization of it, within the university this was seen as an occasion for enlarging its domain. The spokesman for mass expansion was the University of California chancellor Clark Kerr, who sang the praises of what he liked to call the "multiversity," a social and cultural institution that had to be many things to many different people. Playing on the title of Karl Polanyi's famous 1944 account of the emergence of a market economy, Kerr said the university was going through a great transformation. "Knowledge is exploding along with population," he said. "There is also an explosion in the need for certain skills." One field that was "ready to bloom"—whether it was a field of knowledge or skills he did not make clear—was the creative arts, "hitherto the ugly ducklings or Cinderellas of the academic world." Kerr acknowledged that

In the arts the universities have been more hospitable to the historian and critic than to the creator; he has found his havens elsewhere. Yet it is the creativity of science that has given science its prestige in the university. Perhaps creativity will do the same for the humanities, though there may be less need to create than has recently been true in science and the tests of value are far less precise. A very important role remains for the historian of past ages of creativity and for the critic of the current productions. But the universities need to find ways also to accommodate pure creative effort if they are to have places on the stage as well as in the wings in the great drama of cultural growth now playing on the American stage.[21]

Kerr's logic is interesting, but it is obscured a little by the exuberance of his rhetoric. The argument of his last sentence goes something like this. If the university is to play a central role in American culture (that is the major premise), and if the arts are at the center (American culture, Kerr said, was currently having a "great period of cultural flowering"), the conclusion is that the university must become an arts center. This is an exception to the general rule that the minor premise is the point at which most arguments go astray. What is perhaps most revealing about Kerr's thinking is his assumption that the major premise is unexceptionable. True, he was speaking in his capacity as a representative of the university. And true, the "explosion" in enrollments suggested that the university *was* destined to play a central role in the American future. But on Kerr's argument the creative arts, including literature, are subordinated to the university's need for public prominence. They become a mere *means* by which the university takes its place at center stage in the American drama. It is not so much the growth in population, knowledge, and skills that is at issue; what is important is the expansion of the university's cultural role.

In the nineteenth century the university transformed itself from a college into a research institution. In the second half of the twentieth century it added the function of providing a haven for the arts. Apologists for the second transformation, like Kerr, made the case that the arts were not so different from scientific research. "At their most creative edge," Wallace Stegner said, "science and art both represent original questionings—pure research—and both rely upon a galvanizing and originating intuition." The last phrase was an attempt to supply a rational defense of poetic inspiration, but the attempt was negligible. Far more compelling were lists of prizes and honors won by the writers connected with a university—in a 1961 anthology of Iowa workshop writing Engle listed two Lamont Poetry Awards, a Pulitzer Prize, and two National Book Awards among the faculty and students—suggesting that the real benefit of creative writing was that it could endow a university with prestige. (Engle was careful to dedicate his anthology to the University of Iowa, praising it as "a creating source.") The comparison of artistic creation to scientific research suggests something else too. As in the nineteenth-century university there was a shift away from teaching. If writing is the equivalent of research the old stumper *Can writing be taught?* is off the point. The question, as Stegner observed, assumes that literary talent, being innate, is sufficient to make someone into a writer. But it is not, talent also needs to be developed. "And this means that in the game of literary futures," Stegner said, "luck, economic and social pressures, personal preferences, and character—a word that few use any more—matter quite as much as talent." Among the things that have to be dealt with if a talented writer is to be developed are "the economic circumstances which must allow for practice and growth, the social pressures for success that must be read in dollars. . . ." Thus the university was advanced as a solution to the economic and social problems of writers. For them meanwhile it was—again in Stegner's words—a place to live and write that would remove at least for a while the economic insecurity that came close to unnerving them. Or as Engle said in explaining why so many of them had taken academic posts or enrolled in graduate workshops after the war: "They have found the campus a suitable combination of security with time to work." Over and over it was said that the primary function of a graduate program in creative writing is to give young writers the time to develop themselves. What went unstated was that this pointed to a new cultural role on the part of the university. It was no longer a mere research institution. It was now also a writers' colony.22

If the university provided them with security and time to work what did writers provide to the university? The reciprocal obligations were minimal. Describing Stanford's fellowship program in creative writing, Stegner said:

> No academic requirements are made of Fellows; they are automatically admissible to Stanford, no matter how bad their academic records, once they have been granted a fellowship, and they have no obligation to attend any classes except the writing workshop. For that they receive academic credit—whether they want it or not, and generally they do not—because some means has to be found for prorating their tuition. They may become degree candidates if they wish, but most do not wish. They write, and they raid the University for books, lectures, music, theater, and companionship, without having to take any more active part in it than they choose to.

Stanford's program was not idiosyncratic. In a letter, the poet Mark Jarman details his two-year education at Iowa:

> We were required to take 48 hours. Each semester, then, we took 12 hours—or at least I did. They did not all have to be in the writers' workshop, but I took all mine there. . . . I really only wanted to write poems and was willing to slight my academic endeavors in order to do so. . . . You could earn six hours for a workshop, three hours for a seminar or independent study. In your final semester, you could earn six hours for working on your thesis. Ergo, my career at Iowa went like this. Fall 1974: Workshop with Marvin Bell; seminar with Stanley Plumly; seminar with Charles Wright. Spring 1975: Workshop with Charles Wright; seminar with Stanley Plumly; independent study with Charles Wright. Fall 1975: Workshop with Donald Justice; seminar with Sandra McPherson; independent study with Stanley Plumly. Spring 1976: Workshop

with Sandra McPherson; thesis work. There were no texts in the workshops except the poems written by the students; these were discussed weekly, and we met only once a week. . . .

The seminars, on Jarman's description, were in contemporary poetry: on forms, the long poem, "the poem with content," women's poetry. The texts were collections of contemporary verse: Theodore Roethke's *Far Field*, Robert Lowell's *Life Studies*, James Wright's *Two Citizens*, Galway Kinnell's *Book of Nightmares*, Philip Levine's *1933*, Mark Strand's *Story of Our Lives*, Louise Glück's *House on Marshland*, and so on. Even here, though, the function of the seminars was to assist the creative effort: Jarman's studies provoked reflection upon narrative poetry, which "influenced what [he] would later write in *The Reaper*," the influential journal of narrative poetry that he founded (with Robert McDowell) at Southern Indiana University in 1981.[23]

By 1970, according to a *Directory of Creative Writing Programs* issued by the College English Association, forty-four colleges in the United States offered master's degrees either in creative writing or in English with a creative thesis: Alaska, Arizona, Arkansas, Auburn, Boston University, Bowling Green, Brown, California (Irvine), Cal State Dominguez Hills, Cal State Long Beach, Central Michigan, Colorado State, Columbia, Cornell, Denver, Florida, Hollins College, Idaho, Indiana, Iowa, Johns Hopkins, Massachusetts (Amherst), Montana, New Hampshire, New Mexico State, North Carolina (Greensboro), North Dakota, Northern Iowa, Ohio, Oregon, San Francisco State, South Dakota, Southern Methodist, Southwestern Louisiana, Stanford, SUNY Brockport, Syracuse, Utah, Vanderbilt, University of Washington, Wayne State, Western Washington, Wichita State, and Wisconsin (Milwaukee). Twenty-seven other schools were listed as having curricula that were "well-developed": Beloit, Bemidji State, Cal State Hayward, Carnegie Mellon, DePauw, Eastern Oregon, Evansville, LSU, Marshall, University of Miami, Michigan State, the New School, North Carolina (Chapel Hill), North Carolina (Wilmington), Northern Arizona, Ohio State, Penn State, Pittsburgh, San Diego State, South Alabama, South Carolina, Stephen F. Austin, Stephens College, SUNY Buffalo, United States International College, Western Carolina, and Western Michigan.[24]

Now of these, twenty-one were "flagship" state universities (15 with master's programs, six with well-developed programs), thirty more were some other kind of state-supported institution (18 in the first category, 12 in the second), seventeen were private nondenominational colleges (11, 9), and three were church schools (1, 2). From these numbers at least three things stand out. First, fewer than 30 percent of the flagship state universities with a well-developed curriculum in creative writing did not also offer a master's degree—there were two-and-a-half times the number of master's programs when compared with non-master's programs. What this suggests is that the campus of prestige was relatively uninterested in housing creative writing unless it could also have the prestige of serving as regional headquarters for creative writing. In at least two states a more obscure campus had clipped in ahead of its older and more glamorous sister. In 1965, Irvine became the first branch of the University of California to offer an advanced degree in creative writing, arguing explicitly that it would "fill a distinct statewide, to say nothing of a regional, need." Wichita State's initial proposal for a degree in creative writing was rejected in 1967—no new programs were approved that year—but five years later the okay was given. Then in 1978 the board of regents turned down a similar proposal by the University of Kansas, keeping Wichita the only program in the state. This leads to a second observation: 42 percent of the schools on the *Directory*'s list were fleet rather than flagship state universities—land-grant institutions, new branch campuses, former teachers colleges, commuter schools. A striking number were altogether new, dating from after the war: Wilmington (founded 1947), Long Beach (1949), U.S. International (1952), Milwaukee (1956), Hayward (1957), Dominguez Hills (1960), and South Alabama (1964). Others were older as institutions but new as universities. In 1964, as Fred Chappell recalls, the transformation of the Woman's College of North Carolina into the University of North Carolina at Greensboro led directly to the establishment of a writing program:

> No one in the English Department—including especially the writers themselves—wanted a graduate creative writing program, but when our state legislature pressed its FIAT button and transformed the confident Woman's College into a highly bewildered university, the English Department was forced to offer graduate programs of some sort.

In similar fashion Bemidji State dropped "Teachers College" in 1957 and by 1967 it was ready to offer creative writing full time, hiring a native son, the Iowa-educated poet William Douglas Elliott, to teach the subject. Central Michigan converted from teachers college to university in 1959, and nine years later—in response to enrollments that surged by 233 percent over the period—it set up a master's program in creative writing. The final observation to make about the list in the CEA *Directory* is the nearly complete absence of creative writing at church schools—except for colleges affiliated with the United Methodist Church, no religious institutions at all were represented—which given the progressivist and humanist background of the subject (to say nothing of its new function as a haven for purely creative writers) is perhaps not too surprising.[25]

Some writing programs were created by a kind of institutional proselytism. In 1984, Donald Justice, who had taught creative writing his entire professional life and had once headed the Iowa Writers' Workshop, noted that "Those who went through Iowa went out and took part in other writing programs—a kind of pyramid scheme, it seems now, looking back." Iowa graduates had fanned out across the country to institute at least twenty-five new programs: Harry Barba (Skidmore), Joe David Bellamy (St. Lawrence University), Jerry Bumpus (Eastern Washington), James Crumley (Colorado State), Bruce Cutler along with Philip Scheider (Wichita State), Stuart Dybek along with Herbert Scott (Western Michigan), William D. Elliott (Bemidji State), James B. Hall (Oregon), William Harrison along with James Whitehead (Arkansas), John Herrmann (Montana), Morgan Gibson (Wisconsin at Milwaukee), Joseph Langland along with Andrew Fetler, Richard Kim, and Robert Tucker (Massachusetts), Daniel Marder along with S. Leonard Rubinstein (Penn State), Joseph Nicholson along with Vincent Stewart (Lock Haven State), Philip F. O'Connor (Bowling Green), Norman Peterson (Southwest Texas State), Thomas Rabbitt (Alabama), Knute Skinner (Western Washington), Richard G. Stern (University of Chicago), Walter Sullivan (Vanderbilt), Loren Taylor (Northern Iowa), Eric Torgersen (Central Michigan), Lewis Turco (SUNY Oswego), and Robert Williams (Hayward State). It is an open question whether, at very many of these schools, creative writing was established in response to an impulse originating from within or whether it sprang from a different source. The founding of programs began to take on the appearance—at least to someone like Justice—of an organized national scheme.[26]

The "pyramid scheme" (to use Justice's phrase) or the "cultural flowering" (to use Clark Kerr's) was part of a larger trend toward state control of the institutions. At the end of the Second World War, half of the American students were in private colleges. From then on private colleges annually lost about 1 percent of the total. Behind the trend was the growth of federal aid to education paid directly to students in the form of grants and loans. Federal aid had begun during the Depression when 620,000 students between 1933 and 1941 received government support to pay college expenses, first from the Federal Emergency Relief Administration and then the National Youth Administration. The real growth of student aid belonged to the postwar era and was fueled by three different factors. First, the launching by the Soviet Union of an unmanned space satellite called Sputnik on October 4, 1957, raised a hue and cry to improve American education, and Congress hurriedly passed the National Defense Education Act (NDEA) to expand and develop the national curriculum in science, mathematics, and foreign languages. Second, teachers of English and the social sciences demanded to know why their studies had been excluded from the public largesse; in 1965 the NDEA was extended to include them. Third, the first wave of the massive generation born since the war—the notorious "baby boom"—began to descend upon college campuses in the mid-sixties. From this time on national expenditures on student aid shot up like an adolescent (see Fig. 5). The rise in student aid, as the economist Thomas Sowell has observed, virtually ensured that universities would expand their programs, be-

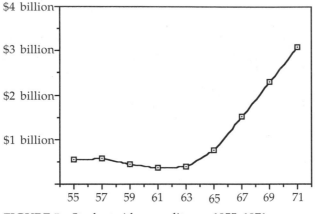

FIGURE 5   Student aid expenditures, 1955–1971

Source: Based on Carnegie Commission on Higher Education, *Higher Education: Who Benefits? Who Pays? Who Should Pay?* (New York: McGraw-Hill, 1973).

cause student aid covered costs over and above the bare cost of tuition. Thus the federal money acted as a powerful incentive to create programs that would raise costs that would bring in more federal money. And writing programs were particularly attractive because, as the English department at Virginia pointed out to the university's administration, they drew upon existing resources and were developed within an academic discipline that was already well-established. New fees could be generated but new facilities were not required and sometimes new faculty was not even needed, at least not immediately.[27]

The growth of creative writing uncannily mimicked the growth of student aid. In 1965—the first year of its existence—Irvine's program had difficulty in filling the twelve slots in its incoming class. The creative arts program at Princeton took off only after Theodore Weiss's arrival in 1966, when within a few years it went from one resident novelist and poet to a staff of twenty-three. Two-and-a-half decades later creative writing had become an industry. Between 1971 and 1989 the number of degrees awarded in the field more than tripled—from 345 to 1107.[28]

By the late sixties and early seventies, then, creative writing was ready and waiting to be professionalized. And so, in due course, a professional organization—the Associated Writing Programs—was founded. The AWP started at Brown University in 1967, and after rough financial times led to a cutback, it moved in 1971 to Washington College in Maryland. The next year the AWP received $10,000 from the National Endowment for the Arts that enabled it to hire its first full-time staff worker and to set up a placement bureau. In the fall of 1972, fifty writers sought its assistance in finding work; within two years the number had grown to 300. The group staged its first independent annual convention—the earlier meetings had been held in concert with the Modern Language Association—in Denver in January 1975. That year the first edition of the *AWP Catalogue* carried listings for 81 writing programs. By the next year the number of job-hunting writers had climbed to 500. The AWP offices were moved again in 1978, this time to Old Dominion University, and the number of writers using its placement bureau reached 950. The growth of the organization can be charted by its budget, which doubled in just two years from 1972 to 1974 and then doubled again between 1974 and 1978.[29]

In 1979 the AWP issued its Guidelines for Creative Writing Programs and Teachers of Creative Writing. These guidelines were an explicit attempt to set the terms of the relationship between writers and their academic employers. "Academic degrees," for instance, "should not be considered a requirement," the organization said. "If however a terminal degree is required, it is recommended that the Master of Fine Arts rather than a Ph.D. be considered the appropriate credential for the teacher of creative writing." The AWP was not setting itself up as an accrediting agency; it was merely acknowledging reality. The very next year, in proposing the establishment of a degree program in creative writing, the English department at Virginia observed that the MFA had become a degree that "is often a prerequisite for employment by schools and colleges seeking to staff courses in creative writing." In defending its proposal to the upper administration, the department said that there were "abundant career opportunities open to those who have earned the MFA in this field. . . ." The department had found, for instance, that of the 51 four-year colleges advertising creative writing positions in the Modern Language Association *Job Information List* for 1979–1980, nineteen specifically required the MFA. There was a clear "preferential pattern," it concluded, "favoring the MFA over the M.A. in creative writing. . . ." What the preferential pattern may have indicated was that academic creative writers were seeking and beginning to attain the exclusive right to judge one another's performance. The AWP noted as much in its guidelines. "AWP believes," it said, "that writing program faculty, who as creative writers are best qualified to make assessments of a candidate's work, should be given the responsibility of making professional decisions about their peers. . . ."[30]

Creative writing was originally an enterprise for bringing the understanding of literature and the use of it into one system. The plan for doing so was not always adequate to the task. And too sometimes the nature of the task was not fully grasped, and those who undertook it nodded long enough to neglect one portion of it. Even then, however, the coherent view of literature sitting at the bottom of creative writing was not abandoned; it was only neglected. The idea of creative writing was to join the study of literary texts to the act of creating them, and the culture would have a place for it as long as these things were put asunder.

In 1976, nearly a century after Barrett Wendell taught the first course in advanced composition at Harvard, the American Philosophical Society re-classified "creative arts" as being separate from the criticism of them.[31] On one hand this registered the fact that creative writing had cut the apron strings, establishing itself as a fully autonomous branch of the curriculum. But on the other hand it suggested that the original intention behind creative writing had been lost sight of. "As things stand now," R. V. Cassill said, "even the best of the writing programs are not integrated with other facets of literary studies. 'Creative writing' is a (usually) suspect *alternative* to 'crit-icism' or 'scholarship.' " What had begun as an alternative to the schisma-tizing of literary study had ended as merely another schism. The poet and critic Robert Pinsky was even harsher, speaking of "what can sometimes seem the sharp distinction" between creative writing and formal literary scholarship—a sharp distinction that had come about to the detriment of both. On one side there is "an immense elaboration of the techniques of com-position" accompanied by "a fatal ignorance of the past"; on the other side an "elaborate sophistication regarding poetic theory" that goes with "a fatal ignorance of composition." The consequence, he said, is "rhetorical pedantry in the poets; and arid nihilism in the critics." Technique had been divorced from theory—composition from the past—as each section of the English de-partment sought to perfect its own specialty.[32]

The mystique of professionalism had obscured the reasons why cre-ative writing was ever taught in the first place. For some it had become a means, not of exposing the lie that literature is a "holy mystery" and teach-ing it instead as something that is unmysteriously *made*, but merely of fur-thering the enterprise with no clearer idea of what it was all about. "Creative writing is the only real growth area in American literary education," said the novelist William Harrison, who founded the program at the University of Arkansas. "Traditionally, English teachers have taught others to be English teachers. This isn't what we do. We teach writers, not critics." The clientele of creative writing had shrunk as the programs had expanded. Harrison was echoed in Arkansas's self-description: "writers who do take the MFA degree are prepared to teach a wide range of courses at the college and university level. The program is well suited to those who wish to become writers who teach." *Writers who teach*—the phrase was telling, and it marked the end of an era. "Finally," Wallace Stegner said, "we are staffed by writers—not teachers who write, but writers who teach, and whose writing is the princi-pal basis for their tenure and promotion." Finally, creative writing had be-come a national staff of writers who teach writers who go on to teach, and to hope for tenure and promotion.[33]

❧ *Notes*

Introduction

[1] Quoted in Samuel Longfellow, *Life of Henry Wadsworth Longfellow* (Boston: Ticknor, 1886), 1: 53–54, 56.

[2] Quoted in Newton Arvin, *Longfellow: His Life and Work* (Boston: Little, Brown, 1963), p. 48. On Longfellow's historical significance see William Charvat, *The Profession of Authorship in America, 1800–1870*, ed. Matthew J. Bruccoli (Columbus: Ohio State University Press, 1968), pp. 106-54.

[3] Robert Hewison, "Iowa Campus," *Times Literary Supplement* (March 13, 1981).

[4] *New York Times* (January 8, 1984). During the academic year 1988–1989 there were 1107 degrees awarded in creative writing—592 bachelor's degrees, 511 master's degrees, and 4 doctorates. See the *Digest of Education Statistics*, 1991 (Washington: Census Bureau, 1991), table 233, p. 243. For the number of creative writing programs see D. W. Fenza and Beth Jarock, eds., *AWP Official Guide to Writing Programs*, 6th ed. (Paradise, Calif.: Dust Books, 1992).

[5] Wallace Stegner, *On the Teaching of Creative Writing*, ed. Edward Connery Latham (Hanover, N.H.: University Press of New England, 1988), p. 51.

[6] J. A. Sutherland, *Fiction and the Fiction Industry* (London: Athlone Press, 1978), p. 150.

[7] Greg Kuzma, "The Catastrophe of Creative Writing," *Poetry* 148 (1986): 349.

[8] Carl Diehl, *Americans and German Scholarship, 1770-1870* (New Haven: Yale University Press, 1978), p. 183.

[9] The books referred to in this paragraph are: Gerald Graff, *Professing Literature: An Institutional History* (Chicago: University of Chicago Press, 1987); Ian Michael, *The Teaching of English from the Sixteenth Century to 1870* (Cambridge: Cambridge University Press, 1987); Kermit Vanderbilt, *American Literature and the Academy: The Roots, Growth, and Maturity of a Profession* (Philadelphia: University of Pennsylvania Press, 1986); James A. Berlin, *Writing Instruction in Nineteenth-Century American Colleges* (Carbondale: Southern Illinois University

Press, 1984); James A. Berlin, *Rhetoric and Reality: Writing Instruction in American Colleges, 1900–1985* (Carbondale: Southern Illinois University Press, 1987); Albert R. Kitzhaber, *Rhetoric in American Colleges, 1850–1900* (Dallas: Southern Methodist University Press, 1990); Nan Johnson, *Nineteenth-Century Rhetoric in North America* (Carbondale: Southern Illinois University Press, 1991); Evan Watkins, *Work Time: English Departments and the Circulation of Cultural Value* (Stanford: Stanford University Press, 1989); Katherine H. Adams, *A History of Professional Writing Instruction in American Colleges: Years of Acceptance, Growth, and Doubt* (Dallas: Southern Methodist University Press, 1993); Susan Miller, *Textual Carnivals: The Politics of Composition* (Carbondale: Southern Illinois University Press, 1991); Anne Ruggles Gere, *Writing Groups: History, Theory, and Implications* (Carbondale: Southern Illinois University Press, 1987); and David R. Russell, *Writing in the Academic Disciplines, 1870–1990: A Curricular History* (Carbondale: Southern Illinois University Press, 1991).

10 For the case against creative writing see Kuzma, "Catastrophe of Creative Writing"; Donald Hall, "Poetry and Ambition," *Kenyon Review* n.s. 5 (1983): 90–104; Bruce Bawer, "Dave Smith's 'Creative Writing,'" *New Criterion* 4 (December 1985): 27–33; Joseph Epstein, "Who Killed Poetry?" *Commentary* 86 (August 1988): 13–20; David Dooley, "The Contemporary Workshop Aesthetic," *Hudson Review* 43 (1990): 259–80; John W. Aldridge, "The New American Assembly-Line Fiction," *American Scholar* 59 (1990): 17–38; Dana Gioia, *Can Poetry Matter? Essays on Poetry and American Culture* (St. Paul: Graywolf, 1992); and R. S. Gwynn, "No Biz Like Po' Biz," *Sewanee Review* 100 (1992): 311–23. For the defense see Stegner, *Teaching Creative Writing*; Richard Hugo, "In Defense of Creative-Writing Classes," in *The Triggering Town: Lectures and Essays on Poetry and Writing* (New York: Norton, 1979), pp. 53–66; Marvin Bell, "The University Is Something Else You Do," in *Old Snow Just Melting: Essays and Interviews* (Ann Arbor: University of Michigan Press, 1983), pp. 104–23; John Barth, "Writing: Can It Be Taught?" *New York Times Book Review* (June 16, 1985); Dave Smith, "Notes on Responsibility and the Teaching of Creative Writing," in *Local Assays: On Contemporary American Poetry* (Urbana: University of Illinois Press, 1985), pp. 215–28; Nancy L. Bunge, *Finding the Words: Conversations with Writers Who Teach* (Athens: Swallow/Ohio University Press, 1985); Joseph M. Moxley, ed., *Creative Writing in America: Theory and Pedagogy* (Urbana: National Council of Teachers of English, 1989); and Jonathan Holden, *The Fate of American Poetry* (Athens: University of Georgia Press, 1992).

11 Kingsley Amis, *Memoirs* (New York: Summit, 1991), p. 196.

12 Lucy S. Dawidowicz, *What Is the Use of Jewish History?* ed. Neal Kozodoy (New York: Schocken, 1992), p. 19.

13 Gerald Graff, letter to the author, November 28, 1993.

14 See Robert Morgan, *Good Measures: Essays, Interviews, and Notes on Poetry* (Baton Rouge: Louisiana State University Press, 1993), p. 18; Robert Scholes, *Textual Power: Literary Theory and the Teaching of English* (New Haven: Yale University Press, 1985), p. 7.

15 Quoted in Sutherland, *Fiction and Fiction Industry*, p. 148.

16 Mark Harris, "What Creative Writing Creates Is Students," *New York Times Book Review* (July 27, 1980).

17 For a discussion of *Wissenschaft* and *Bildung* see Fritz Ringer, "The Origins of Mannheim's Sociology of Knowledge," in *The Social Dimensions of Science*, ed. Ernan McMullin (Notre Dame: University of Notre Dame Press, 1992), pp. 47–67. For a searching meditation on the distinction between the two ideas see Mark R. Schwehn, *Exiles from Eden: Religion and the Academic Vocation in America* (Oxford: Oxford University Press, 1993).

18 Karl Mannheim is the source of the commonplace that genres of knowledge and principles of reasoning are culturally and historically relative, "a function" (in his words) "of the generally prevailing social situation." See *Ideology and Utopia: An Introduction to the Sociology of Knowledge*, tr. Louis Wirth and Edward Shils (New York: Harcourt, Brace, 1936). The literature in the sociology of knowledge is vast. For useful surveys of the field see the bibliographies accompanying Michael Mulkay, "Sociology of Science in the West," *Current Sociology* 28 (1982): 1–184; and Steven Shapin, "History of Science and Its Social Reconstructions," *History of Science* 20 (1982): 157-211. These sources—along with others—are cited by Ernan McMullin in the Introduction to *The Social Dimensions of Science*. Representative book-length works include Mulkay's *Social Process of Innovation* (London: Macmillan, 1972); Diana Crane, *Invisible Colleges: Diffusion of Knowledge in Scientific Communities* (Chicago: University of Chicago Press, 1972); and Barry Barnes, *Interests and the Growth of Knowledge* (London: Routledge, 1977). In the history of universities a central work is Burton J. Bledstein, *The Culture of Professionalism: The Middle Class and the Development of Higher Education in America* (New York: Norton, 1976). An even stronger influence on thinking about professionalization in the human sciences has been Magali Sarfatti Larson, *The Rise of Professionalism: A Sociological Analysis* (Berkeley: University of California Press, 1977). According to Andrew Abbott, a tendency in recent sociology toward the "unmasking" of professions' ideological claims reached its "final form" in Larson's book. For a critique of this tendency see Abbott, *The System of Professions: An Essay on the Division of Expert Labor* (Chicago: University of Chicago Press, 1988), pp. 12–19. In literary study, the most important example of such unmasking may be Michael Warner, "Professionalization and the Rewards of Literature," *Criticism* 27 (1985): 1–28. But see also Brian McCrea, *Addison and Steele Are Dead: The English Department, Its Canon, and the Professionalization of Literary Criticism* (Newark: University of Delaware Press, 1990); Alvin Kernan, *The Death of Literature* (New Haven: Yale University Press, 1990); and Bruce Robbins, *Secular Vocations: Intellectuals, Professionalism, Culture* (London: Verso, 1993).

19 Steven Turner, "The Prussian Professoriate and the Research Imperative, 1790–1840," in *Epistemological and Social Problems of the Sciences in the Early Nineteenth Century*, ed. Hans Niels Jahnke and Michael Otte (Dordrecht: D. Reidel, 1981), pp. 111, 117.

20 On the Authors League see Richard Fine, *James M. Cain and the American Authors' Authority* (Austin: University of Texas Press, 1992), pp. 62–68.

21 For a discussion of professional schools see Everett C. Hughes, "Education for a Profession," in *The Sociological Eye: Selected Papers* (Chicago: Aldine-Atherton, 1971), pp. 387–96.

22 Scholes, *Textual Power*, p. 33.

23 Christy Friend, "The Excluded Conflict: The Marginalization of Composition and Rhetoric Studies in Graff's *Professing Literature*," *College English* 54 (1992): 276–82. I might have overlooked this article if not for Kenneth Womack.

24 Howard Nemerov, "An Interview" in *Trace* (1960), quoted in Richard Ellmann and Robert O'Clair, eds., *Norton Anthology of Modern Poetry*, 2nd ed. (New York: Norton, 1988), p. 1018; Allen Tate, "We Read as Writers," *Princeton Alumni Weekly* 40 (March 8, 1940), quoted in Wilbur L. Schramm, "Imaginative Writing," in *Literary Scholarship: Its Aims and Methods*, ed. Norman Foerster (Chapel Hill: University of North Carolina Press, 1941), p. 179; Paul Engle, "Introduction: The Writer and the Place," in *Midland: Twenty-five Years of Fiction and Poetry Selected from the Writing Workshops of the State University of Iowa*, ed. Engle (New York: Random House, 1961), pp. xxix–xxx.

25 By *constructivism* I mean the philosophical doctrine that the objects of human knowledge—materials and methods both—are not given but constructed. Despite its unfortunate connotation of social constructionism and other varieties of fashionable relativism, the term is appropriate because it links the classical idea of *poesis* (a reminder that writing is making) with late nineteenth-century idealism, which argued that the indispensable and necessary attributes of anything do not exist apart from the use that is made of it. There is no essential difference between literature and non-literature; it is a product of human judgment. Thus in my usage constructivism stands at the opposite pole from essentialism. Also from what I have elsewhere called scholarly interpretivism: see D. G. Myers, "The Lesson of Creative Writing's History," *AWP Chronicle* 26 (February 1994): 1, 12–14.

26 Berlin, *Rhetoric and Reality*, p. 1.

27 Watkins, *Work Time*, p. 102.

28 Watkins, p. 258.

29 Miller, *Textual Carnivals*, pp. 51, 53.

30 Miller, p. 6.

31 Jerry Herron, *Universities and the Myth of Cultural Decline* (Detroit: Wayne State University Press, 1988), p. 117.

32 W. B. Stanford, *Enemies of Poetry* (London: Routledge & Kegan Paul, 1980), p. 157; George E. Woodberry, *The Appreciation of Literature* (New York: Harcourt Brace, 1907), p. 14.

33 Smith, "Notes on Responsibility," p. 221.

34 Or so at least it is argued by philosophers of history as different as Michael Oakeshott and Michel Foucault. Oakeshott contends that a search for origins betrays a "practical" attitude toward the past, seeking justification and support for a present condition of things. Foucault asserts that it is "an attempt to capture the exact essence of things," treating the past as set apart from the world of flux and change. See Oakeshott, "The Activity of Being a Historian," in *Rationalism in Politics and Other Essays*, ed. Timothy Fuller (Indianapolis: Liberty, 1991), pp. 151–83, esp. 168–69; and Foucault, "Nietzsche, Genealogy, History," in *Language, Counter-Memory, Practice: Selected Essays and Interviews*, ed. Donald F. Bouchard (Ithaca: Cornell University Press, 1977), pp. 139–64, esp. 142–44.

35 Stephen Wilbers, *The Iowa Writers' Workshop* (Iowa City: University of Iowa Press, 1980), pp. 19–20.

36 Hugo, "Defense of Creative Writing," p. 53.

37 Michael Drayton, "To My Most Dearley-Loved Friend Henery Reynolds Esquire," in *The Works of Michael Drayton,* ed. J. William Hebell (Oxford: Shakespeare Head, 1932), 3: 226; Ben Jonson, *Discoveries,* in *The Complete Poems,* ed. George Parfitt (New Haven: Yale University Press, 1975), p. 448.

Chapter 1
When Philology Was in Flower

1 This account is adapted from William Belmont Parker, *Edward Rowland Sill: His Life and Work* (Boston: Houghton Mifflin, 1915), pp. 13–21.

2 Quoted in Newton Arvin, "The Failure of E. R. Sill," in *American Pantheon,* ed. Daniel Aaron and Sylvan Schendler (New York: Delta, 1966), p. 179.

3 Quoted in the Introduction to *The Prose of Edward Rowland Sill* (Boston: Houghton Mifflin, 1900), p. xxx.

4 Sill, "Should a College Educate?" in *Prose,* pp. 308–9.

5 Charles W. Eliot, "Liberty in Education," reprinted in *American Higher Education: A Documentary History,* ed. Richard Hofstadter and Wilson Smith (Chicago: University of Chicago Press, 1961), 2: 708.

6 "Education," *Atlantic Monthly* 33 (1874): 636.

7 President Daniel Read quoted in Jonas Viles, *The University of Missouri: A Centennial History* (Columbia: University of Missouri Press, 1939), p. 142.

8 Charles H. Grandgent, "The Modern Languages," in *The Development of Harvard University since the Inauguration of President Eliot, 1869–1929,* ed. Samuel Eliot Morison (Cambridge: Harvard University Press, 1930), p. 67.

9 Clifford S. Griffin, *The University of Kansas: A History* (Lawrence: University Press of Kansas, 1974), p. 143.

10 Quoted in Walter Havinghurst, *The Miami Years, 1809–1969* (New York: Putnam's, 1969), p. 112.

11 Quoted in Walter C. Bronson, *The History of Brown University, 1764–1914* (Providence: By the University, 1914), p. 269.

12 Frederick Rudolph, *Curriculum: A History of the American Undergraduate Course of Study since 1636* (San Francisco: Jossey-Bass, 1977), p. 57.

13 Edward Dwight Eaton, *Historical Sketches of Beloit College* (New York: A. S. Barnes, 1928), p. 75; Robert S. Fletcher and Malcolm O. Young, eds., *Amherst College: Biographical Record of the Graduates and Non-Graduates* (Amherst: By the College, 1921); Howard H. Peckham, *The Making of the University of Michigan, 1817–1967* (Ann Arbor: University of Michigan Press, 1967), pp. 56, 80; George Wilson Pierson, *Yale College: An Educational History, 1871–1921* (New Haven: Yale University Press, 1952), p. 377; Joseph T. Durkin, S.J., *Georgetown University: The Middle Years, 1840–1900* (Washington: Georgetown University

Press, 1963), p. 65; E. Bird Johnson, ed., *Forty Years of the University of Minnesota* (Minneapolis: General Alumni Association, 1910); Leal A. Headley and Merrill F. Jarchow, *Carleton: The First Century* (Northfield. Carleton College, 1966), p. 181; Alfred Sandlin Reid, *Furman University: Toward a New Identity, 1925–1975* (Durham: Duke University Press, 1970), p. 15; William H. S. Demarest, *A History of Rutgers College, 1706–1924* (New Brunswick: Rutgers College, 1924), p. 451; Daniel Walker Hollis, *University of South Carolina: College to University* (Columbia: University of South Carolina Press, 1956), 2: 92; Paul K. Conkin, *Gone With the Ivy: A Biography of Vanderbilt University* (Knoxville: University of Tennessee Press, 1985), p. 66; Griffin, *University of Kansas*, p. 143; Egbert R. Isbell, *A History of Eastern Michigan University, 1849–1965* (Ypsilanti: Eastern Michigan University Press, 1971), pp. 234–35; Theodore Francis Jones, ed., *New York University, 1832–1932* (New York: New York University Press, 1933), p. 141; Wayland Fuller Dunaway, *History of the Pennsylvania State College* (State College: Pennsylvania State College, 1946), p. 176; *Historical Catalogue of Brown University, 1764–1914* (Providence: By the University, 1914); Winton U. Solberg, *The University of Illinois, 1867–1894: An Intellectual and Cultural History* (Urbana: University of Illinois Press, 1968), p. 109; Allan Nevins, *Illinois* (New York: Oxford University Press, 1917), p. 185.

14 S. E. Ochsenford, *Muhlenberg College: A Quarter-Century Memorial Volume, Being a History of the College and a Record of Its Men* (Allentown: Muhlenberg College, 1892), p. 126. Italics have been added.

15 Philip Alexander Bruce, *History of the University of Virginia, 1819–1919*, vol. 3: *The Lengthened Shadow of One Man* (New York: Macmillan, 1921), 3: 379–80.

16 Graff, *Professing Literature*, p. 41.

17 This account is adapted from Hugh Hawkins, *Pioneer: A History of the Johns Hopkins University, 1874–1889* (Ithaca: Cornell University Press, 1960), pp. 162–68.

18 Quoted in Thomas Jefferson Wertenbaker, *Princeton: 1746–1896* (Princeton: Princeton University Press, 1946), p. 304.

19 Grant Showerman, *With the Professor* (New York: Henry Holt, 1910), p. 49.

20 On Corson see Waterman Thomas Hewitt, *Cornell University: A History* (New York: University Publishing Society, 1905), pp. 36–47.

21 Irving Babbitt, *Literature and the American College: Essays in Defense of the Humanities* (Boston: Houghton Mifflin, 1908), pp. 120–21; Henry Nettleship, "Classical Education in the Past and at Present," in *Lectures and Essays* (Oxford: Clarendon, 1895), p. 215; Diehl, *Americans and German Scholarship*, p. 23. For recent discussions of the theoretical issues involved see Jan Ziolkowski, ed., *On Philology* (University Park: Pennsylvania State University Press, 1990).

22 Geoffrey Sampson, *Schools of Linguistics* (Stanford: Stanford University Press, 1980), p. 17. On the comparative method see Henry M. Hoenigswald, "Fallacies in the History of Linguistics: Notes on the Appraisal of the Nineteenth Century," in *Studies in the History of Linguistics: Traditions and Paradigms*, ed. Dell Hymes (Bloomington: Indiana University Press, 1974), p. 348.

23 Anthony Grafton, *Defenders of the Text: The Traditions of Scholarship in an Age of Science, 1450–1800* (Cambridge: Harvard University Press, 1991), pp. 216–17.

On philology as a cultural study see Raimo Antilla, "Linguistics and Philology," in *Linguistics and Neighboring Disciplines*, ed. Renate Bartsch and Theo Vennemann (Amsterdam: North-Holland, 1975), p. 153.

24 William Dwight Whitney, "Logical Consistency in Views of Language," *American Journal of Philology* 1 (1880): 332.

25 On the history of nineteenth-century linguistics Holger Pedersen, *The Discovery of Language: Linguistic Science in the Nineteenth-Century*, tr. John Webster Spargo (Bloomington: Indiana University Press, 1931), has largely been superseded. See Olga Amsterdamska, *Schools of Thought: The Development of Linguistics from Bopp to Saussure* (Dordrecht: D. Reidel, 1987); Julie Tetel Andresen, *Linguistics in America, 1769–1924: A Critical History* (London: Routledge, 1990); and Diehl, *Americans and German Scholarship*.

26 George Melville Bolling, "Linguistics and Philology," *Language* 5 (1929): 30.

27 On the research ideal in German philology and science see Diehl, *Americans and German Scholarship*, p. 10. For an excellent account of the "Germanization" of American higher education see Jurgen Herbst, *The German Historical School in American Scholarship: A Study in the Transfer of Culture* (Ithaca: Cornell University Press, 1965), pp. 30–40.

28 Showerman, *With the Professor*, p. 51.

29 Basil Gildersleeve, *Selections from the Brief Mention*, ed. C. W. E. Miller (Baltimore: Johns Hopkins University Press, 1930), pp. 48, 110.

30 Elizabeth Renker, "Resistance and Change: The Rise of American Literature Studies," *American Literature* 64 (1992): 348, 350.

31 Ernst Robert Curtius, *European Literature and the Latin Middle Ages*, tr. Willard Trask (Princeton: Princeton University Press, 1953), p. 38.

32 C. S. Lewis, "The Idea of an 'English School,' " in *Representations and Other Essays* (London: Oxford University Press, 1939), pp. 74–75.

33 Gildersleeve, *Selections from Brief Mention*, p. 114.

34 Phillips Brooks, "The Purposes of Scholarship," in *Essays and Addresses*, ed. John Cotton Brooks (New York: Dutton, 1895), pp. 257, 269.

35 Barrett Wendell, *Stelligeri and Other Essays concerning America* (New York: Scribner's, 1893), p. 206.

36 Adams Sherman Hill, *Our English* (New York: Harper, 1888), p. 75.

37 Quoted in Hollis, *University of South Carolina*, 2: 74.

38 Louise Pound, "The American Dialect Society: A Historical Sketch," Publication of the American Dialect Society 17 (Greensboro: Woman's College of the University of North Carolina, 1952), p. 4.

39 Laura Sanderson Hines, "The Study of English Literature," *Education* 9 (1888): 229. Italics have been added.

40 Frank W. Noxon, "College Professors Who Are Men of Letters," *Critic* 42 (1903): 125. Cited in Warner, "Professionalization and the Rewards of Literature."

41 Brander Matthews, *Gateways to Literature and Other Essays* (New York: Scribner's, 1912), pp. 66–67; Barrett Wendell, *The Privileged Classes* (New York: Scribner's, 1908), p. 217; Wendell, *The Mystery of Education and Other Academic Performances* (New York: Scribner's, 1909), p. 88.

42 Katharine Lee Bates, "Knowledge versus Feeling," *Poet-Lore* 6 (1894): 384; Francis H. Stoddard, "Literary Spirit in the Colleges," *Educational Review* 6 (1894): 126.

43 Poem 1126 (*c.* 1868) in *The Complete Poems of Emily Dickinson*, ed. Thomas H. Johnson (Boston: Little, Brown, 1960), pp. 505–6. I am grateful to Krista May for bringing this poem to my attention.

44 Ralph Waldo Emerson, "The American Scholar," in *Selected Writings*, ed. Brooks Atkinson (New York: Modern Library, 1964), p. 51.

45 B. L. Packer, *Emerson's Fall: A New Interpretation of the Major Essays* (New York: Continuum, 1982), p. 114. I am indebted to Kenneth M. Price for this reference.

46 Emerson, "American Scholar," p. 49.

47 Emerson, p. 45.

48 Stanley Cavell, "Emerson's Aversive Thinking," in *Romantic Revolutions: Criticism and Theory*, ed. Kenneth R. Johnston et al. (Bloomington: Indiana University Press, 1990), p. 229.

49 Showerman, *With the Professor*, p. 69.

50 Philip Larkin, "An Interview with *Paris Review*," in *Required Writing: Miscellaneous Pieces, 1955–1982* (London: Faber & Faber, 1983), p. 69. Italics in the original.

Chapter 2
The Founding of English Composition

1 Henry A. Beers, *Initial Studies in American Letters* (New York: Chautauqua Press, 1891), pp. 121–22.

2 See Gilbert Ryle, "On Knowing How and Knowing That," in *Collected Papers* (New York: Barnes & Noble, 1972), 2: 212–25. On my argument literary constructivism has been a historical effort to unite Ryle's knowing *how* and knowing *that*.

3 Frederic Ives Carpenter, "The Study of Literature," *Poet-Lore* 6 (1893): 379.

4 L. May McLean, "Rhetoric in Secondary Schools," *Education* 18 (1897): 158.

5 C. H. Ward, "Fluency First," *Education* 38 (1917): 103.

6 Eugene Bouton, "The Study of English," *Education* 5 (1884): 103.

7 Nan Johnson, *Nineteenth-Century Rhetoric*, pp. 80–81, 91.

8 Albert R. Kitzhaber, *Rhetoric in American Colleges*, pp. 41–43.

9 Henry Allyn Frink, "Rhetoric and Public Speaking in the American College," *Education* 13 (1892): 129.

10 For a fascinating account of the ancient saying see William Ringler, *"Poeta Nascitur Non Fit*: Some Notes on the History of an Aphorism," *Journal of the History of Ideas* 2 (1941): 497–504. Sir Francis Galton published his *Hereditary Genius: An Inquiry into Its Laws and Consequences* in 1869. On Galton's place in the history of thinking about human creativity see R. Ochse, *Before the Gates of Excellence: The Determinants of Creative Genius* (Cambridge: Cambridge University Press, 1990). For a more technical discussion see J. Phillippe Rushton, "Sir Francis Galton, Epigenetic Rules, Genetic Similarity Theory, and Human Life-History Analysis," *Journal of Personality* 58 (1990): 117–40.

11 Bouton, "Study of English," 101–2.

12 Mary A. Ripley, "About English," *Education* 9 (1889): 535.

13 Samuel Thurber, "An Address to Teachers of English," *Education* 18 (1898): 524.

14 Gertrude Buck, "What Does 'Rhetoric' Mean?" *Educational Review* 22 (1901): 199–200.

15 McLean, "Rhetoric in Secondary Schools," pp. 159–60.

16 Stegner, *On the Teaching of Creative Writing*, pp. 45–46. Aiken is quoted in W. Jackson Bate et al., eds., *Harvard Scholars in English, 1890–1990* (Cambridge: Harvard University, 1992), p. 19. Laurence R. Veysey also points out the relationship of Harvard composition to creative writing in *The Emergence of the American University* (Chicago: University of Chicago Press, 1965), pp. 187–88. I am grateful to Jennifer R. Goodman for putting *Harvard Scholars in English* into my hands.

17 Charles W. Eliot, "Inaugural Address as President of Harvard," in *American Higher Education*, 2: 203.

18 Quoted in Le Baron Russell Briggs, *To College Teachers of English Composition* (Boston: Houghton Mifflin, 1928), p. 13.

19 Le Baron Russell Briggs, *Men, Women and Colleges* (Boston: Houghton Mifflin, 1925), p. 44.

20 Quoted in Thomas R. Lounsbury, "Compulsory Composition in Colleges," *Harper's* 123 (1911): 868. On Child see Jo McMurtry, *English Language, English Literature: The Creation of an Academic Discipline* (Hamden, Conn.: Archon Books, 1985), pp. 65–110; Bate, ed., *Harvard Scholars*, pp. 1–7; and Graff, *Professing Literature*, pp. 40–41 and passim. For mentioning the burden of correcting undergraduate compositions Graff is taken to task by Friend, "Excluded Conflict," 279. Michael J. Bell defends Child's populism in " 'No Borders to the Ballad Maker's Art': Francis James Child and the Politics of the People," *Western Folklore* 47 (1988): 285–307. On Chamberlain as a teacher of college rhetoric see Willard M. Wallace, *Soul of the Lion: A Biography of General Joshua L. Chamberlain* (New York: Thomas Nelson, 1960), p. 29.

21 On Hill's conception of rhetoric and for biographical data see Paul E. Ried, "The First and Fifth Boylston Professors: A View of Two Worlds," *Quarterly Journal of Speech* 74 (1988): 229–40. See also Kitzhaber, *Rhetoric in American Colleges*, pp. 60–63.

22 Johnson, *Nineteenth-Century Rhetoric*, pp. 82–83, 97, 221, and passim.

23 John F. Genung, *The Practical Elements of Rhetoric with Illustrative Examples* (Boston: Ginn, 1886), p. 1.

24 Adams Sherman Hill, *The Principles of Rhetoric*, new ed. (New York: American Book Co., 1895), p. 111. The first edition was published in 1878.

25 Johnson, *Nineteenth-Century Rhetoric*, p. 173.

26 Hill, *Principles*, p. 18.

27 See the first chapter of the *Principles*, pp. 1–24. The quoted passages are from pp. 18, 24.

28 Briggs, *To College Teachers*, pp. 2–3.

29 Hill, *Our English*, pp. 79–83.

30 Hill, *Our English*, pp. 88–97.

31 Kitzhaber, *Rhetoric in American Colleges*, p. 61; Rollo W. Brown, *Dean Briggs* (New York: Harper, 1926), p. 54.

32 Quoted from Wendell's memoir of his father in M. A. DeWolfe Howe, *Barrett Wendell and His Letters* (Boston: Atlantic Monthly Press, 1924), pp. 37–38. Howe's book remains the best source for information about Wendell. But see also Robert T. Self, *Barrett Wendell* (Boston: Twayne, 1975). On Wendell as a theorist of rhetoric see Kitzhaber, *Rhetoric in American Colleges*, pp. 66–69; Berlin, *Writing Instruction in Nineteenth-Century American Colleges*, chapter 6; and—the best short account—Wallace W. Douglas, "Barrett Wendell," in *Traditions of Inquiry*, ed. John C. Brereton (New York: Oxford University Press, 1985), pp. 3–25.

33 Bate, ed., *Harvard Scholars*, p. 9.

34 See Dolly Svobodny, ed., *Early American Textbooks, 1775–1900* (Washington: U.S. Department of Education, 1985).

35 Howe, *Wendell and His Letters*, pp. 40–41.

36 George Santayana, *The Middle Span* (New York: Scribner's, 1945), p. 171.

37 Lane Cooper, "On the Teaching of Written Composition," *Education* 30 (1910): 430.

38 Barrett Wendell, "English Work in the Secondary Schools," *School Review* 1 (1893): 659.

39 Wendell, *Privileged Classes*, p. 237.

40 Letter to Frederic Schenck (June 1915) in Howe, *Wendell and His Letters*, p. 269; Wendell, *Mystery of Education*, p. 117.

41 The phrase is that of Professor David B. Frankenburger in an article describing the English program at the University of Wisconsin in *English in American Universities*, ed. William Morton Payne (Boston: D. C. Heath, 1895), p. 135. This book consists of articles published in the *Dial* in 1894. The classic source on the revolt against formalism in American thinking is Morton G. White's *Social Thought in America* (Boston: Beacon Press, 1949). For more recent accounts of much of the same material see Jeffrey T. Bergner, *The Origin of Formalism in Social Science* (Chicago: University of Chicago Press, 1981), and Dorothy Ross,

The Origins of American Social Science (Cambridge: Cambridge University Press, 1991). Lawrence A. Cremin examines the revolt against formalism in educational thinking in *The Transformation of the School: Progressivism in American Education, 1876–1957* (New York: Alfred A. Knopf, 1961).

42 Wendell, *Mystery of Education*, pp. 27, 210; *Privileged Classes*, pp. 94, 223.

43 Wendell, "English Work in Secondary Schools," pp. 659–60.

44 Katharine Lee Bates, "English at Wellesley College," in Payne, ed., *English in American Universities*, pp. 145–46; John Erskine, *The Memory of Certain Persons* (Philadelphia: J. B. Lippincott, 1947), p. 97; W. E. Mead, "The Graduate Study of Rhetoric," *PMLA* 16 (1901): xxvi.

45 Berlin, *Writing Instruction in Nineteenth-Century American Colleges*, pp. 74–75.

46 Wendell, "English Work in Secondary Schools," p. 667.

47 Barrett Wendell, *English Composition: Eight Lectures Given at the Lowell Institute* (New York: Scribner's, 1891), pp. 8–9.

48 Wendell, *English Composition*, pp. 2, 26, 28, 67.

49 Alexander Bain, *On Teaching English* (1887), quoted in Frank Aydelotte, "The History of English as a College Subject in the United States," in *The Oxford Stamp and Other Essays* (New York: Oxford University Press, 1917), pp. 187–88.

50 Wendell, *English Composition*, p. 265.

51 George E. Woodberry, *Studies of a Litterateur* (New York: Harcourt Brace, 1921), p. 7.

52 Wendell, *English Composition*, p. 212.

53 Wendell, *English Composition*, p. 40.

54 See James D. Hart, *The Oxford Companion to American Literature* (New York: Oxford University Press, 1941). On Briggs's class in versification see Brown, *Dean Briggs*, pp. 67–68. This biography is the best source of information on Briggs.

55 Le Baron Russell Briggs, *School, College and Character* (Boston: Houghton Mifflin, 1901), p. 133; Briggs, *To College Teachers*, p. 17.

56 Briggs, *Men, Women and Colleges*, pp. 82–83.

57 J. Donald Adams, *Copey of Harvard: A Biography of Charles Townsend Copeland* (Boston: Houghton Mifflin, 1960), p. 156.

58 John Reed, *Insurgent Mexico*, ed. Albert L. Michaels and James W. Wilkie (New York: Simon & Schuster, 1969), p. 37. Originally published in 1914.

59 Quoted in Bate, ed., *Harvard Scholars*, p. 19.

60 John Jay Chapman, "President Eliot," in *Memories and Milestones* (New York: Moffat, Yard, 1915), p. 186.

61 Bernard DeVoto, "English A," *American Mercury* 13 (1928) : 207.

62 Wendell, *Mystery of Education*, p. 178.

Chapter 3
The Problem of Writing in a Practical Age

1 Anonymous, *The Literary Guillotine* (New York: John Lane, 1903), pp. 255–56.

2 Editorial, *Writer* 1 (1887–88): 196.

3 Henry Seidel Canby, "Anon Is Dead," in *American Estimates* (New York: Harcourt Brace, 1929), p. 17; Henry Mills Alden, *Magazine Writing and the New Literature* (New York: Harper, 1908), p. 86; George E. Woodberry, "Literature in the Marketplace," *Forum* 11 (1891): 659–60. On the literary community of nineteenth-century America see Jane Tompkins, *Sensational Designs: The Cultural Work of American Fiction, 1790–1860* (New York: Oxford University Press, 1985).

4 Woodberry, "Literature in the Marketplace," 654–55; Howard Mumford Jones, *The Age of Energy: Varieties of American Experience, 1865–1915* (New York: Viking, 1971), p. 223; John Tebbel, *Between the Covers: The Rise and Transformation of Book Publishing in America* (New York: Oxford University Press, 1987), p. 81.

5 Katharine Lee Bates, *American Literature* (New York: Macmillan, 1897), pp. 128, 135.

6 On copyright see Mark Rose, *Authors and Owners: The Invention of Copyright* (Cambridge: Harvard University Press, 1993). On the collapse of Harper & Brothers see Eugene Exman, *The House of Harper: One Hundred and Fifty Years of Publishing* (New York: Harper & Row, 1967), pp. 171–83; and Tebbel, *Between the Covers*, pp. 94–98. Howells is quoted in both books. On the new publishing practices see Tebbel, pp. 82–84.

7 Ellen B. Ballou, *The Building of the House: Houghton Mifflin's Formative Years* (Boston: Houghton Mifflin, 1970), pp. 421, 425–26.

8 Ballou, *Building of the House*, p. 432; Exman, *House of Harper*, pp. 178, 192, 206.

9 Quoted in James Playsted Wood, *Magazines in the United States: Their Social and Economic Influence* (New York: Ronald Press, 1949), p. 112.

10 On Aldrich as the editor of the *Atlantic Monthly* see M. A. DeWolfe Howe, *The Atlantic Monthly and Its Makers* (Boston: Atlantic Monthly Press, 1919), pp. 77–78; and Ballou, *Building of the House*, pp. 353–80.

11 See Wood, *Magazines in the United States*, p. 149.

12 Hamilton Wright Mabie, *American Ideals, Character and Life* (New York: Macmillan, 1913), p. 29.

13 Gioia, *Can Poetry Matter?* p. 34.

14 Ballou, *Building of the House*, p. 413.

15 Wendell, *English Composition*, p. 49.

16 Henry Seidel Canby, *College Sons and College Fathers* (New York: Harper, 1915), pp. 164–68.

17 Irving King, "Professionalism and Truth-Seeking," *School Review* 16 (1908): 248.

18 Mabie, *American Ideals*, p. 230.

19 C. E. Heisch, *The Art and Craft of the Author* (New York: Grafton Press, 1906), p. 1.

20 Albert Jay Nock, "Absurdity of Teaching English," *Bookman* 69 (1929): 114.

21 Wendell, *Privileged Classes*, pp. 168, 229; Wendell, *Mystery of Education*, pp. 47, 164–65.

22 Lane Cooper, "On the Teaching of Written Composition," 424–28.

23 William Lyon Phelps, "Two Ways of Teaching English," *Century* 51 (1896): 793; Lounsbury, "Compulsory Composition," 873, 876.

24 W. Otto Birk, "Have All Our Methods of Teaching English Composition Failed?" *School and Society* 13 (1921): 385.

25 Sarah Foss Wolverton, "The Professional Scullery," *Educational Review* 60 (1920): 412.

26 Henry Seidel Canby, "Writing English," *Harper's* 128 (1914): 782.

27 C. H. Ward, "What Is English?" *Educational Review* 51 (1916): 171.

28 Ward, "What Is English?" 178.

29 Charles E. Whitmore, "What Ails Collegiate English?" *Educational Review* 64 (1922): 384.

30 Whitmore, "What Ails Collegiate English?" 384, 386.

31 On the splitting of composition and literature into separate departments see Wayland Fuller Dunaway, *History of the Pennsylvania State College* (State College: Pennsylvania State College, 1946), p. 261; and John K. Bettersworth, *People's University: The Centennial History of Mississippi State* (Jackson: University Press of Mississippi, 1980), p. 198. On the drift away from courses in the daily theme see Cooper, "On the Teaching of Written Composition," 422; and DeVoto, "English A," 207.

32 Fred Lewis Pattee, *The Development of the American Short Story: An Historical Survey* (New York: Harper, 1923), p. 365.

33 N. Alvin Pedersen, "Writing Themes for Magazines and Newspapers," *Education* 39 (1918): 220.

34 Lewis Worthington Smith, *The Writing of the Short Story* (Boston: D. C. Heath, 1902).

35 George P. Krapp, "Teaching of English Literature," in *A Cyclopedia of Education*, ed. Paul Monroe (New York: Macmillan, 1913), 4: 53; Frank Norris, "Frank Norris' Weekly Letter" (1901), reprinted in *The Literary Criticism of Frank Norris*, ed. Donald Pizer (Austin: University of Texas Press, 1964), p. 9.

36 Pattee, *Development of the American Short Story*, pp. 364–65; Horace E. Scudder quoted in Ballou, *Building of the House*, p. 444. On the short-story boom see Andrew Levy, *The Culture and Commerce of the American Short Story: America's Workshop*, Cambridge Studies in American Literature and Culture 68 (Cambridge: Cambridge University Press, 1993); and Ray B. West, *Short Story in America, 1900–1950* (Chicago: Henry Regnery, 1952). The first correspondence school opened for business in Scranton, Pennsylvania, in 1891; univer-

sity extension in America began at the University of Chicago the next year. From the beginning, both forms of education provided a home for practical instuction in literary writing. Little has been written on the history of correspondence schools. See John S. Noffsinger, *Correspondence Schools, Lyceums, Chatauquas* (New York: Macmillan, 1926); Walton S. Bittner and Hervey F. Mallory, *University Teaching by Mail: A Survey of Correspondence Instruction Conducted by American Universities* (New York: Macmillan, 1933); and Borje Holmberg, *Growth and Structure of Distance Education* (Wolfeboro, N.H.: Croom Helm, 1986).

37 Wisner Payne Kinne, *George Pierce Baker and the American Theatre* (Cambridge: Harvard University Press, 1954), p. 102.

38 Quoted in Kinne, *George Pierce Baker and the American Theatre*, p. 242.

39 George Piece Baker, *Dramatic Technique* (Boston: Houghton Mifflin, 1919), p. iv.

40 Bronson Howard quoted in Kinne, *George Pierce Baker and the American Theatre*, p. 87.

41 Baker, *Dramatic Technique*, p. v.

42 Baker, *Dramatic Technique*, pp. 2–3, 509–12, 517.

43 Baker, *Dramatic Technique*, pp. 1, 510. For an alternative account of the 47 Workshop see Adams, *History of Professional Writing Instruction*, pp. 79–86.

44 Brander Matthews, "English at Columbia College," in Payne, ed., *English in American Universities*, p. 41; Brander Matthews, *These Many Years: Recollections of a New Yorker* (New York: Scribner's, 1917), p. 394; Brander Matthews, *A Study of Versification* (Boston: Houghton Mifflin, 1911), pp. vi, 266. On Matthews see Lawrence J. Oliver, *Brander Matthews, Theodore Roosevelt, and the Politics of American Literature, 1880–1920* (Knoxville: University of Tennessee Press, 1992).

45 Matthews, *Study of Versification*, p. 2; Matthews, *These Many Years*, p. 408.

46 Lewis Worthington Smith and James E. Thomas, *A Modern Composition and Rhetoric* (Boston: Benjamin A. Sanborn, 1900), p. 357; Matthews, *These Many Years*, p. 394; Adams, *History of Professional Writing Instruction*, p. 73; Charles W. Kent, "English at the University of Virginia," in Payne, ed., *English in American Universities*, p. 69; Martin W. Sampson, "English at the University of Indiana," in Payne, ed., *English in American Universities*, p. 94.

47 Sampson, "English at Indiana," p. 93; Charles Mills Gayley, "English at the University of California," in Payne, ed., *English in American Universities*, p. 107.

48 Bessie Tift College catalogue quoted in De Forest O'Dell, *The History of Journalism Education in the United States*, Contributions to Education 635 (New York: Teachers College, 1935), p. 51; W. E. Mead, "Graduate Study of Rhetoric," xxiv–v.

49 H. C. Chatfield-Taylor, "Wanted: Ateliers of Fiction," *Bookman* 16 (1903): 455–57.

50 John Jay Chapman discusses the problem of an elitist art education in a democratic country in "Art and Art Schools," in *Memories and Milestones* (New York: Moffat, Yard, 1915), pp. 3–16.

51 On Page see Burton J. Hendrick, *The Training of an American: The Earlier Life and Letters of Walter H. Page, 1855–1913* (Boston: Houghton Mifflin, 1928); John Milton Cooper, *Walter Hines Page: The Southerner as American, 1855–1918* (Chapel Hill: University of North Carolina Press, 1977); and Robert J. Rusnak, *Walter Hines Page and the* World's Work, *1900–1913* (Washington: University Press of America, 1982).

52 Walter Hines Page, "On Writing," in *A Publisher's Confession* (Garden City: Doubleday, Page, 1923), pp. 216–17. Originally delivered as an address in August 1907 at the University of Chicago, the essay was then published as "The Writer and the University" in the *Atlantic Monthly* later that year.

53 Page, "On Writing," p. 223.

54 Page, p. 235.

55 Page, pp. 232, 234.

56 Krapp, "Teaching of English Literature," p. 53; Henry Van Dyke, "Reading and Writing in the Teaching of English," *School Review* 15 (1907): 326; Marion Dexter Learned, "Linguistic Study and Literary Creation," President's Address 1909, *PMLA* 25 (1910): lxiv.

57 "About Training Writers," *World's Work* 15 (1907): 9506–07.

58 On the founding of journalism schools see O'Dell, *History of Journalism Education*, pp. 55–91; and Adams, *History of Professional Writing Instruction*, pp. 99–122. For the number of early programs see Albert Alton Sutton, *Education for Journalism in the United States from Its Beginning to 1940*, Northwestern University Studies in the Humanities 14 (Evanston: Northwestern University, 1945), table 1, p. 19.

Chapter 4
Index of Adagios

1 Hart Crane, Letters to Charlotte Rychtarik (July 21 and September 23, 1923), in *The Letters of Hart Crane, 1916–1932*, ed. Brom Weber (Berkeley: University of California Press, 1952), pp. 141–42, 148; Edwin Arlington Robinson, "Hillcrest," in *Collected Poems* (New York: Macmillan, 1937), p. 16.

2 George E. Woodberry, "Professional Poetry," *Atlantic Monthly* 55 (1885): 561–65.

3 John Erskine, *George Woodberry, 1855–1930: An Appreciation* (New York: New York Public Library, 1930), p. 3; Harold Kellock, "Woodberry—A Great Teacher," *Nation* 130 (1930): 121; George E. Woodberry, "A New Defense of Poetry," in *Heart of Man and Other Papers* (New York: Harcourt Brace, 1920), p. 137.

4 Robinson, *Collected Poems*, pp. 15–17. I have modernized the punctuation. The reading of "Hillcrest" that follows is not much more than an expansion and elaboration of Yvor Winters's interpretation in his *Edwin Arlington Robinson*, rev. ed. (Norfolk: New Directions, 1971), pp. 27–31.

5 On Robinson's life the best source remains Hermann Hagedorn, *Edwin Arlington Robinson: A Biography* (New York: Macmillan, 1938). See also Hoyt C.

Franchere, *Edwin Arlington Robinson* (New York: Twayne, 1968); Louis O. Coxe, *Edwin Arlington Robinson: The Life of Poetry* (New York: Pegasus, 1969); and David H. Burton, *Edwin Arlington Robinson: Stages in a New England Poet's Search* (Lewiston, N.Y.: Edwin Mellen, 1987).

6 My account of the Carmel artists' colony is wholly dependent upon Franklin Walker, *The Seacoast of Bohemia* (Santa Barbara: Peregrine Smith, 1973). See also Albert Parry, *Garrets and Pretenders: A History of Bohemianism in America*, rev. ed. (New York: Dover, 1960); Kevin Starr, *Americans and the California Dream, 1850–1915* (Oxford: Oxford University Press, 1973); John Brazil, "George Sterling: Art, Politics, and the Retreat to Carmel," *Markham Review* 8 (1979): 27–33; Thomas E. Benediktsson, *George Sterling* (Boston: Twayne, 1980); and Esther Lanigan Stineman, *Mary Austin: Song of a Maverick* (New Haven: Yale University Press, 1989).

7 Walker, *Seacoast of Bohemia*, pp. 31, 74, 92; Benediktsson, *George Sterling*, p. 38.

8 Joseph Noel, *Footloose in Arcadia: A Personal Record of Jack London, George Sterling, Ambrose Bierce* (New York: Carrick & Evans, 1940), pp. 87, 114, 128–29; Walker, *Seacoast of Bohemia*, p. 10. There is no published biography of Sterling. The best source for his life is the Twayne study by Thomas E. Benediktsson, whose unpublished 1974 University of Washington Ph.D. dissertation is a full-length biography.

9 Stineman, *Mary Austin*, pp. 86–87; Walker, *Seacoast of Bohemia*, pp. 15–16, 46, 96.

10 Walker, *Seacoast of Bohemia*, pp. 49, 56; Benediktsson, *George Sterling*, p. 39; Noel, *Footloose in Arcadia*, pp. 250–51.

11 William Rose Benét, *The Dust Which Is God* (New York: Dodd, Mead, 1941), p. 75. Cited in Walker, *Seacoast of Bohemia*, p. 68.

12 Jack London, *The Valley of the Moon* (New York: Grosset & Dunlap, 1913), p. 406. Cited in Walker, *Seacoast of Bohemia*, pp. 90–91.

13 Mary Austin, *Earth Horizon: An Autobiography* (Boston: Houghton Mifflin, 1932), p. 301.

14 Michael Williams, later editor of the *Commonweal*, quoted in Walker, *Seacoast of Bohemia*, p. 63.

15 Walker, *Seacoast of Bohemia*, pp. 38, 92, 104.

16 Walker, *Seacoast of Bohemia*, pp. 86–89, 92, 94.

17 Charles Angoff, Foreword to *George Sterling: A Centenary Memoir-Anthology* (South Brunswick: A. S. Barnes, 1969), p. 7.

18 London, *Valley of the Moon*, p. 409. Cited in Walker, *Seacoast of Bohemia*, pp. 90–91.

19 The argument of this paragraph owes much to John Brazil, "George Sterling: Art, Politics, and the Retreat to Carmel." Brazil argues that Sterling's retreat to Carmel was an effort to resolve the tension between his social and aesthetic values, and that the effort failed. See also Brazil's unpublished Ph.D. dissertation *Literature, Self, and Society: The Growth of a Political Aesthetic in Early San Francisco* (Yale University, 1976).

20 Walker, *Seacoast of Bohemia*, p. 104.

21 Van Wyck Brooks, *Autobiography* (New York: E. P. Dutton, 1965), pp. 195–96. Cited in Walker, *Seacoast of Bohemia*, p. 113.

22 On her reasons for leaving Carmel see Austin, *Earth Horizon*, p. 308, and Stineman, *Mary Austin*, p. 105. On Sterling's death, which occurred on the occasion of a visit by H. L. Mencken (who discovered the body), see Benediktsson, *George Sterling*, pp. 58–60.

23 Robinson Jeffers, "People and a Heron," in *The Selected Poetry* (New York: Random House, 1951), p. 166. The poem originally appeared in the volume *Roan Stallion* (1925). On Jeffers see Melba B. Bennett, *The Stone Mason of Tor House: The Life and Times of Robinson Jeffers* (Los Angeles: Ward Ritchie Press, 1966); William Everson, *Robinson Jeffers: Fragments of an Older Fury* (Berkeley: Oyez, 1968) and *The Excesses of God: Robinson Jeffers as a Religious Figure* (Stanford: Stanford University Press, 1988); Robert Zaller, *The Cliffs of Solitude: A Reading of Robinson Jeffers* (Cambridge: Cambridge University Press, 1983); and David Copland Morris, "Ideology and Environment: The Challenge of Robinson Jeffers's 'Inhumanism,' " *American Poetry* 5 (1988): 32–52.

24 David Haward Bain, *Whose Woods These Are: A History of the Bread Loaf Writers' Conference* (Hopewell, N.J.: Ecco Press, 1993), p. 12.

25 As far as I know there are no published histories of either the MacDowell Colony or Yaddo, although for an informal memoir of the latter see Marjorie Waite, *Yaddo: Yesterday and Today* (Saratoga Springs: s.n., 1933).

26 President Paul Dwight Moody quoted in Thedore Morrison, *Bread Loaf Writers' Conference: The First Thirty Years, 1926–1955* (Middlebury, Vt.: Middlebury College Press, 1976), p. 6.

27 Morrison, *Bread Loaf*, p. 9.

28 Bain, *Whose Woods These Are*, pp. 16–17.

29 Morrison, *Bread Loaf*, p. 11.

30 Edward Shils, "Ideology and Civility," in *The Intellectuals and the Powers and Other Essays* (Chicago: University of Chicago Press, 1972), pp. 57–58. The essay was originally published in the *Sewanee Review* in 1958.

31 Ezra Pound, "The Mourn of Life," reprinted in Noel Stock, *The Life of Ezra Pound* (New York: Avon Books, 1970), pp. 53–54.

32 Stock, *Ezra Pound*, pp. 54–71.

33 J. V. Cunningham, "Graduate Training in English," in *The Collected Essays* (Chicago: Swallow Press, 1976), p. 272.

34 David D. Henry, *William Vaughn Moody: A Study* (Boston: Bruce Humphries, 1934), p. 20; Daniel Gregory Mason, ed., *Some Letters of William Vaughn Moody* (Boston: Houghton Mifflin, 1913), p. 14. Robert Morss Lovett, who taught at the University of Chicago from 1893 to 1921, was another "creative soul" who opposed the philologizing of English study. See Graff, *Professing Literature*, p. 82. Moody's reference to Philology and Minerva may be a half-remembered allusion to Martianus Capella's fifth-century treatise *De nuptiis Philologiae et Murcurii*. See Curtius, *Latin Literature and the Latin Middle Ages*, pp. 38–39, and

Bruce A. Kimball, *Orators and Philosophers: A History of the Idea of Liberal Education* (New York: Teachers College Press, 1986), pp. 30–31. According to Kimball, the effort to wed eloquence (Mercury) to learning (Philology) has been one of the fundamental objectives of liberal education. Moody's image of the divorce may be another way of saying that by the 1890s liberal education—at least in its literary branch—was *defined* by the conflict between the pedant and the creative soul.

35 My account of Moody's academic career is based upon Maurice F. Brown, *Estranging Dawn: The Life and Works of William Vaughn Moody* (Carbondale: Southern Illinois University Press, 1973).

36 Brown, *Estranging Dawn*, p. 27; Mason, *Some Letters*, pp. 9, 16.

37 Mason, pp. 23–24, 26; Brown, *Estranging Dawn*, pp. 52–53.

38 Brown, pp. 64–65, 71.

39 Brown, pp. 67, 72, 79, 92, 98.

40 Brown, pp. 103–7, 130, 163.

41 John M. Manly, Introduction to *The Poems and Plays of William Vaughn Moody* (Boston: Houghton Mifflin, 1912), p. xiv.

42 Brown, *Estranging Dawn*, pp. 172, 223, 242.

43 Quoted in Manly, Introduction to *Poems and Plays of William Vaughn Moody*, p. xvi.

44 Joyce Kilmer, "The Abolition of Poets," in *The Circus and Other Essays and Fugitive Pieces* (New York: George H. Doran, 1916), pp. 61, 63.

45 Alfred Noyes, *Two Worlds for Memory* (Philadelphia: J. B. Lippincott, 1953), p. 99.

46 Noyes, pp. 99–100; Andrew Turnbull, *Scott Fitzgerald* (New York: Scribner's, 1962), p. 62; F. Scott Fitzgerald, *Correspondence*, ed. Matthew J. Bruccoli and Margaret M. Duggan (New York: Random House, 1980), p. 311; Edmund Wilson, *Letters on Literature and Politics*, ed. Elena Wilson (New York: Farrar, Straus & Giroux, 1977), p. 81.

47 See Stock, *Ezra Pound*, p. 64.

48 Robert Frost, *Selected Letters*, ed. Lawrance Thompson (New York: Holt, Rinehart & Winston, 1964), p. 158. Cited in William H. Pritchard, *Frost: A Literary Life Reconsidered* (Oxford: Oxford University Press, 1984), pp. 57–58. My account of Frost at Amherst owes much to Pritchard.

49 Lawrance Thompson, *Robert Frost: The Years of Triumph, 1915–1938* (New York: Holt, Rinehart & Winston, 1970), p. 83.

50 Alexander Meiklejohn, *The Experimental College*, ed. John Walker Powell (Cabin John, Md.: Seven Locks Press, 1981), pp. x, 113. Originally published in 1932. Frost taught at the Pinkerton Academy from 1906 to 1911 and at the New Hampshire State Normal School at Plymouth from 1911 to 1912. For a neat summary of Frost's teaching philosophy—a question on which Thompson's biography is not particularly helpful—see Pritchard, *Frost*, pp. 58–65.

51 Marion Hawthorne Hedges, "Creative Teaching," *School and Society* 7 (1918): 117–18; Robert S. Newdick, "Robert Frost and the American College," *Journal of Higher Education* 7 (1936): 241; Pritchard, *Frost*, p. 126. Hedges, the author of *Dan Minturn* (1927), a novel about Minnesota state government, is named by Walter B. Rideout as a practitioner of *The Radical Novel in the United States, 1900–1954* (Cambridge: Harvard University Press, 1956).

52 James Kraft, "Biographical Introduction" to Witter Bynner, *Selected Poems*, ed. Richard Wilbur (New York: Farrar, Straus & Giroux, 1978), pp. xxxiii, xliii–v, l.

53 In February 1919 Bynner, a pacifist, signed a petition asking for the release of conscientious objectors to the First World War who had been jailed. A local citizens' group retaliated by demanding that the university investigate him. In a face-to-face encounter, Henry A. Melvin (a justice of the California Supreme Court) attacked Bynner as "pro-German" and a "Goddamn traitor," and punched him. Bynner later described it as "the most unpleasant conflict I've ever experienced." In a letter he told Carl Sandburg that he was "practically run out of the University," although Dean Gayley—despite his own pro-British sentiments—staunchly supported Bynner. The incident had a bizarre sequel. Justice Melvin killed himself the next year. See Witter Bynner, *Selected Letters*, ed. James Kraft (New York: Farrar, Straus & Giroux, 1981), pp. 67–73.

54 Witter Bynner, "On Teaching the Young Laurel to Shoot," in *Prose Pieces*, ed. James Kraft (New York: Farrar, Straus & Giroux, 1979), pp. 366–71. Originally published in the *New Republic* in 1923. "Encouraging" may not be the exact word for Eda Lou Walton's attitude toward Henry Roth: she was his lover *and* his teacher, and she introduced him into a *ménage à trois*. Roth was bitter about it in later years. See Jonathan Rosen, "The 60-Year Itch," *Vanity Fair* 57 (February 1994).

55 Bynner, "On Teaching the Young Laurel to Shoot," pp. 368–69.

56 Leonard Bacon, *Ph.D.s: Male and Female He Created Them* (New York: Harper, 1925), pp. 27, 42–55.

57 Horace, *Ars Poetica* 309, tr. Norman J. DeWitt, in *Criticism: Major Statements*, 3rd ed., ed. Charles Kaplan and William Anderson (New York: St. Martin's, 1991), p. 103.

58 Newdick, "Robert Frost and the American College," 239.

Chapter 5
The Sudden Adoption of Creative Work

1 On Mearns see Timothy Heyward Smith, *Hughes Mearns: The Theory and Practice of Creative Education*, unpublished Ed.D. dissertation (Rutgers University, 1968); John Carr Duff, "Hughes Mearns: Pioneer in Creative Education," *Clearing House* 40 (1966): 419–20; and Myra Cohn Livingston, *The Child as Poet: Myth or Reality* (Boston: Horn Book, 1984), pp. 128–30. Although I did not come across her book until late in my research, Livingston predates me in discussing Mearns as "a pioneer in his work with creativity" (p. 5). Still, I believe that I am the first to have designated Mearns as *the* pioneer of creative writing. An offhand remark by Harrison Hayford first led me to him.

2 Randall Jarrell, *Pictures from an Institution* (New York: Alfred A. Knopf, 1954), p. 80; Hughes Mearns, *Creative Power* (Garden City: Doubleday, Doran, 1929), p. 47; Harold Rugg and Ann Shumaker, *The Child-Centered School: An Appraisal of the New Education* (Yonkers: World, 1928), pp. 63, 250. On Rugg and Shumaker's interpretation of progressive education as the teaching of creative self-expression see Cremin, *Transformation of the School*, p. 183; on their book as a primer of progressive methods see Diane Ravitch, *The Troubled Crusade: American Education, 1945–1980* (New York: Basic Books, 1983), pp. 52–53.

3 On Smyth see Graff, *Professing Literature*, pp. 274–75.

4 William Stanley Braithwaite, ed., *Anthology of Magazine Verse for 1922 and Yearbook of American Poetry* (Boston: Small, Maynard, 1922). Braithwaite, a black poet, also edited anthologies of Renaissance, Victorian, and Georgian poetry, but he never edited an anthology of black poetry. Nor did he ever write about the black experience in his own poetry. Jean Wagner argues that his entire career represents a denial of his race. See *Black Poets of the United States: From Paul Laurence Dunbar to Langston Hughes*, tr. Kenneth Douglas (Urbana: University of Illinois Press, 1973), pp. 127–28. It would be the sheerest speculation to suggest that Braithwaite's interest in poetry written by white children in a private school might be further evidence of racial self-denial.

5 Hughes Mearns, ed., *Lincoln Verse, Story, and Essay*, first series (New York: The Lincoln School of Teachers College, 1923), pp. vii, xv. In the first article ever published in the *English Journal* on creative writing, Jane Souba—a high school teacher in Minneapolis—cites *Lincoln Verse* as the precedent. And she distinguishes creative writing from its predecessors in this way: "Practical writing puts the emphasis on the material. Creative writing puts it where it belongs, on the pupil" (593). See Jane Souba, "Creative Writing in High School," *English Journal* 14 (1925): 591–602.

6 Rugg and Shumaker, *Child-Centered School*, pp. 251–52.

7 Trentwell Mason White, "Concerning the Subject of Creative Writing," *Education* 59 (1938): 129.

8 See Ravitch, "The Rise and Fall of Progressive Education," in *The Troubled Crusade*, pp. 43–80. The most thorough treatments of the progressive education movement are Cremin, *Transformation of the School*, and Arthur Zilversmit, *Changing Schools: Progressive Education Theory and Practice, 1930–1960* (Chicago: University of Chicago Press, 1993).

9 This account is deeply indebted to Herbert M. Kliebard, *The Struggle for the American Curriculum, 1893–1958* (Boston: Routledge & Kegan Paul, 1986), pp. 30–58. Kliebard likes neither the term *progressive education*, which he calls "vague" and "essentially undefinable," nor assertions of Dewey's influence on American education, which he describes as "seriously overestimated or grossly distorted."

10 John Dewey, "Interest in Relation to Training of the Will," in *John Dewey on Education: Selected Writings*, ed. Reginald D. Archambault (New York: Modern Library, 1964), p. 266. First published in 1896. On the history of "interest" in American educational thinking see Daniel Tanner and Laurel Tanner, *History of the School Curriculum* (New York: Macmillan, 1990), pp. 151–54. For a philosophical critique see Alan R. White, "Dewey's Theory of Interest," in *John*

Dewey Reconsidered, ed. R. S. Peters (London: Routledge & Kegan Paul, 1977), pp. 35–55.

11 Abraham Flexner, "A Modern School," in *A Modern College and a Modern School* (Garden City: Doubleday, Page, 1923), pp. 90, 98, 100, 108–9. First published in the *American Review of Reviews* in 1916. When asked about the source of his ideas, Flexner cited the influence of Dewey and Charles W. Eliot. On Flexner and the Lincoln School see Cremin, *Transformation of the School*, pp. 280–91, and Tanner and Tanner, *History of the School Curriculum*, pp. 115–16, 167–74.

12 Duff, "Hughes Mearns," 419.

13 Lionel Trilling, "On the Teaching of Modern Literature," in *Beyond Culture: Essays on Literature and Learning* (New York: Viking, 1968), p. 5; John Dewey, "Culture and Cultural Values," in *A Cyclopedia of Education*, ed. Paul Monroe (New York: Macmillan, 1911), 2: 238; William Hughes Mearns, "Our Medieval High Schools: Shall We Educate Children for the Twelfth or the Twentieth Century?" *Saturday Evening Post* (March 2, 1912): 19. Italics have been added to the passage from Mearns.

14 John Dewey, *Democracy and Education: An Introduction to the Philosophy of Education* (New York: Macmillan, 1916), pp. 260–61; John Dewey, "Culture and Industry in Education," *Educational Bi-Monthly* 1 (1906): 8–9.

15 Rugg and Shumaker, *Child-Centered School*, pp. 62, 246; Fred Newton Scott, "English Composition as a Mode of Behavior," *English Journal* 11 (1922): 468.

16 Mearns, *Creative Power*, pp. 246, 256–57.

17 Lawrence H. Conrad, *Teaching Creative Writing* (New York: D. Appleton-Century, 1937), p. 12.

18 Rugg and Shumaker, *Child-Centered School*, p. 253; Hughes Mearns, *Creative Youth: How a School Environment Set Free the Creative Spirit* (Garden City: Doubleday, Page, 1925), p. 28.

19 William Webster Ellsworth, *Creative Writing: A Guide for Those Who Aspire to Authorship* (New York: Funk & Wagnalls, 1929), p. 23. Italics have been added.

20 James Berlin argues that the familiar division of the subject into "forms of discourse"—exposition, argument, description, and narration—is an eighteenth-century conception of rhetoric that was influenced by faculty psychology, a view of the human mind as split into separate cells that carry out separate mental functions. See Berlin, *Writing Instruction in Nineteenth-Century American Colleges*, pp. 19–34. In other words, these authors take an already artificial four-part division and reduce it even further.

21 Bernard L. Jefferson and Harry Houston Peckham, *Creative Prose Writing* (New York: Doubleday, Doran, 1926), pp. vi, 207; Adele Bildersee, *Imaginative Writing: An Illustrated Course for Students* (Boston: D. C. Heath, 1927), pp. 40, 226.

22 George E. Gardner, "Should Power to Create or Capacity to Appreciate Be the Aim in the Study of English?" *Education* 13 (1894): 137.

23 Clara F. Stevens, "College English," *Education* 27 (1906): 103–4. Similarly, Eleanora F. Dean—a high school teacher in St. Paul—urged the teaching of versification, "but the purpose of making good readers of poetry and not poets

must be kept in mind" (125). See Eleanora F. Dean, "The Teaching of Versification in the High School," *English Journal* 5 (1916): 119–30.

24 John Hooper, *Poetry in the New Curriculum: A Manual for Elementary Teachers* (Brattleboro, Vt.: Stephen Daye, 1932), p. 38; Conrad, *Teaching Creative Writing*, p. 23.

25 Hughes Mearns, "Educating the New Child," *North American Review* 230 (1930): 697, 700; Mearns, *Creative Power*, pp. 6–7, 9; Mearns, *Creative Youth*, pp. 17–18. On Cardinal Newman as an advocate of liberalism against utilitarianism see Jaroslav Pelikan, *The Idea of the University: A Reexamination* (New Haven: Yale University Press, 1992).

26 Mearns, *Creative Youth*, p. 57; Hughes Mearns, "English as an Expression of the Activities of Everyday Life," *Journal of Educational Method* 2 (1923): 286; Mearns, *Creative Power*, pp. 14–15, 119–20; Dewey, *Democracy and Education*, p. 42. The italics in the passage from Dewey are in the original.

27 Mearns, *Creative Power*, p. 187; Hughes Mearns, "Creative Education in College Years," *Progressive Education* 23 (1946): 269; Braithwaite quoted in Mearns, *Creative Youth*, p. 3; Hughes Mearns, *The Creative Adult: Self-Education in the Art of Living* (New York: Doubleday, Doran, 1940), p. 263; Hughes Mearns, "Golden Lads and Girls," *Survey* 50 (1926): 320.

28 Bildersee, *Imaginative Writing*, p. ix; Ellsworth, *Creative Writing*, p. 15; Iowa Writers' Workshop, informational brochure (Iowa City: University of Iowa, n.d.). David Greenhood, who had been Witter Bynner's student at Berkeley, says the belief that no one can be taught to write is the professional writer's "professional adage." See *The Writer on His Own* (Albuquerque: University of New Mexico Press, 1971), p. 55.

29 Martha Peck Porter, *The Teacher in the New School* (Yonkers: World, 1931), p. 167; Percival C. Chubb, *The Teaching of English in the Elementary and Secondary School*, rev. ed. (New York: Macmillan, 1929), p. 403; John Dewey, "Individuality and Experience," in *Dewey on Education*, p. 154.

30 Mearns, *Creative Power*, p. 257. By "the modern discovery of the child as artist," Mearns was referring in particular to the child poets Hilda Conkling, who published the first of three volumes in 1920 at the age of ten, and Nathalia Crane, a Jewish girl living in Brooklyn who published the first of three in 1924 at eleven. In a review of Crane's *Singing Crow and Other Poems*, Mearns said that "[t]he clairvoyant power of the poet is not a question of age; it is simply a matter of gift. And this gift is an untutored thing, arising from sources in the spirit beyond our understanding." See *Progressive Education* 4 (1927): 134. Crane later went on to become an English professor at San Diego State and was embarrassed by her childhood poetry. Conkling's story is sadder. Her poems were really a collaborative effort between her and her mother Grace Conkling, an English professor at Smith College. She "talked" her poems at bedtime, and afterward her mother transcribed them, punctuated them, and arranged them into lines of free verse. When a well-wisher asked how she wrote, Hilda replied, "You'll have to ask my mother." In later years, Conkling felt that her early "gift" for poetry was a handicap from which it had taken a lifetime to recover—she described herself as handicapped for reality. It might be asked, though, whether the handicap was her gift for poetry or an almost symbiotic relationship with her mother. By her own account Hilda was her mother's con-

stant companion until Grace's death in 1958. Until then Grace made all of Hilda's decisions. In her preface to *Poems by a Little Girl* (1920), Amy Lowell drew attention to this aspect of the relationship between mother and daughter, quoting two lines: "If I sing, you listen;/ If I think, you know." The second line especially suggests the child's fantasy of perfect union with the mother. Hilda did not leave home until 20, never went to college, never married, never settled on a career—all this despite an IQ of 186. See Livingston, *The Child as Poet*, pp. 53–68, 94–97.

31 Mearns, *Creative Youth*, p. 29; Hughes Mearns, "The Creative Spirit and Its Significance for Education," in *Creative Expression*, ed. Gertrude Hartman and Ann Shumaker, 2nd ed. (Milwaukee: E. H. Hale, 1938), pp. 19–20; John Barth, "Writing: Can It Be Taught?"

32 Lois Whitney, "English Primitivistic Theories of Epic Origins," *Modern Philology* 21 (1924): 337–78. Hurd is quoted from the notes to his 1751 edition of Horace's *Epistola and Augustum*. Bishop Percy claimed that "Nature and common sense had supplied to these old simple bards the want of critical art, and taught them some of the most essential rules of Epic Poetry. . . ." Addison agreed that "these great natural geniuses . . . were never disciplined and broken by rules of art. . . ." And Ferguson contrasted the primitive poet's "supernatural instinct" to the classical poet's judgment and reflection.

33 Gertrude Buck, *The Metaphor: A Study in the Psychology of Rhetoric* (Ann Arbor: Inland Press, ?1899), pp. 42, 69.

34 Mearns, *Creative Power*, p. 260; Hughes Mearns, "Creative Learning," in *Challenges to Education, War and Post-War*, 30th Annual Schoolmen's Week Proceedings (Philadelphia: University of Pennsylvania, 1943), p. 159.

35 Mearns, "Creative Spirit and Its Significance," p. 20; Mearns, "Creative Learning," pp. 159, 165; Mearns, *Creative Youth*, pp. 50n, 55–56.

36 Mearns, *Creative Youth*, p. 61; Mearns, *Creative Power*, p. 27; W. C. Brownell, *Standards* (New York: Scribner's, 1917), p. 70.

37 Mearns, *Creative Youth*, p. 79; J. E. Spingarn, "The New Criticism," in *Creative Criticism and Other Essays*, new and enlarged ed. (New York: Harcourt Brace, 1931), pp. 36–37. Spingarn, an interesting figure, was first president of the National Association for the Advancement of Colored People. See Barbara Joyce Ross, *J. E. Spingarn and the Rise of the NAACP, 1911–1939* (New York: Atheneum, 1972).

38 Mearns, ed., *Lincoln Verse*, p. xiv; Mearns, "Educating the New Child," 700; Conrad, *Teaching Creative Writing*, p. 25.

39 Hooper, *Poetry in the New Curriculum*, p. 14; Porter, *Teacher in the New School*, pp. 176–77; Mearns, ed., *Lincoln Verse*, p. vii; Conrad, *Teaching Creative Writing*, pp. 48, 52.

40 John Dewey, "Individuality and Experience" and "The School and Society," in *Dewey on Education*, pp. 151, 300–301, 303. Italics in the original. For a treatment of the broader issues see Feodor F. Cruz, *Dewey's Theory of Community* (New York: Lang, 1987). On manual arts training see Cremin, *Transformation of the School*, pp. 23–57.

41 Hughes Mearns, "The Changing Elementary Schools," *Saturday Evening Post* 185 (January 4, 1913): 7; Porter, *Teacher in the New School*, p. 149. The "project" as a teaching unit was first described in a 1916 article in *School and Society* by David Snedden, who traced it back to the teaching of vocational agriculture. The "project method" was named and popularized two years later in an essay—originally published in the *Teachers College Record*, then reissued as a pamphlet in an edition of 60,000 copies—by William H. Kilpatrick, a professor at Teachers College, Columbia, and a disciple of Dewey. For historical perspectives see Kliebard, *Struggle for the American Curriculum*, pp. 156–79, and Tanner and Tanner, *History of the School Curriculum*, pp. 157–62. I am grateful to Anne D. Hall for pointing out the anti-empiricism implicit in many "creative" school projects.

42 Mearns, *Creative Power*, p. 144; Mearns, *Creative Youth*, pp. 24, 34.

43 Hooper, *Poetry in the New Curriculum*, pp. 16, 26; J. V. Cunningham, "How Shall the Poem Be Written?" in *Collected Essays* (Chicago: Swallow Press, 1976), p. 259; Hughes Mearns, "Poetry Is When You Talk to Yourself," in *Challenges to Education*, p. 155.

44 Diana Trilling, *The Beginning of the Journey: The Marriage of Diana and Lionel Trilling* (New York: Harcourt Brace, 1993), p. 86.

45 See Logan Pearsall Smith, *Words and Idioms: Studies in the English Language* (London: Constable, 1925), pp. 94–95.

46 Rollo Walter Brown, *The Creative Spirit: An Inquiry into American Life* (New York: Harper, 1925), p. 15.

47 As early as 1914, in his paper "On Narcissism," Freud was quoting Heine on "the psychogenesis of the Creation: God is imagined as saying: 'Illness was no doubt the final cause of the whole urge to create. By creating, I could recover; by creating, I became healthy.' " Quoted in John Frosch, *The Psychotic Process* (New York: International Universities Press, 1983), p. 110. More recently the psychoanalytic theorist Otto Kernberg has argued that creativity is a sign of healthy ego development, showing that a person has learned to direct his or her energies to productive ends: "Creative enjoyment and creative achievement are the main aspects of sublimatory capacity; they may be the best indicators of the extent to which a conflict-free ego sphere is available, and their absence, therefore, is an important indicator of ego weakness." See Kernberg, "Borderline Personality Organization," in *Essential Papers on Borderline Disorders: One Hundred Years at the Border*, ed. Michael H. Stone (New York: New York University Press, 1986), p. 298. For a more extended and less technical discussion of the same principle see James F. Masterson, "The Creative Solution," in *The Search for the Real Self: Unmasking the Personality Disorders of Our Age* (New York: Free Press, 1988), pp. 208–30.

48 The first four antonyms are taken from *The Creative Life* by Ludwig Lewisohn, who explains his title by saying that the creative is a way of life "at which the repressed dentist or deacon looks with the malice of envy. . . ." And then Lewisohn breaks into apostrophe: "O excellent dentist or deacon in Youngstown or Natchez, your young son who scribbles verses and consorts with tramps and will hear nothing of dentistry and dogma may but be following a law of being that transcends all that you have and are, know and believe." See Ludwig Lewisohn, *The Creative Life* (New York: Boni & Liveright, 1924), p.

24. For the last three antonyms and their use in revealing the need for institutional reform see Brown, *Creative Spirit*, pp. 220–21.

49 Brown, *Creative Spirit*, p. 187.

50 Mearns said the "highest approval" in a creative writing class must be reserved for "that work which bears the mark of original invention." And the teacher will recognize this work "instinctively, by feel, as it were. . . ." See *Creative Power*, pp. 41, 43.

51 Mearns, "Golden Lads," 333.

Chapter 6
Criticism Takes Command

1 William McFee, "The Cheer-Leader in Literature," in *Contemporary American Criticism*, ed. James Cloyd Bowman (New York: Henry Holt, 1926), pp. 241–54. Delivered at the annual convention of the Modern Language Association in December 1925, the article was subsequently published in *Harper's* in 1926. In his 1571 commentary on the *Poetics*, Lodovico Castelvetro says that the theory of the *furor poeticus* "originated with the people and the poets agreed to it for the sake of their interests. . . ." Those who read poetry with astonishment "reckon [it] as a miracle and a special gift of God that . . . they do not know how to attain by their own natural powers. . . ." The belief is wrong, but it is flattering to the poets and so they nourish it, making it appear as a condition of poetry. See Allan H. Gilbert, ed., *Literary Criticism Since Plato* (New York: American Book Co., 1940), pp. 310–11.

2 Paul Kaufman, "Promethean Fire: A Challenge to the American College," *School and Society* 28 (1928): 121–27.

3 Snow Longley Housh, "Report of Creative Writing in Colleges," *English Journal*, coll. ed. 20 (1931): 672; Matthew Wilson Black, "Creative Writing in the College," in Hartman and Shumaker, *Creative Expression*, p. 248; John T. Frederick, "The Place of Creative Writing in American Schools," *English Journal*, coll. ed. 22 (1933): 11.

4 Norman Foerster to Alice Worsley, typescript of interview notes in the Norman Foerster Papers, Cecil H. Green Library, Stanford University. Despite also being a founder of American literary studies and having an award from the Modern Language Association named after him, Foerster has not been the subject of many scholarly investigations. See Louis J. A. Mercier, "Humanistic Education: The Critique of Norman Foerster," in *American Humanism and the New Age* (Milwaukee: Bruce, 1948), pp. 165–88; Frances Mary Flanagan, *The Educational Role of Norman Foerster*, Ph.D. dissertation (University of Iowa, 1971); Wilbers, *Iowa Writers' Workshop*, pp. 71–79 and passim; Gilbert Bruce Kelly, *Norman Foerster and American New Humanist Criticism*, Ph.D. dissertation (University of Nebraska, 1983); and Vanderbilt, *American Literature and the Academy*, pp. 357–59 and passim. Perhaps needless to say, I am profoundly indebted to Stephen Wilbers's book, without which I might never even have learned of Foerster's work at Iowa.

5 Norman Foerster, "Reconstructing the Ph.D. in English," *Nation* 108 (1919): 748.

6 Janet Piper, *The Iowa Writers' Workshop in Retrospect: A Respository of Relevant Writing* (Austin: privately printed, ?1981), unpaginated.

7 Donald A. Stauffer, ed., *The Intent of the Critic* (Princeton: Princeton University Press, 1941), p. 38.

8 J. David Hoeveler, *The New Humanism: A Critique of Modern America, 1900–1940* (Charlottesville: University Press of Virginia, 1977), p. 19. On the humanist movement as a whole Hoeveler remains the best guide, but see also Thomas R. Nevin, *Irving Babbitt: An Intellectual Study* (Chapel Hill: University of North Carolina Press, 1984).

9 Wilbers, *Iowa Writers' Workshop*, p. 79.

10 Norman Foerster, *The American Scholar: A Study in* Litterae Inhumaniores (Chapel Hill: University of North Carolina Press, 1929), pp. 42, 44; Austin Warren, letter of April 1930 in the Foerster papers; Foerster to Worsley in the Foerster papers.

11 Kay quoted in Flanagan, *Educational Role of Norman Foerster*, p. 101; Greenlaw quoted by Foerster to Worsley in the Foerster papers; Jessup quoted in Flanagan, p. 106; Foerster to Kay, 1937 annual report on the School of Letters in the Foerster papers; Foerster quoted in Wilbers, *Iowa Writers' Workshop*, p. 44.

12 Bate, ed., *Harvard Scholars in English*, p. 85.

13 David Roberts, *Jean Stafford: A Biography* (London: Chatto & Windus, 1988), pp. 113, 125.

14 Henry Seidel Canby, "The American Scholar," in *American Estimates*, pp. 133, 142–43.

15 Randall Stewart quoted in Thomas Daniel Young, *Gentleman in a Dustcoat: A Biography of John Crowe Ransom* (Baton Rouge: Louisiana State University, 1976), p. 142. George P. Krapp repeats the phrase *wissenschaftlichte Methode* to describe philology in "Teaching of English Literature," p. 50.

16 Allen Tate, "We Read as Writers," quoted in Wilbur L. Schramm, "Imaginative Writing," in Foerster, ed., *Literary Scholarship: Its Aims and Methods*, p. 179; Norman Foerster, *Toward Standards: A Study of the Present Critical Moment in American Letters* (New York: Farrar & Rinehart, 1930), p. 42; Norman Foerster, *The American State University: Its Relation to Democracy* (Chapel Hill: University of North Carolina Press, 1937), p. 217; Norman Foerster, "The Study of Letters," in *Literary Scholarship: Its Aims and Methods*, p. 20.

17 Brander Matthews, "Can English Literature Be Taught?" *Educational Review* 3 (1892): 340; Henry Seidel Canby, "Literature and Universities," in *Definitions: Essays in Contemporary Criticism*, Second series (New York: Harcourt Brace, 1924), p. 214; W. C. Brownell, *Criticism* (New York: Scribner's, 1914), p. 4; Trilling, *Beginning of the Journey*, p. 83; Jay B. Hubbell, *The Enjoyment of Literature* (New York: Macmillan, 1929), pp. 147–48. The best account of criticism's takeover of university literary study is Graff's *Professing Literature*. But see also John Fekete, *The Critical Twilight: Explorations in the Ideology of Anglo-American Literary Theory from Eliot to McLuhan* (London: Routledge & Kegan Paul, 1977); Grant Webster, *The Republic of Letters: A History of Postwar American Literary Opinion* (Baltimore: Johns Hopkins University Press, 1979); Vincent B. Leitch, *American Literary Criticism from the Thirties to the Eighties* (New York:

Columbia University Press, 1988); and Mark Jancovich, *The Cultural Politics of the New Criticism* (Cambridge: Cambridge University Press, 1993).

18 Cleanth Brooks told me in conversation in November 1992 that Ransom's book was not a manifesto, although "most people took the title to mean 'He has founded a school.' " On Ransom see Young, *Gentleman in a Dustcoat*, and Cleanth Brooks, "John Crowe Ransom as I Remember Him," *American Scholar* 58 (1989): 211–33. On the year 1928 in Winters's development see Grosvenor Power, *Language as Being in the Poetry of Yvor Winters* (Baton Rouge: Louisiana State University Press, 1980). On Blackmur see Russell A. Fraser, *A Mingled Yarn: The Life of R. P. Blackmur* (New York: Harcourt Brace Jovanovich, 1981) and Edward T. Cone et al., ed., *The Legacy of R. P. Blackmur: Essays, Memoirs, Texts* (New York: Ecco Press, 1987). On *Hound and Horn* see Mitzi B. Hamovitch, ed., *The* Hound and Horn *Letters* (Athens: University of Georgia Press, 1982). On the *Partisan Review* see James B. Gilbert, *Writers and Partisans: A History of Literary Radicalism in America* (New York: Wiley, 1968), and Terry A. Cooney, *The Rise of the New York Intellectuals:* Partisan Review *and Its Circle* (Madison: University of Wisconsin Press, 1986). On the *Southern Review* see Thomas W. Cutrer, *Parnassus on the Mississippi: The* Southern Review *and the Baton Rouge Literary Community* (Baton Rouge: Louisiana State University Press, 1984), and Cleanth Brooks and Robert Penn Warren, "The Origin of the *Southern Review*," *Southern Review* 22 (1986): 214–17. On literary magazines in general see Frederick J. Hoffman, *The Little Magazine: A History and Bibliography* (Princeton: Princeton University Press, 1946), and G. A. M. Janssens, *The American Literary Review: A Critical History, 1920–1950* (The Hague: Mouton, 1968). On Brooks see Lewis W. Simpson, ed., *The Possibilites of Order: Cleanth Brooks and His Works* (Baton Rouge: Louisiana State University Press, 1976), and Mark Royden Winchell's 1996 biography from the University Press of Virginia. On Kittredge see Clyde K. Hyder, *George Lyman Kittredge: Teacher and Scholar* (Lawrence: University Press of Kansas, 1962).

19 Stephen Greenblatt, "Shakespeare Bewitched," in *New Historical Literary Study: Essays on Reproducing Texts, Representing History*, ed. Jeffrey N. Cox and Larry J. Reynolds (Princeton: Princeton University Press, 1993), p. 112.

20 Cleanth Brooks and Robert Penn Warren, *Understanding Poetry: An Anthology for College Students* (New York: Henry Holt, 1938), p. iv.

21 Monroe K. Spears, *Dionysius and the City: Modernism in Twentieth-Century Poetry* (Oxford: Oxford University Press, 1970), pp. 197–98; John Crowe Ransom, *The New Criticism* (Norfolk: New Directions, 1941), pp. 41, 94.

22 R. P. Blackmur, *New Criticism in the United States* (Tokyo: Kenkyshua, 1959), p. 16; Donald Davidson, *Southern Writers in the Modern World* (Athens: University of Georgia Press, 1958), p. 21; Allen Tate, "American Poetry Since 1920," in *The Poetry Reviews of Allen Tate, 1924–1944*, ed. Ashley Brown and Frances Neel Cheney (Baton Rouge: Louisiana State University, 1983), p. 81. Blackmur's *New Criticism* was originally delivered as a lecture in Japan at the Nagano Summer Seminar in American Literature in July 1956. Tate's "American Poetry" first appeared in the *Bookman* in 1929. I owe to Grant Webster the insight that new critical practice had its roots in the Fugitives' conversations about poetry. See his *Republic of Letters*, p. 96. Davidson is quoted there and also—more fully—in Young, *Gentleman in a Dustcoat*, p. 122, which contains an account of the Fugitives' beginnings. See also Louise Cowan, *The Fugitive Group: A Literary*

History (Baton Rouge: Louisiana State University Press, 1959); John L. Stewart, *The Burden of Time: The Fugitives and Agrarians* (Princeton: Princeton University Press, 1965); and Paul K. Conkin, *The Southern Agrarians* (Knoxville: University of Tennessee Press, 1988).

23 Alfred Kazin, "The Writer and the University," in *The Inmost Leaf: A Selection of Essays* (New York: Harcourt Brace, 1955), p. 242.

24 See R. S. Crane, "Criticism as Inquiry; or, The Dangers of the 'High Priori Road,' " in *The Idea of the Humanities and Other Essays Critical and Historical* (Chicago: University of Chicago Press, 1967), 2: 44.

25 George Spran, *The Meaning of Literature* (New York: Scribner's, 1925), p. 47.

26 Thomas P. Beyer, "The Creative Life at Hamline," in *Hamline History*, ed. Charles Nelson Pace (St. Paul: Hamline University Alumni Association, 1939), pp. 112–13.

27 R. P. Blackmur, "A Feather-Bed for Critics: Notes on the Profession of Writing," in *The Expense of Greatness* (New York: Arrow Editions, 1940), p. 302.

28 Irving Babbitt, "On Being Creative," in *On Being Creative and Other Essays* (Boston: Houghton Mifflin, 1932), p. 23; Foerster, *Toward Standards*, p. 64; Foerster in the University of North Carolina *Daily Tar Heel*, March 27, 1932 (clipping in Foerster papers).

29 Foerster, "The Study of Letters," p. 6; Foerster, *Toward Standards*, p. 13; Norman Foerster, "Literary Scholarship and Criticism," *English Journal*, coll. ed. 25 (1936): 228.

30 Foerster, "Language and Literature," in *University of Iowa Studies*, Series on Aims and Progress of Research 33, ed. John William Ashton (Iowa City: University of Iowa, 1931), p. 115; Foerster, *American Scholar*, p. 60; Foerster, *American State University*, p. 124; Foerster, *American Criticism*, pp. 107, 235; Brown, *Creative Spirit*, p. 188.

31 Henry Seidel Canby, "Education for Authors," in *American Estimates* (New York: Harcourt Brace, 1929), pp. 220–21; Foerster, *American Scholar*, pp. 60, 66; Norman Foerster, "Author and Alma Mater," typescript of an unpublished essay in the Foerster papers; Norman Foerster, *American Criticism: A Study in Literary Theory from Poe to the Present* (Boston: Houghton Mifflin, 1928), p. 228; Norman Foerster, "Language and Literature," p. 115; Norman Foerster, "A University Prepared for Victory," in *The Humanities after the War*, ed. Foerster (Princeton: Princeton University Press, 1944), pp. 29–30.

32 Norman Foerster, "The Education of a Writer," typescript of an unpublished essay in the Foerster papers.

33 Foerster, "Education of a Writer"; Foerster, *American State University*, p. 198; Paul Elmer More, "Academic Leadership," in *Shelburne Essays* (Boston: Houghton Mifflin, 1915), 9: 45–46.

34 Brownell, *Standards*, p. 94; Irving Babbitt, *Democracy and Leadership* (Indianapolis: Liberty, 1979), pp. 267, 338; Foerster, *American Criticism*, pp. 260, 340; Foerster, *Toward Standards*, p. 66; Irving Babbitt, "Genius and Taste," in *Criticism in America: Its Function and Status*, ed. J. E. Spingarn (New York:

Harcourt Brace, 1924), p. 164. *Democracy and Leadership* was first published in 1924.

35 Babbitt, "On Being Creative," p. 15; Foerster, *American Criticism*, p. 243.

36 Norman Foerster, progress report of November 1941 to Dean Harry K. Newburn in the Foerster papers; Foerster quoted in a March 1931 press release in the Foerster papers; R. S. Crane, letter of October 1940 in the Foerster papers; Foerster, *American State University*, p. 125.

37 Foerster, "Author and Alma Mater"; Foerster, "Study of Letters," p. 27.

38 Foerster, *American State University*, p. 221n; Wilbur L. Schramm, "Imaginative Writing," p. 181.

39 Foerster to Dean Newburn in the Foerster papers.

40 Piper, *Iowa Writers' Workshop in Retrospect*, unpaginated. On Edwin Ford Piper see Wilbers, *Iowa Writers' Workshop*, pp. 13–15 and passim.

41 Newton Arvin, "Individualism and the American Writer," in *Literary Opinion in America*, rev. ed., ed. Morton Dauwen Zabel (New York: Harper, 1951), pp. 544, 548. Originally published in the *Nation* in 1931.

42 Roy W. Cowden in a roundtable discussion "Should the University Encourage Creative Arts?" in *A University between Two Centuries: The Proceedings of the 1937 Celebration of the University of Michigan*, ed. Wilfred B. Shaw (Ann Arbor: University of Michigan Press, 1937), p. 186; Kent Sagendorph, *Michigan: The Story of the University* (New York: E. P. Dutton, 1948), p. 308.

43 Foerster to Worsley in the Foerster papers. The circumstances behind Foerster's resignation seem to have been these. Harry K. Newburn, recently appointed as dean of liberal arts at Iowa, proposed to eliminate all classes in history and foreign languages from the university's graduation requirements. Foerster countered with a proposal to eliminate all requirements in social science. Newburn was a social scientist. Whether he sought Foerster's removal or Foerster volunteered to resign is unclear. Originally Foerster had hoped, as he wrote to his old friend the classicist Gerald F. Else in May 1944, to "stay on for a few years as a professor concerned with graduate students and my own studies" (letter in the Foerster papers). In the end he found it impossible to do so.

44 Margaret Deland quoted in Ellsworth, *Creative Writing*, p. 33; Amy Kaplan, "Edith Wharton's Profession of Authorship," *ELH* 53 (1986): 435, 441; Elaine Showalter, *Sister's Choice: Tradition and Change in American Women's Writing* (Oxford: Clarendon, 1991), p. 105. Of course my argument in this paragraph about the exclusion of women is the merest echo of Jane Tompkins's argument in *Sensational Designs*.

45 Mary Roberts was awarded an M.A. for *Paisley Shawl*, a collection of poems. See Wilbers, *Iowa Writers' Workshop*, p. 57 n. 22.

46 Bildersee, *Imaginative Writing*, pp. 20, 112, 116–17.

47 Brenda Ueland, *Help from the Nine Muses*, reprinted as *If You Want to Write* (St. Paul: Graywolf, 1987), pp. 99–100; Sandra M. Gilbert, "Literary Paternity," in *Critical Theory Since 1965*, ed. Hazard Adams and Leroy Searle (Tallahassee: Florida State University Press, 1986), p. 494. Ueland's book was originally pub-

lished in 1938, Gilbert's essay—later the first chapter of *The Madwoman in the Attic*—in 1979.

48 Dorothea Brande, *Becoming a Writer* (Los Angeles: Jeremy P. Tarcher, 1981), pp. 22, 161, 168. Originally published in 1934.

49 Margaret Widdemer, *Do You Want to Write?* (New York: Farrar & Rinehart, 1937), pp. 51, 57; O. M. Cheney, *Economic Survey of the Book Industry, 1930–1931* (New York: National Association of Book Publishers, 1931), pp. 37–38. Widdemer's book was originally delivered as a series of broadcasts over the NBC radio network under the direction of its Women's Activities Section.

50 Esther L. Schwartz, *So You Want to Write! How to Make Money by Publishing* (New York: Phoenix, 1936), pp. 3, 40.

51 Schwartz, p. 16.

52 Lionel Trilling, "The Lesson and the Secret," in *Of This Time, Of That Place and Other Stories* (New York: Harcourt Brace Jovanovich, 1979), p. 67. Originally published in *Harper's Bazaar* in 1945.

Chapter 7
The Elephant Machine

1 Wallace Stegner, "Writing as Graduate Study," *College English* 11 (1950): 430.

2 Allen Tate, "What Is Creative Writing?" *Wisconsin Studies in Contemporary Literature* 5 (1964): 184. On Engle see Wilbers, *Iowa Writers' Workshop*, pp. 83–108. It was Janet Piper who said that Engle had been carefully groomed for the job of director. See Piper, *Iowa Writers' Workshop in Retrospect*, unpaginated. In the third edition of the *AWP Catalogue of Writing Programs* (1980), 101 institutions are listed as offering advanced degrees in creative writing or an M.A. in English with the option of a creative thesis. I stumbled upon the term "elephant machine" in George Riemer, *How They Murdered the Second "R"* (New York: Norton, 1969), p. 236.

3 Warren Kliewer, "Allen Tate as a Teacher," in *Allen Tate and His Work: Critical Evaluations*, ed. Radcliffe Squires (Minneapolis: University of Minnesota Press, 1972), p. 42; Wallace Stegner, "To a Young Writer," in *One Way to Spell Man* (Garden City: Doubleday, 1982), p. 31; Saul Bellow, *It All Adds Up: From the Dim Past to the Uncertain Future* (New York: Viking, 1994), p. 282. Stegner's essay was originally published in the *Atlantic* in 1959. On the distinction between discipline and profession see Everett C. Hughes, "Is Education a Discipline?" in *The Sociological Eye*, pp. 408–16. On the relationship between knowledge and professionalization see Christopher Jencks and David Riesman, *The Academic Revolution* (Garden City: Doubleday, 1968), pp. 199–207.

4 Ezra Pound, *Patria Mia* (1950), quoted in Robert N. Wilson, *Man Made Plain: The Poet in Contemporary Society* (Cleveland: Howard Allen, 1958), pp. 153–54; Paul Engle, "Introduction: The Writer and the Place," in *Midland*, p. xxx.

5 Theodore Weiss, "A Personal View: Poetry, Pedagogy, Per-Versities," in *The American Writer and the University*, ed. Ben Siegel (Newark: University of Delaware Press, 1989), p. 154; Walter Van Tilburg Clark, "The Teaching and Study of Writing," *Western Review* 14 (1950): 170. According to one of his stu-

dents, Yvor Winters shared Weiss's view of the relationship between poets and the university. "The analogy Winters used to offer was with the English clergy in the 17th century," Donald Justice recalled. "Poets like Herbert and Herrick were members of an institution that gave them and their poetry a kind of credit in society." See "An Interview with Donald Justice," *Sequoia* 28 (Autumn 1984): 28.

6 Proposal: Master of Fine Arts in Creative Writing, Western Michigan University, 1981. I am indebted to Michele McLaughlin-Dondero for a copy of this proposal.

7 For example, Paul Murray Kendall of Ohio University said creative writing would lead to "a heightening of perception leading to deeper realization of the value of experience and a more knowing and sensitive exploration of that experience. . . ." Quoted in Richard Scowcroft, "Courses in Creative Writing," in *The College Teaching of English*, ed. John C. Gerber, National Council of Teachers of English Curriculum Series 4 (New York: Appleton-Century-Crofts, 1965), p. 135. Almost verbatim, Kendell reasserts what Barrett Wendell had given as the aesthetic benefit of a writing course ("the deliberate cultivation of perception"). Somewhat differently, the poet Reed Whittemore hoped creative writing would serve as propaedeutic to the study of poetry. After taking a course or two, students "would all have been indoctrinated in the disciplines and conventions of verse and would not have to question them—at least not for every class and every poem—before going on to see how well or badly the disciplines and conventions had been observed, used, capitalized upon." Reed Whittemore, "Aesthetics in the Sonnet Shop," *American Scholar* 28 (1959): 350.

8 Richard Fine, *James M. Cain and the American Authors' Authority*, p. 58; Ronald A. May, letter to the author, December 4, 1986; Vincent McHugh, *Primer of the Novel* (New York: Random House, 1950), p. 268.

9 U.S. Bureau of Labor Statistics, unpublished tabulations, August 1987, in *Encyclopedia Britannica*, 15th ed., s.v. "Economic Growth and Planning"; John Brooks, *The Great Leap: The Past Twenty-five Years in America* (New York: Harper & Row, 1966), p. 132; William Jackson Lord, *How Authors Make a Living* (1962), quoted in Robert Byrne, *Writing Rackets* (New York: Lyle Stuart, 1969), pp. 135–36.

10 Wallace Stegner, "Can Teachers Be Writers?" *Intermountain Review* 1 (January 1, 1937): 3; Wilson, *Man Made Plain*, pp. 151–52.

11 Howard Nemerov, *A Howard Nemerov Reader* (Columbia: University of Missouri Press, 1991), p. 287; Stegner, "To a Young Writer," p. 30; Barbara Tuchman, "The Historian as Artist," in *Practicing History: Selected Essays* (New York: Alfred A. Knopf, 1981), p. 46; Bellow, *It All Adds Up*, p. 279.

12 Fred Chappell, "Welcoming Remarks," *Greensboro Review* no. 52 (Summer 1992): 83; Ray B. West, "A University Writing Program," *Western Review* 14 (1950): 238. Chappell offered his remarks November 9, 1991, at the Peter Taylor Homecoming on the Greensboro campus. Thanks to Steve Gilliam for this citation.

13 Nemerov, *Nemerov Reader*, p. 310; Ian Hamilton, *Robert Lowell: A Biography* (New York: Random House, 1982), p. 168; *Historical Statistics of the United States, Colonial Times to 1870* (Washington: U.S. Bureau of the Census, 1975), series R 192–217; Norman Podhoretz, *Making It* (New York: Harper, 1980), p. 41; Fredric

Jameson, *Marxism and Form: Twentieth-Century Dialectical Theories of Literature* (Princeton: Princeton University Press, 1971), p. 416. Podhoretz's autobiography was first published in 1967

14 Bellow, *It All Adds Up*, p. 311; Stegner, "One Way to Spell Man," in *One Way to Spell Man*, pp. 5, 11–12; Alan Swallow, "The Word," in *The Nameless Sight: Poems 1937–1956* (Denver: Alan Swallow, 1956), p. 30; Cleanth Brooks, "Irony as a Principle of Structure," in Zabel, ed., *Literary Opinion in America*, pp. 729–41; Tate, "What Is Creative Writing?" 181. Stegner's essay was originally published in the *Saturday Review* in 1958.

15 Judson Jerome, "The Career of Poetry and William Dickey: A Case Study," in *The Poet and the Poem* (Cincinnati: Writer's Digest, 1963), p. 184; Helen C. White, "Creative Writing in the University," *Wisconsin Studies in Contemporary Literature* 5 (1964): 40; John Paul Russo, "The Tranquilized Poem: The Crisis of the New Criticism in the 1950s," *Texas Studies in Language and Literature* 30 (1988): 198–229; Reed Whittemore, "The Line of an American Poet," in *The Feel of Rock: Poems of Three Decades* (Washington: Dryad Press, 1982), p. 24. Whittemore's poem originally appeared in *An American Takes a Walk* (1956).

16 Stegner, "One Way to Spell Man," pp. 10, 16; Paul Engle and Warren Carrier, eds., *Reading Modern Poetry* (Chicago: Scott, Foresman, 1955), p. xi; John Matthias, "Poet-Critics of Two Generations," in *Reading Old Friends: Essays, Reviews, and Poems on Poetics, 1975–1990* (Albany: State University of New York Press, 1992), p. 176.

17 Karl Shapiro, *A Primer for Poets* (Lincoln: University of Nebraska Press, 1953), p. 66; Donald Barthelme quoted in Susan Squire, "The Best Writing Workshop West of Iowa City," *Los Angeles Times Magazine* (August 9, 1987); West, "University Writing Program," 240.

18 Jean Stafford, "Wordman, Spare That Tree!" *Saturday Review/World* 1 (July 13, 1974): 17; James Whitehead interviewed in John Graham, *Craft So Hard to Learn: Conversations with Poets and Novelists about the Teaching of Writing*, ed. George Garrett (New York: William Morrow, 1972), p. 68; Dorothea Brande, *Becoming a Writer*, pp. 99–104; R. V. Cassill, *Writing Fiction* (New York: Pocket Books, 1962), p. 9; James K. Folsom, "Evaluating Creative Writing," in *Writing and Literature in the Secondary School*, ed. Edward J. Gordon (New York: Holt, Rinehart & Winston, 1965), pp. 137–38. On the circumstances surrounding Cassill's leaving Iowa for Brown see Wilbers, *Iowa Writers' Workshop*, pp. 109–16.

19 Nemerov, *Nemerov Reader*, pp. 308–9; Keith W. Olson, "The G.I. Bill and Higher Education: Success and Surprise," *American Quarterly* 25 (1973): 596–610. Whatever the consequence of hiring writers "to put up against the veterans," Olson argues that in general it is wrong to suggest that the G.I. Bill brought about deep and lasting changes in the university curriculum. "Because they received preferential administrative treatment, and because they shared with non-veterans similar attitudes toward college, society and courses of study," Olson says, "veterans demanded no changes in the basic structure or values of higher education. And colleges during the veteran era simply were too busy to study and restructure themselves" (607). Olson wishes to defend veterans against the glib accusation that they received a watered-down university education: "easy" curricula were not needed, he says, because the veterans academically outperformed their younger peers (604–5).

20 President's Commission on Higher Education, *Higher Education for American Democracy* (New York: Harper & Row, 1947), 1: 101; Oscar Handlin and Mary F. Handlin, *The American College and American Culture: Socialization as a Function of Higher Education* (New York: McGraw-Hill, 1970), pp. 72, 84. On the postwar expansion see David Dodds Henry, *Challenges Past, Challenges Present: An Analysis of American Higher Education Since 1930* (San Francisco: Jossey-Bass, 1975).

21 Clark Kerr, *The Uses of the University* (New York: Harper & Row, 1966), pp. 110–13. Originally delivered as the Godkin Lectures at Harvard in 1963.

22 Stegner, "One Way to Spell Man," p. 8; Engle, "Introduction: The Writer and the Place," in *Midland*, pp. xiii, xxx; Wallace Stegner, "What Besides Talent?" *Author and Journalist* 41 (March 1956): 13; Stegner, "To a Young Writer," p. 26.

23 Wallace Stegner, "The University and the Creative Arts," *Arts in Society* 2 (Spring–Summer 1963): 34; Mark Jarman, letter to the author, February 18, 1987.

24 Donald A. Sears, ed., *Directory of Creative Writing Programs in the United States and Canada* (Fullerton: College English Association, 1970).

25 Proposal for a Program of Graduate Study in Creative Writing, University of California, Irvine, May 1965, p. 38; Wichita State University *Alumni Report* (November–December 1984); Chappell, "Welcoming Remarks," 82. I am grateful to Scott Nelson for a copy of the UCI proposal and to Rae Goldsmith for information about Central Michigan.

26 "An Interview with Donald Justice," 28; Wilbers, Iowa *Writers' Workshop*, pp. 137–38.

27 David Riesman, *On Higher Education: The Academic Enterprise in an Era of Rising Student Consumerism* (San Francisco: Jossey-Bass, 1980), p. 107; Henry, *Challenges Past, Challenges Present*, pp. 24–25, 111, 116–33; Thomas Sowell, "The Scandal of College Tuition," *Commentary* 94 (August 1992): 24; Proposal for the Degree of Master of Fine Arts in Creative Writing, University of Virginia, June 1980, p. 2. For a copy of the Virginia proposal I owe thanks to George Garrett. The other great event of 1957—the graver, although it was overshadowed by Sputnik, which was launched twelve days later—was the forcible desegregation of Little Rock Central High School on September 23. This ought to have been of deeper concern to English teachers: most of the African American children who began to attend the formerly whites-only schools were tragically unprepared to handle the language academically. Yet Sputnik and the NDEA exercised the broader influence upon English teaching. Emphasis was placed upon the literacy needs of a modern technological society and the need to transmit the democratic values contained in the nation's cultural heritage. See John S. Simmons et al., "The Swinging Pendulum: Teaching English in the USA, 1945–1987," in *Teaching and Learning English Worldwide*, ed. James Britton et al. (Clevedon: Multilingual Matters, 1990), pp. 97–99.

28 Randall Black, "Magic Words," *UCI Journal* (Spring 1991): 9; Theodore Weiss, "A Personal View," p. 152. In 1971, there were 154 bachelor's degrees awarded in creative writing, 185 master's degrees, and six doctorates. See Mary Evans Hooper, *Earned Degrees Conferred, 1970–71* (Washington: U.S. Department of Health, Education and Welfare, 1973), table 8, p. 470. For the number of degrees in creative writing awarded during the 1988–89 academic year see *Digest of Education Statistics, 1991*, table 233, p. 243.

29 Kathy Walton, "A Brief History of the Associated Writing Programs," type-script on AWP letterhead dated March 1980. I am beholden to D. W. Fenza for a copy of this typescript

30 Ellen Bryant Voigt and Marvin Bell, "AWP Guidelines for Creative Writing Programs and Teachers of Creative Writing," *AWP Newsletter* 19 (September/October 1987): 12–13; Proposal for the Master of Fine Arts in Creative Writing, University of Virginia, pp. 1, 9–10. The AWP Guidelines were originally drafted in September 1979 and signed by a committee the members of which included Max Apple, George Cuomo, George P. Elliott, Daniel Halpern, John Clellon Holmes, David Madden, William Matthews, Philip F. O'Connor, Susan Shreve, David J. Smith, James Whitehead, Dara Wier, Charles Wright, and Al Young.

31 Fritz Machlup, *Knowledge: Its Creation, Distribution, and Economic Significance,* vol. 2: *The Branches of Learning* (Princeton: Princeton University Press, 1982), pp. 101–2.

32 R. V. Cassill, "Teaching Literature as an Art," in *In an Iron Time: Statements and Reiterations* (West Lafayette: Purdue University Studies, 1969), p. 43; Robert Pinsky, "The Interest of Poetry," *PN Review* no. 17 (1980): 34.

33 *Springdale* (Ark.) *News*, February 27, 1977; The Programs in Creative Writing and Translation, informational brochure (Fayetteville: University of Arkansas, n.d.); Stegner, "The University and the Creative Arts," 34.

Bibliography

Abbott, Andrew. *The System of Professions: An Essay on the Division of Expert Labor*. Chicago: University of Chicago Press, 1988.

Adams, J. Donald. *Copey of Harvard: A Biography of Charles Townsend Copeland*. Boston: Houghton Mifflin, 1960.

Adams, Katherine H. *A History of Professional Writing Instruction in American Colleges: Years of Acceptance, Growth, and Doubt*. Dallas: Southern Methodist University Press, 1993.

Alden, Henry Mills. *Magazine Writing and the New Literature*. New York: Harper, 1908.

Amis, Kingsley. *Memoirs*. New York: Summit, 1991.

Amsterdamska, Olga. *Schools of Thought: The Development of Linguistics from Bopp to Saussure*. Dordrecht: D. Reidel, 1987.

Andresen, Julie Tetel. *Linguistics in America, 1769–1924: A Critical History*. London: Routledge, 1990.

Angoff, Charles. *George Sterling: A Centenary Memoir-Anthology*. South Brunswick: A. S. Barnes, 1969.

Anonymous. *The Literary Guillotine*. New York: John Lane, 1903.

Antilla, Raimo. "Linguistics and Philology." In *Linguistics and Neighboring Disciplines*. Ed. Renate Bartsch and Theo Vennemann. Amsterdam: North-Holland, 1975. Pp. 145–55.

Arvin, Newton. "Individualism and the American Writer." 1931. In Zabel. Pp. 544–49.

———. *Longfellow: His Life and Work*. Boston: Little, Brown, 1963.

———. "The Failure of E. R. Sill." In *American Pantheon*. Ed. Daniel Aaron and Sylvan Schendler. New York: Dell, 1966. Pp. 174–93.

Austin, Mary. *Earth Horizon: An Autobiography*. Boston: Houghton Mifflin, 1932.

Aydelotte, Frank. "The History of English as a College Subject in the United States." In *The Oxford Stamp and Other Essays*. New York: Oxford University Press, 1917. Pp. 187–88.

Babbitt, Irving. *Literature and the American College: Essays in Defense of the Humanities*. Boston: Houghton Mifflin, 1908.

———. "Genius and Taste." In *Criticism in America: Its Function and Status*. Ed. J. E. Spingarn. New York: Harcourt Brace, 1924. Pp. 152–75.

———. *Democracy and Leadership*. 1924. Reprint. Indianapolis: Liberty, 1979.

———. "On Being Creative." In *On Being Creative and Other Essays*. Boston: Houghton Mifflin, 1932. Pp. 1–33.

Bacon, Leonard. *Ph.D.s: Male and Female He Created Them*. New York: Harper, 1925.

Baker, George Pierce. *Dramatic Technique*. Boston: Houghton Mifflin, 1919.

Bain, David Haward. *Whose Woods These Are: A History of the Bread Loaf Writers' Conference, 1926–1992.* Hopewell, N.J.: Ecco, 1993.

Ballou, Ellen B. *The Building of the House: Houghton Mifflin's Formative Years.* Boston: Houghton Mifflin, 1970.

Barth, John. "Writing: Can It Be Taught?" *New York Times Book Review* (June 16, 1985).

Bate, W. Jackson, et al., eds. *Harvard Scholars in English, 1890 to 1990.* Cambridge: Harvard University, 1991.

Bates, Katharine Lee. "Knowledge versus Feeling." *Poet-Lore* 6 (1894): 383–86.

———. "Wellesley College." In Payne. Pp. 141–48.

———. *American Literature.* New York: Macmillan, 1897.

Bawer, Bruce. "Dave Smith's 'Creative Writing.' " *New Criterion* 4 (December 1985): 27–33.

Beers, Henry A. *Initial Studies in American Letters.* New York: Chautauqua Press, 1891.

Bellow, Saul. *It All Adds Up: From the Dim Past to the Uncertain Future.* New York: Viking, 1994.

Benediktsson, Thomas E. *George Sterling.* Boston: Twayne, 1980.

Benét, William Rose. *The Dust Which Is God.* New York: Dodd, Mead, 1941.

Berlin, James A. *Writing Instruction in Nineteenth-Century American Colleges.* Carbondale: Southern Illinois University Press, 1984.

———. *Rhetoric and Reality: Writing Instruction in American Colleges, 1900–1985.* Carbondale: Southern Illinois University Press, 1987.

Bettersworth, John K. *People's University: The Centennial History of Mississippi State.* Jackson: University Press of Mississippi, 1980.

Beyer, Thomas P. "The Creative Life at Hamline." In *Hamline History.* Ed. Charles Nelson Pace. St. Paul: Hamline University Alumni Association, 1939. Pp. 106–17.

Bildersee, Adele. *Imaginative Writing: An Illustrated Course for Students.* Boston: D. C. Heath, 1927.

Birk, W. Otto. "Have All Our Methods of Teaching English Composition Failed?" *School and Society* 13 (1921): 383–85.

Black, Matthew Wilson. "Creative Writing in the College." In Hartman and Shumaker. Pp. 245–52.

Black, Randall. "Magic Words." *UCI* (University of California, Irvine) *Journal* (Spring 1991): 9–10.

Blackmur, R. P. "A Feather-Bed for Critics: Notes on the Profession of Writing." In *The Expense of Greatness.* New York: Arrow Editions, 1940. Pp. 277–305.

———. *New Criticism in the United States.* Tokyo: Kenkyshua, 1959.

Bledstein, Burton J. *The Culture of Professionalism: The Middle Class and the Development of Higher Education in America.* New York: Norton, 1976.

Bolling, George Melville. "Linguistics and Philology." *Language* 5 (1929): 27–32.

Bouton, Eugene. "The Study of English." *Education* 5 (1894): 91–104.

Braithwaite, William Stanley, ed. *Anthology of Magazine Verse for 1922 and Yearbook of American Poetry.* Boston: Small, Maynard, 1922.

Brande, Dorothea. *Becoming a Writer.* 1934. Reprint. Los Angeles: Jeremy P. Tarcher, 1981.

Brazil, John. "George Sterling: Art, Politics, and the Retreat to Carmel." *Markham Review* 8 (1979): 27–33.

Briggs, Le Baron Russell. *School, College and Character.* Boston: Houghton Mifflin, 1901.

———. *Men, Women and Colleges.* Boston: Houghton Mifflin, 1925.

———. *To College Teachers of English Composition.* Boston: Houghton Mifflin, 1928.

Bronson, Walter C. *The History of Brown University, 1764–1914.* Providence: By the University, 1914.

Brooks, Cleanth. "Irony as a Principle of Structure." 1949. In Zabel. Pp. 729–41.

Brooks, Cleanth, and Robert Penn Warren. *Understanding Poetry: An Anthology for College Students*. New York: Henry Holt, 1938.

Brooks, John. *The Great Leap: The Past Twenty-five Years in America*. New York: Harper & Row, 1966.

Brooks, Phillips. "The Purposes of Scholarship." In *Essays and Addresses*. Ed. John Cotton Brooks. New York: E. P. Dutton, 1895. Pp. 247–72.

Brooks, Van Wyck. *Autobiography*. New York: E. P. Dutton, 1965.

Brown, Maurice F. *Estranging Dawn: The Life and Works of William Vaughn Moody*. Carbondale: Southern Illinois University Press, 1973.

Brown, Rollo Walter. *The Creative Spirit: An Inquiry into American Life*. New York: Harper, 1925.

Brownell, W. C. *Criticism*. New York: Scribner's, 1914.

_____. *Standards*. New York: Scribner's, 1917.

Bruce, Philip Alexander. *History of the University of Virginia, 1819–1919*. Vol. 3: *The Lengthened Shadow of One Man*. New York: Macmillan, 1921.

Buck, Gertrude. *The Metaphor: A Study in the Psychology of Rhetoric*. Ann Arbor: Inland, ?1899.

_____. "What Does 'Rhetoric' Mean?" *Educational Review* 22 (1901): 197–200.

Bynner, Witter. "On Teaching the Young Laurel to Shoot." 1923. In *Prose Pieces*. Ed. James Kraft. New York: Farrar, Straus & Giroux, 1979. Pp. 366–71.

_____. *Selected Poems*. Ed. Richard Wilbur. New York: Farrar, Straus & Giroux, 1978.

_____. *Selected Letters*. Ed. James Kraft. New York: Farrar, Straus & Giroux, 1981.

Byrne, Robert. *Writing Rackets*. New York: Lyle Stuart, 1969.

Canby, Henry Seidel. "Writing English." *Harper's* 128 (1914): 778–84.

_____. "Current Literature and the Colleges." In *College Sons and College Fathers*. New York: Harper, 1915. Pp. 159–83.

_____. "Literature and Universities." In *Definitions: Essays in Contemporary Criticism*. Second series. New York: Harcourt Brace, 1924. Pp. 212–14.

_____. "Anon Is Dead." In *American Estimates*. New York: Harcourt Brace, 1929. Pp. 17–28.

_____. "The American Scholar." In *American Estimates*. Pp. 129–43.

_____. "Education for Authors." In *American Estimates*. Pp. 219–21.

Carpenter, Frederic Ives. "The Study of Literature." *Poet-Lore* 6 (1893): 378–81.

Cassill, R. V. *Writing Fiction*. New York: Pocket Books, 1962.

_____. "Teaching Literature as an Art." In *In an Iron Time: Statements and Reiterations*. West Lafayette: Purdue University Studies, 1969. Pp. 31–47.

Cavell, Stanley. "Emerson's Aversive Thinking." In *Romantic Revolutions: Criticism and Theory*. Ed. Kenneth R. Johnston et al. Bloomington: Indiana University Press, 1990. Pp. 219–49.

Chapman, John Jay. "Art and Art Schools." In *Memories and Milestones*. New York: Moffat, Yard, 1915. Pp. 3–16.

_____. "President Eliot." In *Memories and Milestones*. Pp. 165–90.

Chappell, Fred. "Welcoming Remarks." *Greensboro Review* no. 52 (Summer 1992): 80–87.

Chatfield-Taylor, H. C. "Wanted: Ateliers of Fiction." *Bookman* 16 (1903): 455–57.

Cheney, O. M. *Economic Survey of the Book Industry, 1930–1931*. New York: National Association of Book Publishers, 1931.

Chubb, Percival C. *The Teaching of English in the Elementary and Secondary School*. Rev. ed. New York: Macmillan, 1929.

Clark, Walter Van Tilburg. "The Teaching and Study of Writing." *Western Review* 14 (1950): 169–75.

Conkin, Paul K. *Gone with the Ivy: A Biography of Vanderbilt University.* Knoxville: University of Tennessee Press, 1985.

Conrad, Lawrence H. *Teaching Creative Writing.* New York: D. Appleton Century, 1937.

Cooper, Lane. "On the Teaching of Written Composition." *Education* 30 (1910): 421–30.

Crane, Hart. *The Letters of Hart Crane, 1916–1932.* Ed. Brom Weber. Berkeley: University of California Press, 1952.

Crane, R. S. "History versus Criticism in the University Study of Literature." In *The Idea of the Humanities and Other Essays Critical and Historical.* Vol. 2. Chicago: University of Chicago Press, 1967. Pp. 3–24.

———. "Criticism as Inquiry; or, The Dangers of the 'High Priori Road.'" In *The Idea of the Humanities.* Vol. 2. Pp. 25–44.

Cremin, Lawrence A. *The Transformation of the School: Progressivism in American Education, 1876–1957.* New York: Alfred A. Knopf, 1961.

Cunningham, J. V. "How Shall the Poem Be Written?" In *The Collected Essays.* Chicago: Swallow, 1976. Pp. 256–71.

———. "Graduate Training in English." In *Collected Essays.* Pp. 272–73.

Curtius, Ernst Robert. *European Literature and the Latin Middle Ages.* Tr. Willard Trask. Princeton: Princeton University Press, 1953.

Davidson, Donald. *Southern Writers in the Modern World.* Athens: University of Georgia Press, 1958.

Dean, Eleanora F. "The Teaching of Versification in the High School." *English Journal* 5 (1916): 119–30.

Demarest, William H. S. *A History of Rutgers College, 1706–1924.* New Brunswick: Rutgers College, 1924.

DeVoto, Bernard. "English A." *American Mercury* 13 (1928): 204–12.

Dewey, John. "Interest in Relation to Training of the Will." 1896. In *John Dewey on Education: Selected Writings.* Ed. Reginald D. Archambault. New York: Modern Library, 1964. Pp. 260–85.

———. "The School and Society." 1899. In *John Dewey on Education.* Pp. 295–310.

———. "Culture and Industry in Education." *Educational Bi-Monthly* 1 (1906): 8–9.

———. "Culture and Cultural Values." 1911. In Monroe. Vol. 2. Pp. 238–39.

———. *Democracy and Education: An Introduction to the Philosophy of Education.* New York: Macmillan, 1916.

———. "Individuality and Experience." 1926. In *John Dewey on Education.* Pp. 149–56.

Dickinson, Emily. *The Complete Poems.* Ed. Thomas H. Johnson. Boston: Little, Brown, 1960.

Diehl, Carl. *Americans and German Scholarship, 1770–1870.* New Haven: Yale University Press, 1978.

Digest of Education Statistics, 1991. Washington: U.S. Census Bureau, 1991.

Dooley, David. "The Contemporary Workshop Aesthetic." *Hudson Review* 43 (1990): 259–80.

Douglas, Wallace W. "Barrett Wendell." In *Traditions of Inquiry.* Ed. John C. Brereton. New York: Oxford University Press, 1985. Pp. 3–25.

Drayton, Michael. "To My Most Dearley-Loved Friend Henery Reymonds Esquire." 1627. In *The Works of Michael Drayton.* Ed. J. William Hebell. Vol. 3. Oxford: Shakespeare Head, 1932. Pp. 226–31.

Duff, John Carr. "Hughes Mearns: Pioneer in Creative Education." *Clearing House* 40 (1966): 419–20.

Dunaway, Wayland Fuller. *History of the Pennsylvania State College.* State College: Pennsylvania State College, 1946.

Durkin, Joseph T., S.J. *Georgetown University: The Middle Years, 1840–1900*. Washington: Georgetown University Press, 1963.

Eaton, Edward Dwight. *Historical Sketches of Beloit College*. New York: A. S. Barnes, 1928.

"Education." Editorial. *Atlantic Monthly* 33 (1874): 635–40.

Eliot, Charles W. "Inaugural Address as President of Harvard." 1869. Reprinted in Hofstadter and Smith. Pp. 601–24.

_____. "Liberty in Education." 1885. Reprinted in Hofstadter and Smith. Pp. 701–14.

Ellsworth, William Webster. *Creative Writing: A Guide for Those Who Aspire to Authorship*. New York: Funk & Wagnalls, 1929.

Emerson, Ralph Waldo. "The American Scholar." 1837. Reprinted in *Selected Writings*. Ed. Brooks Atkinson. New York: Modern Library, 1964. Pp. 45–63.

Engle, Paul, ed. *Midland: Twenty-five Years of Fiction and Poetry Selected from the Writing Workshops of the State University of Iowa*. New York: Random House, 1961.

Engle, Paul, and Warren Carrier, eds. *Reading Modern Poetry*. Chicago: Scott, Foresman, 1955.

Epstein, Joseph. "Who Killed Poetry?" *Commentary* 86 (August 1988): 13–20.

Erskine, John. *George Woodberry, 1855–1930: An Appreciation*. New York: New York Public Library, 1930.

_____. *The Memory of Certain Persons*. Philadelphia: J. B. Lippincott, 1947.

Exman, Eugene. *The House of Harper: One Hundred and Fifty Years of Publishing*. New York: Harper & Row, 1967.

Fenza, D. W., and Beth Jarock, eds. *AWP Official Guide to Writing Programs*. Sixth ed. Paradise, Calif.: Dust Books, 1992.

Fine, Richard. *James M. Cain and the American Authors' Authority*. Austin: University of Texas Press, 1992.

Fitzgerald, F. Scott. *Correspondence*. Ed. Matthew J. Bruccoli and Margaret M. Duggan. New York: Randon House, 1980.

Flanagan, Frances Mary. *The Educational Role of Norman Foerster*. Ph.D. dissertation. University of Iowa, 1971.

Fletcher, Robert S., and Malcolm O. Young, eds. *Amherst College: Biographical Record of the Graduates and Non-Graduates*. Amherst: By the College, 1921.

Flexner, Abraham. "A Modern School." In *A Modern College and a Modern School*. Garden City: Doubleday, Page, 1923. Pp. 84–142.

Foerster, Norman. Foerster Papers. Cecil H. Green Library. Stanford University.

_____. "Reconstructing the Ph.D. in English." *Nation* 108 (1919): 747–50.

_____. *American Criticism: A Study in Literary Theory from Poe to the Present*. Boston: Houghton Mifflin, 1928.

_____. *The American Scholar: A Study in* Litterae Inhumaniores. Chapel Hill: University of North Carolina Press, 1929.

_____. *Toward Standards: A Study of the Present Critical Moment in American Letters*. New York: Farrar & Rinehart, 1930.

_____. "Language and Literature." In *University of Iowa Studies*. Series on Aims and Progress of Research 33. Ed. John William Ashton. Iowa City: University of Iowa, 1931.

_____. "Literary Scholarship and Criticism." *English Journal*, coll. ed. 25 (1936): 224–32.

_____. *The American State University: Its Relation to Democracy*. Chapel Hill: University of North Carolina Press, 1937.

_____. "The Study of Letters." In Foerster, ed., *Literary Scholarship: Its Aims and Methods*. Pp. 3–31.

_____. "A University Prepared for Victory." In *The Humanities after the War*. Ed. Norman Foerster. Princeton: Princeton University Press, 1944. Pp. 26–31.

———, ed. *Literary Scholarship: Its Aims and Methods*. Chapel Hill: University of North Carolina Press, 1941.

Folsom, James K. "Evaluating Creative Writing." In *Writing and Literature in the Secondary School*. Ed. Edward J. Gordon. New York: Holt, Rinehart & Winston, 1965. Pp. 123–38.

Frederick, John T. "The Place of Creative Writing in American Schools." *English Journal*, coll. ed. 22 (1933): 8–16.

Friend, Christy. "The Excluded Conflict: The Marginalization of Composition and Rhetoric Studies in Graff's *Professing Literature*." *College English* 54 (1992): 276–86.

Frink, Henry Allyn. "Rhetoric and Public Speaking in the American College." *Education* 13 (1892): 129–141.

Frost, Robert. *Selected Letters*. Ed. Lawrance Thompson. New York: Holt, Rinehart & Winston, 1964.

Gardner, George E. "Should Power to Create or Capacity to Appreciate Be the Aim in the Study of English?" *Education* 15 (1894): 133–40, 221–29.

Gayley, Charles Mills. "English at the University of California." In Payne. Pp. 99–109.

Genung, John F. *The Practical Elements of Rhetoric with Illustrative Examples*. Boston: Ginn, 1886.

Gere, Anne Ruggles. *Writing Groups: History, Theory, and Implications*. Carbondale: Southern Illinois University Press, 1987.

Gilbert, Sandra M. "Literary Paternity." 1979. In *Critical Theory Since 1965*. Ed. Hazard Adams and Leroy Searle. Tallahassee: Florida State University Press, 1986. Pp. 486–96.

Gildersleeve, Basil. *Selections from the Brief Mention*. Ed. C. W. E. Miller. Baltimore: Johns Hopkins University Press, 1930.

Gioia, Dana. *Can Poetry Matter? Essays on Poetry and American Culture*. St. Paul: Graywolf, 1992.

Graff, Gerald. *Professing Literature: An Institutional History*. Chicago: University of Chicago Press, 1987.

Grafton, Anthony. *Defenders of the Text: The Traditions of Scholarship in an Age of Science, 1450–1800*. Cambridge: Harvard University Press, 1991.

Graham, John. *Craft So Hard to Learn: Conversations with Poets and Novelists about the Teaching of Writing*. Ed. George Garrett. New York: William Morrow, 1972.

Grandgent, Charles H. "The Modern Languages." In *The Development of Harvard University since the Inauguration of President Eliot, 1869–1929*. Ed. Samuel Eliot Morison. Cambridge: Harvard University Press, 1930. Pp. 65–105.

Greenhood, David. *The Writer on His Own*. Albuquerque: University of New Mexico Press, 1971.

Griffin, Clifford S. *The University of Kansas: A History*. Lawrence: University Press of Kansas, 1974.

Hagedorn, Hermann. *Edwin Arlington Robinson: A Biography*. New York: Macmillan, 1938.

Hall, Donald. "Poetry and Ambition," *Kenyon Review* n.s. 5 (1983): 90–104.

Hamilton, Ian. *Robert Lowell: A Biography*. New York: Random House, 1982.

Harris, Mark. "What Creative Writing Courses Create Is Students." *New York Times Book Review* (July 27, 1980).

Hartman, Gertrude, and Ann Shumaker, eds. *Creative Expression*. 2nd ed. Milwaukee: E. H. Hale, 1938.

Havinghurst, Walter. *The Miami Years, 1809–1969*. New York: Putnam's, 1969.

Hawkins, Hugh. *Pioneer: A History of the Johns Hopkins University, 1874–1889*. Ithaca: Cornell University Press, 1960.

Headley, Leal A., and Merrill E. Jarchow. *Carleton: The First Century.* Northfield: Carleton College, 1966.

Hedges, Marion Hawthorne. "Creative Teaching." *School and Society* 7 (1918): 117–18.

Heisch, C. E. *The Art and Craft of the Author.* New York: Grafton, 1906.

Henry, David Dodds. *Challenges Past, Challenges Present: An Analysis of American Higher Education Since 1930.* San Francisco: Jossey-Bass, 1975.

Herbst, Jurgen. *The German Historical School in American Scholarship: A Study in the Transfer of Culture.* Ithaca: Cornell University Press, 1965.

Herron, Jerry. *Universities and the Myth of Cultural Decline.* Detroit: Wayne State University Press, 1988.

Hewison, Robert. "Iowa Campus." *Times Literary Supplement* (March 13, 1981).

Hill, Adams Sherman. *Our English.* New York: Harper, 1888.

———. *The Principles of Rhetoric.* 1878. New ed. New York: American Book Co., 1895.

Hines, Laura Sanderson. "The Study of English Literature." *Education* 9 (1888): 229–35.

Historical Catalogue of Brown University, 1764–1914. Providence: By the University, 1914.

Historical Statistics of the United States, Colonial Times to 1970. Washington: U.S. Bureau of the Census, 1975.

Hoenigswald, Henry M. "Fallacies in the History of Linguistics: Notes on the Appraisal of the Nineteenth Century." In *Studies in the History of Linguistics: Traditions and Paradigms.* Ed. Dell Hymes. Bloomington: Indiana University Press, 1974. Pp. 346–58.

Hoeveler, J. David. *The New Humanism: A Critique of Modern America, 1900–1940.* Charlottesville: University Press of Virginia, 1977.

Hofstadter, Richard, and Wilson Smith, eds. *American Higher Education: A Documentary History.* Chicago: University of Chicago Press, 1961.

Hollis, Daniel Walker. *University of South Carolina.* Vol. 2: *College to University.* Columbia: University of South Carolina Press, 1956.

Hooper, John. *Poetry in the New Curriculum: A Manual for Elementary Teachers.* Brattleboro, Vt.: Stephen Daye, 1932.

Hooper, Mary Evans. *Earned Degrees Conferred, 1970–71.* Washington: U.S. Department of Health, Education and Welfare, 1973.

Housh, Snow Longley. "Report of Creative Writing in Colleges." *English Journal,* coll. ed. 20 (1931): 672–78.

Hubbell, Jay B. *The Enjoyment of Literature.* New York: Macmillan, 1929.

Hugo, Richard. "In Defense of Creative-Writing Classes." In *The Triggering Town: Lectures and Essays on Poetry and Writing.* New York: Norton, 1979. Pp. 53–66.

Jarrell, Randall. *Pictures from an Institution.* New York: Alfred A. Knopf, 1954.

Jeffers, Robinson. *The Selected Poetry.* New York: Random House, 1951.

Jefferson, Bernard L., and Harry Houston Peckham. *Creative Prose Writing.* New York: Doubleday, Doran, 1926.

Jencks, Christopher, and David Riesman. *The Academic Revolution.* Garden City: Doubleday, 1968.

Jerome, Judson. "The Career of Poetry and William Dickey: A Case Study." In *The Poet and the Poem.* Cincinnati: Writer's Digest, 1963. Pp. 176–84.

Johnson, E. Bird, ed. *Forty Years of the University of Minnesota.* Minneapolis: General Alumni Association, 1910.

Johnson, Nan. *Nineteenth-Century Rhetoric in North America.* Carbondale: Southern Illinois University Press, 1991.

Jones, Howard Mumford. *The Age of Energy: Varieties of American Experience, 1865–1915.* New York: Viking, 1971.

Jones, Theodore Francis, ed. *New York University, 1832–1932*. New York: New York University Press, 1933.

Jonson, Ben. *Discoveries*. 1640. In *The Complete Poems*. Ed. George Parfitt. New Haven: Yale University Press, 1975. Pp. 375–458.

Justice, Donald. "An Interview." *Sequoia* 28 (1984): 18–28.

Kaplan, Amy. "Edith Wharton's Profession of Authorship." *ELH* 53 (1986): 433–57.

Kaufman, Paul. "Promethean Fire: A Challenge to the American College." *School and Society* 28 (1928): 121–28.

Kellock, Harold. "Woodberry—A Great Teacher." *Nation* 130 (1930): 120–22.

Kent, Charles W. "English at the University of Virginia." In Payne. Pp. 65–70.

Kernan, Alvin. *The Death of Literature*. New Haven: Yale University Press, 1990.

Kerr, Clark. *The Uses of the University*. New York: Harper & Row, 1966.

Kilmer, Joyce. "The Abolition of Poets." In *The Circus and Other Essays and Fugitive Pieces*. New York: George H. Doran, 1916. Pp. 60–69.

Kimball, Bruce A. *Orators and Philosophers: A History of the Idea of Liberal Education*. New York: Teachers College Press, 1986.

King, Irving. "Professionalism and Truth-Seeking." *School Review* 16 (1908): 241–51.

Kinne, Wisner Payne. *George Pierce Baker and the American Theatre*. Cambridge: Harvard University Press, 1954.

Kitzhaber, Albert R. *Rhetoric in American Colleges, 1850–1900*. Dallas: Southern Methodist University Press, 1990.

Kliebard, Herbert M. *The Struggle for the American Curriculum, 1893–1958*. Boston: Routledge & Kegan Paul, 1986.

Kliewer, Warren. "Allen Tate as a Teacher." In *Allen Tate and His Work: Critical Evaluations*. Ed. Radcliffe Squires. Minneapolis: University of Minnesota Press, 1972. Pp. 42–49.

Krapp, George P. "Teaching of English Literature." 1913. In Monroe. Vol. 4. Pp. 49–55.

Kuzma, Greg. "The Catastrophe of Creative Writing." *Poetry* 148 (1986): 342–54.

Larkin, Philip. "An Interview with *Paris Review*." In *Required Writing: Miscellaneous Pieces, 1955–1982*. London: Faber & Faber, 1983. Pp. 57–76.

Larson, Magali Sarfatti. *The Rise of Professionalism: A Sociological Analysis*. Berkeley: University of California Press, 1977.

Learned, Marion Dexter. "Linguistic Study and Literary Creation." President's Address 1909. *PMLA* 25 (1910): xlvi–lxv.

Lewis, C. S. "The Idea of an 'English School.'" In *Representations and Other Essays*. London: Oxford University Press, 1939. Pp. 59–77.

Lewisohn, Ludwig. *The Creative Life*. New York: Boni & Liveright, 1924.

Livingston, Myra Cohn. *The Child as Poet: Myth or Reality*. Boston: Horn Book, 1984.

London, Jack. *The Valley of the Moon*. New York: Grosset & Dunlap, 1913.

Longfellow, Samuel. *Life of Henry Wadsworth Longfellow*. Boston: Ticknor, 1886.

Lounsbury, Thomas R. "Compulsory Composition in Colleges." *Harper's* 123 (1911): 866–80.

Mabie, Hamilton Wright. *American Ideals, Character and Life*. New York: Macmillan, 1913.

McFee, William. "The Cheer-Leader in Literature." In *Contemporary American Criticism*. Ed. James Cloyd Bowman. New York: Henry Holt, 1926. Pp. 239–55.

McHugh, Vincent. *Primer of the Novel*. New York: Random House, 1950.

McLean, L. May. "Rhetoric in Secondary Schools." *Education* 18 (1897): 158–65.

Machlup, Fritz. *Knowledge: Its Creation, Distribution, and Economic Significance*. Vol. 2: *The Branches of Learning*. Princeton: Princeton University Press, 1982.

Manly, John M., ed. *The Poems and Plays of William Vaughn Moody*. Boston: Houghton Mifflin, 1912.

Mason, Daniel Gregory, ed. *Some Letters of William Vaughn Moody*. Boston: Houghton Mifflin, 1913.

Matthews, Brander. "Can English Literature Be Taught?" *Educational Review* 3 (1892): 337–47.

_____. *Aspects of Fiction and Other Ventures in Criticism*. New York: Harper, 1896.

_____. *A Study of Versification*. Boston: Houghton Mifflin, 1911.

_____. *Gateways to Literature and Other Essays*. New York: Scribner's, 1912.

_____. *These Many Years: Recollections of a New Yorker*. New York: Scribner's, 1917.

Matthias, John. "Poet-Critics of Two Generations." In *Reading Old Friends: Essays, Reviews, and Poems on Poetics, 1975–1990*. Albany: State University of New York Press, 1992. Pp. 161–78.

Mead, W. E. "The Graduate Study of Rhetoric." *PMLA* 16 (1901): xx–xxxii.

Mearns, [William] Hughes. "Our Medieval High Schools: Shall We Educate Children for the Twelfth or the Twentieth Century?" *Saturday Evening Post* (March 2, 1912): 19.

_____. "The Changing Elementary Schools." *Saturday Evening Post* 185 (January 4, 1913): 6–7, 27.

_____, ed. *Lincoln Verse, Story, and Essay*. First series. New York: The Lincoln School of Teachers College, 1923.

_____. "English as an Expression of the Activities of Everyday Life," *Journal of Educational Method* 2 (1923): 285–88.

_____. *Creative Youth: How a School Environment Set Free the Creative Spirit*. Garden City: Doubleday, Page, 1925.

_____. "Golden Lads and Girls." *Survey* 50 (1926): 319–20, 333.

_____. Review of *The Singing Crow and Other Poems* by Nathalia Crane. *Progressive Education* 4 (1927): 134–35.

_____. *Creative Power*. Garden City: Doubleday, Doran, 1929.

_____. "Educating the New Child." *North American Review* 230 (1930): 696–703.

_____. "The Creative Spirit and Its Significance for Education." In Hartman and Shumaker. Pp. 14–21.

_____. *The Creative Adult: Self-Education in the Art of Living*. New York: Doubleday, Doran, 1940.

_____. "Creative Learning." In *Challenges to Education, War and Post-War*. 30th Annual Schoolmen's Week Proceedings. Philadelphia: University of Pennsylvania, 1943. Pp. 157–66.

_____. "Poetry Is When You Talk to Yourself." In *Challenges to Education*. Pp. 154–57.

_____. "Creative Education in College Years." *Progressive Education* 23 (1946): 268–69, 279.

Meiklejohn, Alexander. *The Experimental College*. 1932. Ed. John Walker Powell. Cabin John, Md.: Seven Locks, 1981.

Michael, Ian. *The Teaching of English from the Sixteenth Century to 1870*. Cambridge: Cambridge University Press, 1987.

Miller, Susan. *Textual Carnivals: The Politics of Composition*. Carbondale: Southern Illinois University Press, 1991.

Monroe, Paul, ed. *A Cyclopedia of Education*. 5 vols. New York: Macmillan, 1911–13.

More, Paul Elmer. "Academic Leadership." In *Shelburne Essays*. Vol. 9. Boston: Houghton Mifflin, 1915. Pp. 39–67.

Morrison, Theodore. *Bread Loaf Writers' Conference: The First Thirty Years, 1926–1955*. Middlebury, Vt.: Middlebury College Press, 1976.

Nemerov, Howard. *A Howard Nemerov Reader*. Columbia: University of Missouri Press, 1991.

Nettleship, Henry. "Classical Education in the Past and at Present." In *Lectures and Essays*. Oxford: Clarendon, 1895. Pp. 208–17.

Nevins, Allan. *Illinois*. New York: Oxford University Press, 1917.

Newdick, Robert S. "Robert Frost and the American College." *Journal of Higher Education* 7 (1936): 237–43.

Nitchie, Elizabeth. *The Criticism of Literature*. New York: Macmillan, 1928.

Nock, Albert Jay. "Absurdity of Teaching English." *Bookman* 69 (1929): 113–19.

Noel, Joseph. *Footloose in Arcadia: A Personal Record of Jack London, George Sterling, Ambrose Bierce*. New York: Carrick & Evans, 1940.

Norris, Frank. "Frank Norris' Weekly Letter." 1901. Reprinted in *The Literary Criticism of Frank Norris*. Ed. Donald Pizer. Austin: University of Texas Press, 1964.

Noxon, Frank W. "College Professors Who Are Men of Letters." *Critic* 42 (1903): 124–35.

Noyes, Alfred. *Two Worlds for Memory*. Philadelphia: J. B. Lippincott, 1953.

Ochsenford, S. E. *Muhlenberg College: A Quarter-Century Memorial Volume, Being a History of the College and a Record of Its Men*. Allentown: Muhlenberg College, 1892.

O'Dell, De Forest. *The History of Journalism Education in the United States*. Contributions to Education 653. New York: Teachers College, Columbia University, 1935.

Olson, Keith W. "The G.I. Bill and Higher Education: Success and Surprise." *American Quarterly* 25 (1973): 596–610.

Packer, B. L. *Emerson's Fall: A New Interpretation of the Major Essays*. New York: Continuum, 1982.

Page, Walter Hines. "The Writer and the University." *Atlantic Monthly* 100 (1907): 685–95.

Parker, William Belmont. *Edward Rowland Sill: His Life and Work*. Boston: Houghton Mifflin, 1915.

Pattee, Fred Lewis. *The Development of the American Short Story: An Historical Survey*. New York: Harper, 1923.

Payne, William Morton, ed. *English in American Universities*. Boston: D. C. Heath, 1895.

Peckham, Howard H. *The Making of the University of Michigan, 1817–1967*. Ann Arbor: University of Michigan Press, 1967.

Pedersen, N. Alvin. "Writing Themes for Magazines and Newspapers," *Education* 39 (1918): 217–24.

Phelps, William Lyon. "Two Ways of Teaching English." *Century* 51 (1896): 793–94.

Pinsky, Robert. "The Interest of Poetry." *PN Review* no. 17 (1980): 34–35.

Piper, Janet. *The University of Iowa Writers' Workshop in Retrospect: A Repository of Relevant Writing*. Austin: privately printed, ?1981.

Porter, Martha Peck. *The Teacher in the New School*. Yonkers: World, 1931.

Pound, Louise. "The American Dialect Society: A Historical Sketch." Publication of the American Dialect Society 17. Greensboro: Woman's College of the University of North Carolina, 1952.

President's Commission on Higher Education. *Higher Education for American Democracy*. 6 vols. New York: Harper & Row, 1947.

Pritchard, William H. *Frost: A Literary Life Reconsidered*. New York: Oxford University Press, 1984.

Ransom, John Crowe. *The New Criticism*. Norfolk: New Directions, 1941.

Reed, John. *Insurgent Mexico*. 1914. Ed. Albert L. Michaels and James W. Wilkie. New York: Simon & Schuster, 1969.

Reid, Alfred Sandlin. *Furman University: Toward a New Identity, 1925–1975*. Durham: Duke University Press, 1970.

Renker, Elizabeth. "Resistance and Change: The Rise of American Literature Studies." *American Literature* 64 (1992): 347–65.

Ried, Paul E. "The First and Fifth Boylston Professors: A View of Two Worlds." *Quarterly Journal of Speech* 74 (1988): 229–40.

Riesman, David. *On Higher Education: The Academic Enterprise in an Era of Rising Student Consumerism.* San Francisco: Jossey-Bass, 1980.

Ringler, William. *"Poeta Nascitur Non Fit:* Some Notes on the History of an Aphorism." *Journal of the History of Ideas* 2 (1941): 497–504.

Ripley, Mary A. "About English." *Education* 9 (1889): 535–40.

Roberts, David. *Jean Stafford: A Biography.* London: Chatto & Windus, 1988.

Robinson, Edwin Arlington. *Collected Poems.* New York: Macmillan, 1937.

Rudolph, Frederick. *Curriculum: A History of the American Undergraduate Course of Study since 1636.* San Francisco: Jossey-Bass, 1977.

Rugg, Harold, and Ann Shumaker. *The Child-Centered School: An Appraisal of the New Education.* Yonkers: World, 1928.

Russell, David R. *Writing in the Academic Disciplines, 1870–1990: A Curricular History.* Carbondale: Southern Illinois University Press, 1991.

Sampson, Geoffrey. *Schools of Linguistics.* Stanford: Stanford University Press, 1980.

Sampson, Martin W. "English at the University of Indiana." In Payne. Pp. 92–98.

Santayana, George. *The Middle Span.* New York: Scribner's, 1945.

Scholes, Robert. *Textual Power: Literary Theory and the Teaching of English.* New Haven: Yale University Press, 1985.

Schramm, Wilbur L. "Imaginative Writing." In Foerster, ed., *Literary Scholarship: Its Aims and Methods.* Pp. 177–213.

Schwartz, Esther L. *So You Want to Write! How to Make Money by Publishing.* New York: Phoenix, 1936.

Scott, Fred N. "English Composition as a Mode of Behavior." *English Journal* 11 (1922): 463–73.

Scowcroft, Richard. "Courses in Creative Writing." In *The College Teaching of English.* Ed. John C. Gerber. National Council of Teachers of English Curriculum Series 4. New York: Appleton-Century-Crofts, 1965. Pp. 131–52.

Sears, Donald A., ed. *Directory of Creative Writing Programs in the United States and Canada.* Fullerton: College English Association, 1970.

Self, Robert T. *Barrett Wendell.* Boston: Twayne, 1975.

Shapiro, Karl. *A Primer for Poets.* Lincoln: University of Nebraska Press, 1953.

Shaw, Wilfred B., ed. "Should the University Encourage Creative Arts?" In *A University between Two Centuries: The Proceedings of the 1937 Celebration of the University of Michigan.* Ann Arbor: University of Michigan Press, 1937. Pp. 183–91.

Showalter, Elaine. *Sister's Choice: Tradition and Change in American Women's Writing.* Oxford: Clarendon, 1991.

Showerman, Grant. *With the Professor.* New York: Henry Holt, 1910.

Sill, Edward Rowland. *The Prose of Edward Rowland Sill.* Boston: Houghton Mifflin, 1900.

Simmons, John S., et al. "The Swinging Pendulum: Teaching English in the USA, 1945–1987." In *Teaching and Learning English Worldwide.* Ed. James Britton et al. Clevedon: Multilingual Matters, 1990. Pp. 89–130.

Smith, Dave. "Notes on Responsibility and the Teaching of Creative Writing." In *Local Assays: On Contemporary American Poetry.* Urbana: University of Illinois Press, 1985. Pp. 215–28.

Smith, Lewis Worthington. *The Writing of the Short Story.* Boston: D. C. Heath, 1902.

――――― , and James E. Thomas. *A Modern Composition and Rhetoric.* Boston: Benjamin A. Sanborn, 1900.

Smith, Logan Pearsall. *Words and Idioms: Studies in the English Language.* London: Constable, 1925.

Smith, Timothy Heyward. *Hughes Mearns: The Theory and Practice of Creative Education*. Ed.D. dissertation. Rutgers University, 1968.

Solberg, Winton U. *The University of Illinois, 1867–1894: An Intellectual and Cultural History*. Urbana: University of Illinois Press, 1968.

Souba, Jane. "Creative Writing in High School." *English Journal* 14 (1925): 591–602.

Spears, Monroe K. *Dionysius and the City: Modernism in Twentieth-Century Poetry*. Oxford: Oxford University Press, 1970.

Spingarn, J. E. "The New Criticism." In *Creative Criticism and Other Essays*. New and enlarged ed. New York: Harcourt Brace, 1931. Pp. 3–38.

Spran, George. *The Meaning of Literature*. New York: Scribner's, 1925.

Squire, Susan. "The Best Writing Workshop West of Iowa City." *Los Angeles Times Magazine* (August 9, 1987).

Stafford, Jean. "Wordman, Spare That Tree!" *Saturday Review/World* 1 (July 13, 1974): 14–17.

Stanford, W. B. *Enemies of Poetry*. London: Routledge & Kegan Paul, 1980.

Stauffer, Donald A., ed. *The Intent of the Critic*. Princeton: Princeton University Press, 1941.

Stegner, Wallace. "Can Teachers Be Writers?" *Intermountain Review* 1 (January 1, 1937): 1, 3.

_____. "Writing as Graduate Study." *College English* 11 (1950): 429–32.

_____. "What Besides Talent?" *Author and Journalist* 41 (March 1956): 11–13, 29.

_____. "One Way to Spell Man." 1958. In *One Way to Spell Man*. Garden City: Doubleday, 1982. Pp. 5–17.

_____. "To a Young Writer." 1959. In *One Way to Spell Man*. Pp. 26–34.

_____. "The University and the Creative Arts." *Arts in Society* 2 (Spring–Summer 1963): 33–34.

_____. *On the Teaching of Creative Writing*. Ed. Edward Connery Latham. Hanover, N.H.: University Press of New England, 1988.

Stevens, Clara F. "College English." *Education* 27 (1906): 101–11.

Stock, Noel. *The Life of Ezra Pound*. New York: Avon Books, 1970.

Stoddard, Francis H. "Literary Spirit in the Colleges." *Educational Review* 6 (1894): 126–35.

Sutherland, J. A. *Fiction and the Fiction Industry*. London: Athlone, 1978.

Sutton, Albert Alton. *Education for Journalism in the United States from Its Beginning to 1940*. Northwestern University Studies in the Humanities 14. Evanston: Northwestern University, 1945.

Svobodny, Dolly, ed. *Early American Textbooks, 1775–1900*. Washington: U.S. Department of Education, 1985.

Swallow, Alan. "The Word." In *The Nameless Sight: Poems 1937–1956*. Denver: Alan Swallow, 1956. P. 30.

Tanner, Daniel, and Laurel Tanner. *History of the School Curriculum*. New York: Macmillan, 1990.

Tate, Allen. "American Poetry Since 1920." 1929. In *The Poetry Reviews of Allen Tate, 1924–1944*. Ed. Ashley Brown and Frances Neel Cheney. Baton Rouge: Louisiana State University, 1983. Pp. 78–88.

_____. "We Read as Writers." *Princeton Alumni Weekly* 40 (March 8, 1940): 505–6.

_____. "What Is Creative Writing?" *Wisconsin Studies in Contemporary Literature* 5 (1964): 181–84.

Tebbel, John. *Between the Covers: The Rise and Transformation of Book Publishing in America*. New York: Oxford University Press, 1987.

Thompson, Lawrance. *Robert Frost: The Years of Triumph, 1915–1938*. New York: Holt, Rinehart & Winston, 1970.

Thurber, Samuel. "An Address to Teachers of English." *Education* 18 (1898): 516–26.

Trilling, Diana. *The Beginning of the Journey: The Marriage of Diana and Lionel Trilling*. New York: Harcourt Brace, 1993.

Trilling, Lionel. "The Lesson and the Secret." 1945. In *Of This Time, Of That Place and Other Stories*. New York: Harcourt Brace Jovanovich, 1979. Pp. 58–71.

_____. "On the Teaching of Modern Literature." In *Beyond Culture: Essays on Literature and Learning*. New York: Viking, 1968. Pp. 3–30.

Tuchman, Barbara. "The Historian as Artist." In *Practicing History: Selected Essays*. New York: Alfred A. Knopf, 1981. Pp. 45–50.

Turnbull, Andrew. *Scott Fitzgerald*. New York: Scribner's, 1962.

Turner, Steven. "The Prussian Professoriate and the Research Imperative, 1790–1840." In *Epistemological and Social Problems of the Sciences in the Early Nineteenth Century*. Ed. Hans Niels Jahnke and Michael Otte. Dordrecht: D. Reidel, 1981. Pp. 109–21.

Ueland, Brenda. *Help from the Nine Muses*. 1938. Reprinted as *If You Want to Write*. St. Paul: Graywolf, 1987.

Vanderbilt, Kermit. *American Literature and the Academy: The Roots, Growth, and Maturity of a Profession*. Philadelphia: University of Pennsylvania Press, 1986.

Van Dyke, Henry. "Reading and Writing in the Teaching of English." *School Review* 15 (1907): 325–32.

Viles, Jonas. *The University of Missouri: A Centennial History*. Columbia: University of Missouri Press, 1939.

Voigt, Ellen Bryant, and Marvin Bell. "AWP Guidelines for Creative Writing Programs and Teachers of Creative Writing." 1979. *AWP Newsletter* 19 (September/October 1987): 12–13

Walker, Franklin. *The Seacoast of Bohemia*. Santa Barbara: Peregrine Smith, 1973.

Wallace, Willard M. *Soul of the Lion: A Biography of General Joshua L. Chamberlain*. New York: Thomas Nelson, 1960.

Ward, C. H. "What Is English?" *Educational Review* 51 (1916): 168–78.

_____. "Fluency First." *Education* 38 (1917): 102–9.

Warner, Michael. "Professionalization and the Rewards of Literature." *Criticism* 27 (1985): 1–28.

Watkins, Evan. *Work Time: English Departments and the Circulation of Cultural Value*. Stanford: Stanford University Press, 1989.

Weiss, Theodore. "A Personal View: Poetry, Pedagogy, Per-Versities." In *The American Writer and the University*. Ed. Ben Siegel. Newark: University of Delaware Press, 1989. Pp. 149–58.

Wendell, Barrett. *English Composition: Eight Lectures Given at the Lowell Institute*. New York: Scribner's, 1891.

_____. "English Work in the Secondary Schools." *School and Society* 1 (1893): 638–50.

_____. *Stelligeri and Other Essays concerning America*. New York: Scribner's, 1893.

_____. *The Privileged Classes*. New York: Scribner's, 1908.

_____. *The Mystery of Education and Other Academic Performances*. New York: Scribner's, 1909.

Wertenbaker, Thomas Jefferson. *Princeton: 1746–1896*. Princeton: Princeton University Press, 1946.

West, Ray B. "A University Writing Program." *Western Review* 14 (1950): 164, 236–40.

_____. *Short Story in America, 1900–1950*. Chicago: Henry Regnery, 1952.

White, Helen C. "Creative Writing in the University." *Wisconsin Studies in Contemporary Literature* 5 (1964): 37–47.

White, Trentwell Mason. "Concerning the Subject of Creative Writing." *Education* 59 (1938): 129–30.

Whitmore, Charles E. "What Ails Collegiate English?" *Educational Review* 64 (1922): 383–86.

Whitney, Lois. "English Primitivistic Theories of Epic Origins." *Modern Philology* 21 (1924): 337–78.

Whitney, William Dwight. "Logical Consistency in Views of Language." *American Journal of Philology* 1 (1880): 327–43.

Whittemore, Reed. "The Line of an American Poet." 1956. In *The Feel of Rock: Poems of Three Decades*. Washington: Dryad Press, 1982. P. 24.

_____. "Aesthetics in the Sonnet Shop." *American Scholar* 28 (1959): 344–54.

Widdemer, Margaret. *Do You Want to Write?* New York: Farrar & Rinehart, 1937.

Wilbers, Stephen. *The Iowa Writers' Workshop*. Iowa City: University of Iowa Press, 1980.

Wilson, Edmund. *Letters on Literature and Politics*. Ed. Elena Wilson. New York: Farrar, Straus & Giroux, 1977.

Wilson, Robert N. *Man Made Plain: The Poet in Contemporary Society*. Cleveland: Howard Allen, 1958.

Winters, Yvor. *Edwin Arlington Robinson*. Rev. ed. Norfolk: New Directions, 1971.

Wolverton, Sarah Foss. "The Professional Scullery." *Educational Review* 60 (1920): 407–16.

Wood, James Playsted. *Magazines in the United States: Their Social and Economic Influence*. New York: Ronald, 1949.

Woodberry, George E. "Professional Poetry." *Atlantic Monthly* 55 (1885): 561–66.

_____. "Literature in the Market-Place." *Forum* 11 (1891): 652–61.

_____. *The Appreciation of Literature*. New York: Harcourt Brace, 1907.

_____. "A New Defense of Poetry." In *The Heart of Man and Other Papers*. New York: Harcourt Brace, 1920. Pp. 51–139.

_____. *Studies of a Litterateur*. New York: Harcourt Brace, 1921.

Young, Thomas Daniel. *Gentleman in a Dustcoat: A Biography of John Crowe Ransom*. Baton Rouge: Louisiana State University Press, 1976.

Zabel, Morton Dauwen, ed. *Literary Opinion in America*. Rev. ed. New York: Harper, 1951.

Ziolkowski, Jan, ed. *On Philology*. University Park: Pennsylvania State University Press, 1990.

❧ *Index*